LOS LOGOS COMPASS

gestalten

Contents

CON
TENTS

/
PREFACE
Pages 4–7

01/
PICTOGRAM
Pages 8–15

02/
PICTO/TEXT
Pages 16–61

03/
LOVE OF LETTERS
Pages 62–121

04/
STROKE OF LUCK
Pages 122–141

05/
SIGNATURE
Pages 142–169

Contents

06/
PRE-SCHOOL
Pages 170–185

07/
MIND THE GAP
Pages 186–203

08/
LIQUID / LIQUID
Pages 204–225

09/
WE ARE FAMILY
Pages 226–243

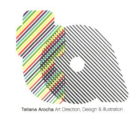

10/
DATA
Pages 244–305

11/
ORNAMENTAL
Pages 306–333

12/
RETRO / NAÏVE
Pages 334–353

13/
TACTILE
Pages 354–369

/
ADDRESS INDEX
Pages 370–383

/
WORK INDEX
Pages 384–407

/PREFACE

BY ROBERT KLANTEN

/ NOW IN ITS FIFTH INCARNATION, THE *LOS LOGOS* SERIES CELEBRATES THE UNIVERSAL APPEAL OF THE LOGO IN ITS COUNTLESS EMBODIMENTS WITH A NEW FORMAT AND APPROACH. CHARTING MAJOR SHIFTS IN THE LOGOSPHERE, IT SERVES AS A GUIDE AND COMPASS TO THE LATEST DEVELOPMENTS.

For a long time, categorization by application—be it art, commercial, or otherwise—made plenty of sense: after all, the resulting visual identities were often linked by a common style or theme, a tenuous red thread of approach and aesthetics. In recent years, however, the tides have turned in logo design and the waters have become decidedly murkier, with plenty of eddies churning up the primordial soup of the respective memes and markers. Dipping into this rich aesthetic gene pool, everyone is free to pick their own tailored blend of specific—and possibly mixed—visual messages.

Here, the division between black and white, culture and corporate, nimble niche and sluggish behemoth no longer holds true: all we see are singular agendas, reflected in the clients' logo choices, or their designers' suggestions. All of a sudden, interesting and radical designs are no longer the domain of niche brands and artsy projects, but a source of instant kudos for anyone in need of radical chic: multinationals like Unilever might opt for a friendly eco touch, new entrepreneurs add instant authenticity with a heraldic marker or two while street-style outlets flirt with a sober purism otherwise associated with insurance companies.

As trite as they might seem, these examples demonstrate two separate—and diametrically opposite—schools of thought: while some logo designers endeavor to enhance and underscore what a brand is all about, others prefer to conjure a new look out of thin air, a visual blueprint and template of what the brand would like to become—or how it would like to be perceived. With this in mind, it no longer makes sense to sort the rich pickings of contemporary logo highlights by goal or application.

/ INSTEAD, THIS PUBLICATION FOCUSES ON CAREFULLY CURATED CLUSTERS SORTED BY STYLE AND TECHNIQUE: WHAT YOU SEE IS WHAT YOU GET, FROM SIMPLE PICTOGRAMS TO ELABORATE CALLIGRAPHY.

Within these shifting tides of design—and among myriads of micro trends—we can detect several strong undercurrents in the overall logo landscape. Most notable of all, traditional image-text combinations, scalable, solid and easy to decipher, enjoy renewed popularity among mainstream firms and avant-garde outlets alike. A steady staple in our visually encoded lives, these often unobtrusive visual markers convey solidity, trustworthiness, and longevity. Tempered by lean times and uncertainty, these logos—and their creators—have grown up a bit, shedding excess flourishes and visual baby fat to provide a counterpoint to life's perceived volatility.

Preface

Nevertheless, there is more to these staples than meets the eye: honed by increased competition, they betray more ambition, craftsmanship, and perfection in every line, letter, and ligature than a first glance might convey.

/

ON THE FLIP SIDE, WE ALSO WITNESS A RETURN AND REGRESSION TO CHILDHOOD INNOCENCE, TO REASSURINGLY FAMILIAR AND NAÏVE DESIGNS THAT LOWER OUR DEFENSES AND PROVIDE A WELCOME COUNTERPOINT TO THE REALITY OF PRAGMATIC CUT-BACKS AND A FICKLE FUTURE. IN THE SAME VEIN, MANY DESIGNERS EXPLORE AND EXPLOIT OUR YEARNING FOR SOLIDITY AND AUTHENTICITY, FOR ALL THINGS "HUMAN" IN A TECHNOLOGY-BASED WORLD, WITH PHYSICAL DESIGNS AND DIY ENDEAVORS.

Although hardly suited to reproduction, the resulting logos celebrate their flaws and delight in mid-twentieth century Modernity with all its quirks, cozy optimism, and gentle color schemes. Appealing to discerning foodies and bespoke beauty addicts alike, the retro chic of silkscreen and letterpress aesthetics suggests a real treat behind the logo—a handmade blend of Sunday's Finest and a sheltered life, of patina-tinged pastel shades and a rose-tinted childhood when the world was in order. By referencing these labor-intensive printing techniques, designers insinuate a weight and history the actual brand might have some catching up to do.

Along similar lines, hand-drawn logos and illustrated letter forms indicate originality: forget Gutenberg— each letter deserves individual attention and its own idiosyncratic flaws and flavors to broadcast the brand's appreciation for kinks and quirks, for that all-important human touch.

/

AT THE SAME TIME, THIS PUBLICATION – AND THE LOGOSPHERE ITSELF – ALSO RECORDS A RISE IN REPETITIVE PATTERNS, IN VISUAL TRANSLATIONS OF NEURAL NETWORKS AND ARTIFICIAL INTELLIGENCE, TAMED FOR THE OCCASION BY APPROPRIATING THE TOOLS AND AESTHETICS OF SCIENTIFIC METHODS AND INFORMATION GRAPHICS.

The corresponding logos invariably start from a substrate of basic shapes or scripts and then evolve a life of their own. Here, Blondie's Parallel Lines might meet before they reach infinity to mingle, merge, or dissolve into patterns—and then resolve into a discernible mark. Treading the thin line between eye strain and eye candy, these predominantly monochrome creations hide visual codes in tiny disturbances, yet also cherish the safety of algorithms, the mathematical backbone of self-determined chaos where a tiny tweak of predetermined parameters can produce delightfully varied outcomes.

And this generative approach lends itself equally well to non-hierarchical logo families. No longer just an outlet for clear sub-brands or products, more and more logo sets explore the concept of aesthetic variations on a theme, without tying the resulting logo palette to specific-use scenarios. These controlled adaptations of predefined standards run the entire gamut of possible permutations. By daring us to spot the common heritage and family resemblance, the missing aesthetic link, they manage to convey a sense of diversity, openness and flexibility.

Against this background of contradictory developments, we certainly "live in the interesting times" once predicted by the well-known Chinese proverb (or curse). Far more than just a collection of landmark logos from the recent past, this revised volume of *Los Logos* has bucked the trend and gone up a size to give each design more room to breathe.

/

A CAREFULLY CURATED SELECTION OF KEY CREATIONS, IT TAKES US BEHIND THE SCENES OF LOGO DESIGN TO EXPLORE THESE PIVOTAL PROCESS AND CHOICES — WITH HAND-PICKED EXAMPLES, BACKGROUND STORIES, AND IN-DEPTH INTERVIEWS, FROM THE VERY FIRST STROKE TO THE FINAL RESULT. AND WHILE THE ECONOMIC CLIMATE MIGHT HAVE FORCED BOTH DESIGNERS AND CLIENTS TO TIGHTEN THEIR COLLECTIVE BELTS, IT HAS ALSO HELPED TO WEED OUT MANY CASES OF HALF-HEARTED TYPOGRAPHY OR UNINSPIRED PLAGIARISM, WHICH CAN ONLY BE A GOOD THING.

Now, with less money for aimless experimentation, each project and identity counts: we place higher demands on shelf-life and execution, but also the unique touches that will help a logo stand out from the crowd. And while some designers take the conservative route with solid, sober lifetime design, others opt for a liberated — and liberating — "no compromise or bust" attitude. After all, what do they have to lose?

So, look closely: the great pool of logo design is teeming with truly stellar examples of either approach.

Ch.01　Pictogram

01/ PICTOGRAM

METAPHORS /
ALL IMAGE /
SIGNS AND
SYMBOLS /
CHARACTERS /

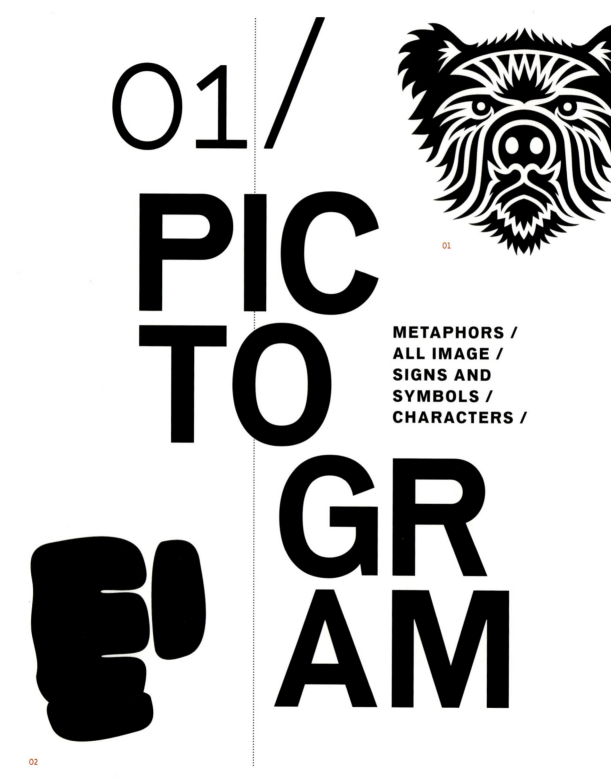

01

02

8

03

Who needs words? Like a perfect game of Pictionary, sketched with a minimum of strokes and even fewer colors (but subject to subsequent polish), a pictogram efficiently communicates the gist of a brand by focusing on what really counts. Boiled down to a central theme, the resulting logo communicates a key visual or idea in a universal language that has literally been around for ages.

Signs and symbols not only precede the written word, but count among the intangible aspects that make us human and unique. Our ability to abstract information and capture it in a durable medium, from naturalistic cave paintings to Egyptian hieroglyphics, allows us to express thoughts and instructions through globally recognized visual aids. From actual characters with character to abstract, unique placeholders, these pictograms reduce meaning to an expressive sign.

It is this abstraction, this mental translation from symbol to fully-fledged idea, to a nugget of information not necessarily mirrored faithfully in the image displayed, that has allowed us to trade across borders and to communicate with others over space and time. Whether monetary token or written script, the symbol is an effective means of exchanging wealth and information.

In logo design, the same principle applies. Brands wear their hearts on their sleeves or—in the case of this music icon for The Gopher Illustrated **p.11.01**—their instruments on their heads. The majority of pictogram-based identities are similarly uncomplicated and almost simplistic in their choice of imagery. We often encounter real depictions of what is on offer—keys and trees, coffee and cup, sun and cloud—occasionally supplemented by elements that anchor the visual testimony in space, point the way, show a path and direction, or emphasis the circle of life in a modern take on yin and yang. This design principle culminates in the ingenious simplicity of our recycling symbol: what goes around comes around.

Because of this blatant simplicity, the humble pictogram tends to be the most "useful" and versatile logo of them all. Easily scalable and variable, often monochrome or based on a minimum of colors, it transcends language and cultural barriers. This makes it especially popular with political parties and religious faiths—just think of the iconic shapes and bumper-sticker appeal of the Islamic crescent moon and Christian fish symbol.

01
xy arts

02
Acme Industries

03
Superlow/
Halvor Bodin

04
Masheen

Easily as evocative, yet infinitely more personal, are logos like Halvor Bodin's **03** broken heart tattoo, which is based on the name of a client's recently deceased mother, and Masheen's **04** graphic battle of the sexes, a logo set designed to illustrate a talk on gender issues by mixing, matching, and pitting the sexes against each other in personal encounters of the universally recognized male and female symbols.

In contrast to these overt and descriptive examples, some designers opt for true abstraction, creating pictogram logos without obvious allusions. A new vessel and visual blank slate, this type of logo is unique to every client—and gives them scope to fill it with life, content, and ideas of their own.

04

Ch.01   Pictogram   Characters

01 Nico Ammann

02 Bo Lundberg & Jan Cafourek

03 Power Graphixx

04 xy arts

05 Sabina Keric

06 Power Graphixx

07 A-Side Studio

08 Andrea Gustafson

09 Ken

10

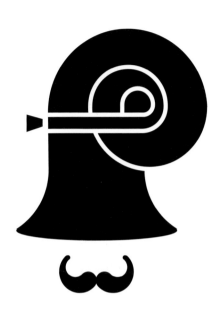
01 modo

02 EL MIRO

03 Fresh Estudio

04 Norwegian Ink

05 Sabina Keric

06 Analog.Systm

07 Edgar Bąk

Ch.01   Pictogram

01 Sawdust

02 atelier aquarium   03 Positron Co Ltd

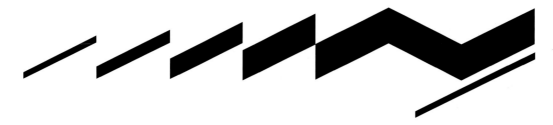

04 Taeko Isu

Pictogram   Ch. 01

01   John L. Nguyen

02   Ali Khorshidpour

03   DTM_INC

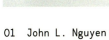

04   John L. Nguyen

05   xyz.ch

06   Jarek Kowalczyk

07   Chris Rubino

08   Ali Khorshidpour

09   THE SKULL DEZAIN

Ch.01   Pictogram

01 Jonathan Calugi   02 Mash   03 Mash

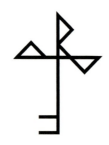

04 Denny Backhaus   05 Acme Industries   06 Edgar Bąk

07 Lifter Baron   08 Fons Hickmann m23   09 cerotreees

10 Acme Industries   11 xy arts   12 Young Jerks

01 Roy Smith

02 COUP

03 Core60

04 Lifter Baron

05 modo

06 xyz.ch

07 xy arts

08 backyard10

Ch.02   Picto/Text

02/ PIC TO /TE XT

**THE CLASSICS /
AMBIGRAMS /
DOPPELGANGER /**

01 SCOP®

02

03 CAPE ANN FARMERS' MARKET

16

04

In times of economic uncertainty, people often turn to what they know, to solid craftsmanship, conservative cuts, and lasting, reliable options—in furniture, finance, fashion, and more.

Along these lines, we are also witnessing the resurgence of a more sober and "dependable" approach to design. In the realm of logos and visual identities, the classic combination of image and text remains a popular fall-back option. A little more explanatory than most, it starts with a strong, solid anchoring visual that is followed by a clarifying phrase—the company's name or a descriptive term—just to be on the safe side.

01
Project 1000 / Stefan Szakal

02
Red Design

03
asmallpercent / Tim Ferguson Sauder

Artist and designer Ji Lee believes there is nothing wrong with this approach, as we should "never be afraid of the obvious." This is a lesson many designers have taken to heart. Here, the Bottletop Band [02] dabbles with a faithful Coca-Cola pastiche, while Mads Burcharth's [05] Codefish logo spells out the programming firm's name in nerd-compatible ASCII code. Stefan Szakal's [01] logo for the children and parents organization Scop ups the cheese factor with its literal take on having a heart for helping hands. So, while some of the most obvious picto/text transliterations might set our collective teeth on edge, they are also immediate, infectious, and effective.

Meanwhile, a wide variety of institutions—from museums and medical practitioners to book shops, political societies, and entire cities—opt for a more restrained, understated picto/text variant to convey a sense of trustworthiness and reliability. Slightly generic, and thus unassailable, these logos give us a combination we know and understand; a familiar staple in our visually encoded lives. Subtle, grounded, and very much subordinated to the client's needs, picto/text logos are therefore rarely designer ego trips and often demonstrate visual parallels.

04
Brusatto

05
Mads Burcharth

Take Tomasz Politański's [p.20] design for the Museum of Art in Lodz, and Geoffrey Brusatto's [04] logo for the Fashion Museum Hasselt—both turn a solid letter M into a monolithic, museum-like structure to create an instantly recognizable, yet edgy vessel for modern art.

05

At the same time, this style of logo also illustrates another phenomenon prevalent among picto/text designers: while serif fonts add a touch of class or allude to the finer things in life—think high-class restaurants, upmarket hotels, and exclusive consultancies—sans-serif typefaces tend to be associated with more contemporary and pragmatic applications. This division is most pronounced in arts and culture, where serifs signify the story told, historical museums, and traditional theaters, while sans-serif fonts reference modern art and contemporary productions.

06, 07
Scandinavian DesignLab

Nevertheless, even within this narrow framework there is plenty of room for clever use of space and imagery. Some designers, for example, escape the constraints of "image above, text below" to experiment with novel and appealing ways to integrate their client's salient characteristics into the logo. Angling for compliments and customers, Tim Ferguson's 03 logo for Cape Ann Farmers' Market is both refreshingly obvious and effective. Scandinavian DesignLab's 06, 07 logo for Danish supermarket chain Super Best gets the mix of simplicity and imagery just right.

Veering even further from the tried and tested, there is a small, but visible group of designers who love to subvert neo-con picto/text associations and mess with our design preconceptions. People in fringe brands and fashion-based industries are discovering the delicious dichotomy of pairing a deliberately plain or "harmless" identity with, say, an extreme-sports message.

06

So look closely. As always, the devil—and the skill—is in the detail!

07

01 designJune

02 Clusta

03 Hugh Frost

04 Jarek Kowalczyk

05 FEED

06 cypher13

07 Celeste Prevost

08 Creative Inc

Ch.02   Picto / Text

MUZEUM SZTUKI

01 Tomasz Politański

02 General Projects

03 Positron Co Ltd

04 Rasmus Snabb

05 Andreas Töpfer & Buchgut

06 La Cáscara Amarga

Picto/Text   Ch. 02

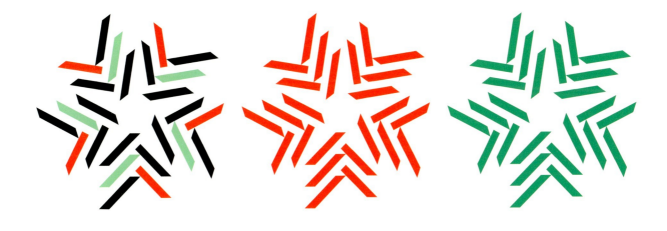

01 **JULIA HEITMANN**
Corporate design/key visual,
Youth Winter Olympic Games
Innsbruck 2012

Triumph at the Olympics, a celebration of sport and human achievement, is the pinnacle of any athlete's career. Hamburg-based designer Julia Heitmann, a former junior world champion rower, knows this from personal experience. Although she missed both Athens 2004 and Beijing 2008 by a hair's breadth, she never lost her love for the Games and for the spirit of endeavor, optimism, and good-natured competition.

For her final year design school project, she decided to create a logo for the upcoming first Youth Winter Olympics that will be taking place in Innsbruck in 2012. Her design pays homage to the Olympics' rich past and heady history, to Otl Aicher's iconic 1972 designs, and to Alpine sports and tourism posters from the 1930s.

Heitmann looked to the city's own color palette for inspiration—Austria's national red, the minty green of Innsbruck's river, a touch of aqua from the fresh mountain air and glacial ice, and the white of the snow that drives the competition. She matched this distinct color scheme with the characteristic spacing of an ice crystal and a shape inspired by the fast-growing spruce, a symbol of aspiration, dynamism and youthful exuberance.

Ch.02 Picto/Text

01 Federico Landini

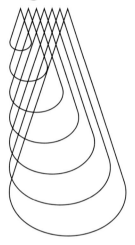

02 Grandpeople

03 Hype Type Studio

04 Struggle inc.

05 Toko

06 Matt W. Moore

07 Maniackers Design

08 Hey Ho

22

Picto/Text   Ch. 02

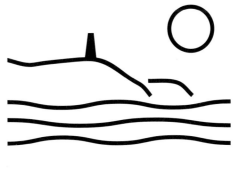

01 Alexander Spliid

02 A-Side Studio

03 The Action Designer

04 Inventaire

05 Janine Rewell

06 The Luxury of Protest

07 FEED

08 Revivify Graphic Design

01   büro uebele visuelle kommunikation

Picto/Text   Ch. 02

01   Joshua Distler

02   Ryan Crouchman

03   cypher13

04   Roy Smith

05   Gabe Ruane

06   Landor Associates

25

Ch.02 Picto/Text

01 **ONLAB**
City of Tramelan

How do you revive an entire community?

Situated in the Bernese Jura, Tramelan is a hub of the Swiss watchmaking industry. Although this tradition is still going strong, the community itself has been shrinking for the past 25 years.

In 2004, Tramelan's officials asked design studio onlab—founder Nicolas Bourquin grew up in the municipality—to join a commission that would investigate Tramelan's future identity and development opportunities.

The resulting report delivered an analysis of the city's (infra)structural, political, economic, social, and cultural situation, its local, regional, and national image, as well as its self-perception.

As part of the resulting extensive restructuring measures, onlab then developed a new visual identity and communications strategy for Tramelan—a fresh new look that conveys the tradition and essence of this Swiss community.

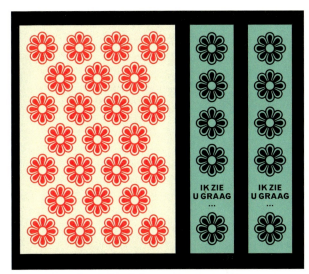

01 Rob van Hoesel

02 Lundgren+Lindqvist

03 Floor Wesseling

Ch.02   Picto/Text

01   Jaime Narváez

02   ehquestionmark

03   Device

04   Fabio Santoro

05   Axel Raidt

06   Reaktor Lab

07   Strohl

08   Joshua Distler

09   Hexanine

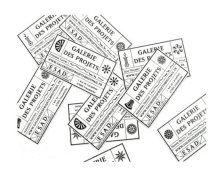
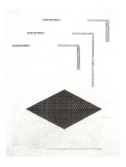

01 Avalanche

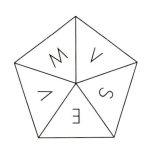

02 SWSP Design   03 Vänskap   04 No-Domain

Ch.02   Picto/Text

01   Mutabor

02   Mutabor

03   Mutabor

04   Mutabor

05   Mutabor

06   Mutabor

07   General Projects

08   Mutabor

09   Mutabor

10   Mutabor

11   Cassie Leedham

01 SWSP Design

02 SWSP Design

03 Benoît Bodhuin

04 TU SAIS QUI™

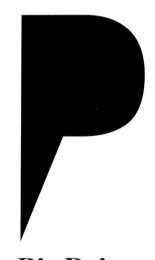

05 Markus Moström

06 Trademark™

07 Jarrik Muller

08 Patrik Ferrarelli

09 Company

Ch.02   Picto / Text

03   asmallpercent

01   Maximilian Baud & Uwe Strasser   02   Landor Associates   04   Bestial Design® Studio

05   asmallpercent   06   INDASTRIACOOLHIDEA   07   Breckon Gráfica

08   EL MIRO   09   Lundgren+Lindqvist   10   Out Of Order

Picto/Text   Ch. 02

02 Alen 'Type08' Pavlovic

01 Ekaterina Tiouleikina

03 Strukt

04 asmallpercent

05 Giorgio Paolinelli

06 asmallpercent

07 Eddie Brown

08 asmallpercent

09 Moxie Sozo

33

Ch.02 Picto/Text

02 Moxie Sozo

03 Core60

01 Graphical House

04 REX

05 Revivify Graphic Design

06 Revivify Graphic Design

07 Revivify Graphic Design

08 Staynice

09 Core60

10 Büro Destruct

11 EMPK

Picto/Text   Ch. 02

01   Brand New History™

02   Moxie Sozo

03   Stefan Romanu

04   EMPK

05   Company

06   Copenheroes

07   Graphical House

08   The Action Designer

09   Staynice

10   Matt W. Moore

11   HoohaaDesign

35

Ch.02   Picto/Text

01   Image Now

02   Matteo Mastronardi

03   Di-Da Komunikakzioa

04   Dimomedia Lab

05   Super Top Secret

06   Di-Da Komunikakzioa

07   nocturn.ro

08   nocturn.ro

09   hintzegruppen

10   Martin Holm

11   strange//attraktor:

Picto/Text   Ch. 02

01 Benjamin Metz

02 Core60   03 X3 Studios

04 Edhv   05 Edhv   06 Company

07 FriendsWithYou   08 Andy Mangold   09 Extraverage

Ch.02   Picto/Text

01 Boldº

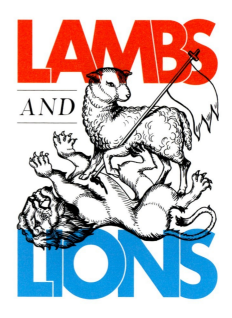
02 Sister Arrow & Hugh Frost

03 The KDU

04 Moxie Sozo

05 V15

06 Büro4

07 Edgar Bąk

08 hintzegruppen

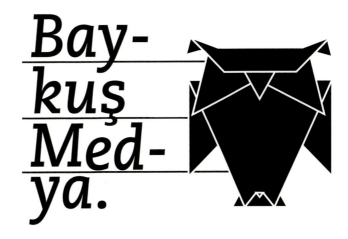

01 Eduardo Vidales

02 Savas Ozay

03 Ian Lynam Design

04 Fieldtrip

05 ehquestionmark

06 Bionic Systems

07 Scandinavian DesignLab

08 Bionic Systems

Ch.02　Picto/Text

01　techvector

02　Pierre Jeanneret

03　Mitchell Paone

04　Graphical House

05　HelloComputer

06　Revivify Graphic Design

Picto/Text   Ch. 02

01 e-Types

02 SWSP Design   03 Mutabor

04 Josiah Jost   05 Face.

06 Bleed   07 Mutabor

Ch.02   Picto/Text

zielo
nypomi
dor

01   Edgar Bąk

*modi
summer*

02   SUNDAY VISION

03   Tomasz Politański

 STATENS
KUNSTRÅD
DANISH ARTS COUNCIL

04   e-Types

ROONEY'S
BOUTIQUE HOTEL

05   Monoblock

06   Deanne Cheuk

NORDEA
FONDEN

07   e-Types

08   The KDU

42

01　Red Design

02　superbüro

03　Coutworks

04　Skin Designstudio

05　Inventaire

06　Inventaire

07　Peter Gregson

08　asmallpercent & Return Design

Ch.02 Picto / Text					Doppelganger

01   Joseph Garner

02   Eddie Brown

03   Revivify Graphic Design

04   Peter Schmidt Group

05   Alessandro Mingione

06   Alphabet Arm Design

07   Revivify Graphic Design

08   Rokac

09   Alen 'Type08' Pavlovic

10   Toko

11   Coley Porter Bell

12   Felix Lobelius

44

01 Felix Sockwell

02 Revivify Graphic Design

03 Floris Voorveld

04 Revivify Graphic Design

05 Roy Smith

06 Ptarmak, Inc.

07 Acme Industries

08 Project 1000

JOHN LANGDON

USA

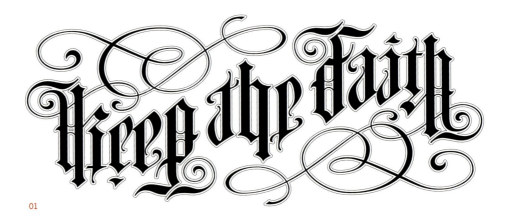

01

US artist and designer John Langdon loves to play with words—and then some. Best-known for his pioneering ambigrams, i.e. words that can be read equally well from more than one point of view, he takes an almost architectural approach to letters in order to charge them with new meaning and a fresh perspective.

—

Your designs suggest not just a love of letters, but of words and language in general. Exploring the hidden subtext, there are many references to mysteries, code-breaking, puzzles, and tricks of the mind—reflected in your collaborations with major feature films like Angels and Demons **or** The Da Vinci Code**…**

I graduated from college with a degree in English and a particular interest in words. I love the historical aspects of language: how words originated and why we use them in the way we do.

At the same time, I love ambiguity. The idea that things can be interpreted—with validity—from more than one (person's) point of view is of great importance in human relationships and it also intrigues me intellectually. My interest in ambiguity and optical illusions seems to make my work appropriate to accompany stories like the ones by Dan Brown. His protagonist, Robert Langdon, is a bit like me in several ways: he is not only a symbologist (while I design symbols), but also very good with language. He can do anagrams in his head!

—

You have been crafting ambigrams for more than 30 years. Did you actually invent this particular type of letter-based trickery?

Yes and no. Ambigrams had been created at least several times before I began doing them. I had seen Raymond Loewy's New Man logo and Richard Hess' Vista logo—both beautifully designed, rotationally symmetrical logos. And they certainly influenced me. But they required almost no manipulation. The words as set in normal typography would be close to being ambigrams.

It was Herb Lubalin and Tom Carnase's invertible 72 logo that made me realize how much could be done with really careful and sensitive drawing. I was already trying to create Escher-like illusions with words when I first saw those logos, and I was under the spell of the yin/yang symbol (and still am). Others who had created ambigrams in the past had done so for a particular purpose. I began doing them as an ongoing artistic expression. And a few years later, I discovered that Scott Kim had also "invented" ambigrams at around the same time that I had.

—

You seem to explore a wide range of different typographical styles and typefaces in your ambigrams—are there any notable preferences or limitations? Which fonts work especially well—and why?

The secret of a high-quality, readable, beautiful ambigram: I never pre-determine the style. The structure and shape of every letter is determined by the manipulations required to make it work in two directions. Once I have the skeletal forms in place for the whole word, then I develop the stylistic details for those forms. I try to invest the ambigram with details that will unify all the differing approaches to the shapes of the letters. I want to disguise, as much as possible, how much I have twisted the letters into cooperating with my goal to create an ambigram.

The letter D has probably caused me more problems in ambigram creation than any other. A lowercase D makes a very nice inverted P,

02

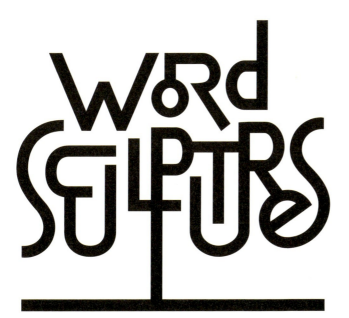

03

and that's about it. For the most part, even when I have used a letter-to-letter solution many times—a lowercase A/lowercase E, for instance—the fact that it is appearing in a different word, surrounded by different letters, means that I have to re-imagine it anew. That's one of the aspects of ambigram design that keeps it fresh and challenging. The most fun comes when the solutions are not one-to-one, letter-to-letter inversions, but when solutions depend on using more than one letter, or parts of more than one letter, to create a single letter in the other direction.

However, there is the intriguing fact that when any other approach falls short of creating a successful ambigram, Gothic Blackletter may do the trick. Its look is familiar enough to most Western readers, yet it naturally has many quirks that are no longer used in conventional typography. Very few readers are familiar with the details of that style. That combination of familiarity and unfamiliarity gives the ambigram designer a lot of freedom to manipulate letters in unorthodox ways.

—

In logo design, do these typefaces reflect the client in some way?

In logo design, every decision should be made to represent the nature of the client. In my opinion, ambigrams are not an ideal approach to a logo, because they cannot be crafted to suit any particular situation. I try to explain to people that the style of an ambigram can't be imposed on the design and most people are pretty understanding. But much of the time, when it comes down to stylistic details, I can nudge the style to make it a little bit more elegant or casual or aggressive or delicate—abstract feelings can be expressed in subtle ways.

—

So, what is the first thing you do when someone asks you to design a logo or ambigram?

I play. I write the word in pencil in as many different ways as I can imagine it. I sketch every pictorial and symbolic image that the name or word brings to mind. I look for similarities among different elements. I look for exploitable ambiguities. Random, non-goal-oriented play is a great way to make discoveries. It is highly effective.

04

05

06

07

At what point does a design stop being legible and trip over into the realm of conceptual exercise? And how do you make sure that you stay on the "right" side of this precarious balance?

Legibility is super-important to me, but I probably fall short of that goal on occasion. I seek and need the spontaneous response of an unsuspecting reader (usually my wife). For me, if an ambigram is not readable, it is a failure. If an observer cannot read it, it doesn't even really qualify as a word. And if it isn't a word, how can it be an ambigram?

Take the *Action Africa* [06] ambigram, for example. It has a high level of readability despite the manipulations. Or the *Cryptic* [07] logo, an absolute favorite of mine. I think the balance between the pictorial image and the readable word is almost perfect. I love the *Lovekraft* [05] ambigram for the intricacy and the beauty of the letterforms and the deviousness of the problem solving.

One of the ways I keep my success rate this high is by refusing to do bad ambigrams. I would rather sacrifice a commission than create something that is unattractive or unreadable.

08

09

Ambigrams Picto/Text Ch. 02

01 903 Creative

02 Hayes Image

03 Tim Bjørn

04 EL MIRO

05 EL MIRO

06 Alessandro Mingione

07 BANK™

08 Joseph Garner

09 Hugo Mulder

10 NALINDESIGN™

11 Inventaire

12 Rokac

Ch.02 Picto/Text

01 Regina

02 Red Design

03 Jesse Kirsch

04 Bestial Design® Studio

05 REX

06 Huschang Pourian

07 FriendsWithYou

08 A-Side Studio

09 Taeko Isu

10 Robi Jõeleht

11 urbn; interaction

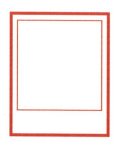
12 adam gf

01 e-Types

02 Dongwoo Kim

03 e-Types

04 Stefan Romanu

05 Projekttriangle Design Studio

06 Kokoro & Moi

07 Toko

08 Graphical House

Ch.02 Picto/Text

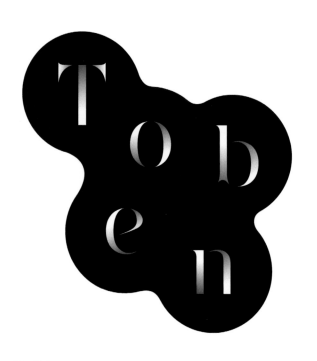

01 Toben

02 Jaime Narváez

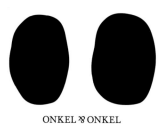

03 Typejockeys

04 Tobias Röttger

05 GVA Studio

06 HelloMe

07 max-o-matic

08 Jürgen Frost

Picto / Text Ch. 02

01 one8one7
02 FriendsWithYou
03 FriendsWithYou

04 Ken Tanabe
05 Form+Format

06 Pop Ovidiu Sebastian
07 Derek A. Friday
08 one8one7

09 Transfer Studio
10 Transfer Studio
11 Creative Inc

53

Ch.02 Picto/Text

01 Benoît Bodhuin

02 Felix Sockwell

03 KesselsKramer

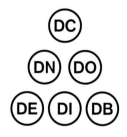

04 Chris Rubino

05 Autobahn

06 Brusatto

07 hintzegruppen

08 Patrik Ferrarelli

09 Gabe Ruane

54

Picto/Text   Ch. 02

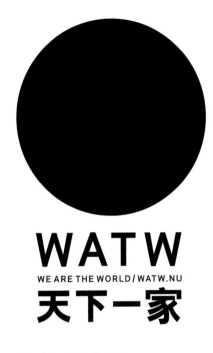
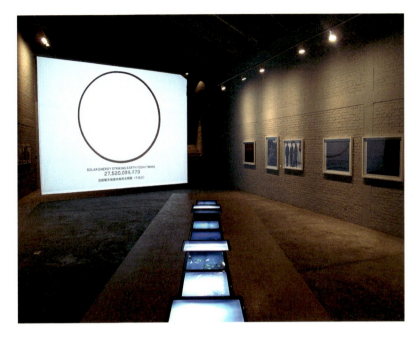

01   Kummer & Herrman

02   André Beato   03   UNIT   04   Áron Jancsó

05   The Pressure   06   General Projects   07   FriendsWithYou

Ch.02 Picto/Text

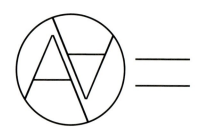  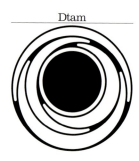

01 Positron Co Ltd   02 gebrauchsgrafikundso   03 Dtam—TM

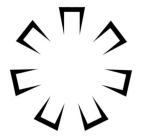  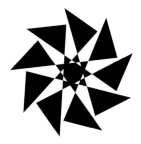

04 vonSüden   05 Ali Khorshidpour   06 Eduardo Vidales

07 R. Vancampenhoudt & Make Agency   08 FEED   09 Autobahn

10 EBSL   11 phospho   12 ilovedust

01 Floor 5

02 Büro Destruct

03 Aldo Lugo

04 Fons Hickmann m23

05 Floor 5

06 Mr. Kone

07 Kelly D. Williams

08 Taeko Isu

Ch.02   Picto/Text   KMS TEAM

KMS TEAM

Munich/Germany

Pages 58–61

A respected heavyweight in the German brand-strategy and communication landscape, Munich-based KMS TEAM focuses on the bigger picture.
The company, whose clients range from Porsche to Vodafone, prefers to develop combined brand and communications strategies—where the logo becomes just one aspect of a mark's overall corporate identity and appeal.

—
What are the ground rules of logo design?

Never copy or imitate. A logo is the main signifier for an entire company or brand, and summarizes its identity in one strong symbol. So first of all—and most importantly—logo design requires a strong sense of empathy to really grasp the essence of a company or brand. The designer has to ask questions and understand the replies, otherwise the result will appear arbitrary and anemic.
To this end, it is vital that the design distils the brand's central premise and has an emotional impact. It has to work instantly.

01

02

03

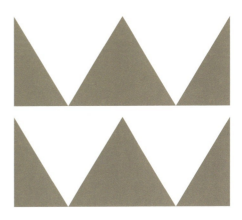

04

05

06

07

During the actual design process, there are several questions that apply to any client or visual identity. Is the design unique and recognizable? Does it work across all media and applications? Is the design system flexible and scalable? Is the design appropriate for all relevant markets?

But none of this matters if you don't invest enough energy into the actual execution. Unfortunately, many good ideas fail due to shoddy craftsmanship.

—
So is the logo just part of a greater package?

At KMS our work rarely starts with the logo. Most of the time our clients sense that their brand isn't optimally positioned. When a fundamental change of strategy is required, updating the logo becomes part of the overall repositioning effort. We always aim for a holistic approach—any corporate design needs to be in line with the company's strategy and overall corporate identity.

08

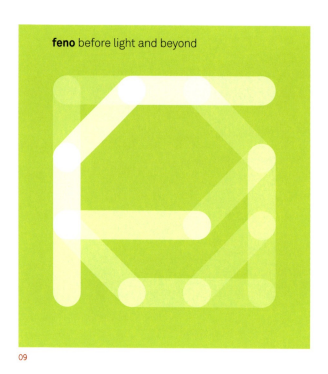
09

10

—
Against this background, could you pick a few examples of KMS logos that work especially well?

Klöpferholz:[13] The clarity of the logo—the letter "K" fashioned from wooden planks—is immediate, catchy, and reflects the client's core business.

Canyon:[02] A radical logo that made its mark in the competitive and fashion-oriented cycling market, despite going against the trend. Still a leader in its field.

Stiftung Warentest (Independent German product-testing organization): A brand derived from T for test and 1 for the best possible ranking. Superimposed, the two elements merge into an iconic symbol that graces millions of tested products and has instant recognition value.

—
Do you ever run into trouble convincing your clients of these ideas?

New design approaches unsettle people, as humans tend to prefer what they know and avoid the unknown. This is a universal fact, so we favor a subtle and sensitive approach—otherwise the desired revolution could quickly become a cautious evolution.

A good example would be the above-mentioned logo for the bicycle manufacturer Canyon. Initially, the owner found our proposal too radical and progressive, while industrial designers considered it too conservative and traditional. Faced with this situation, it was vital that the owner found the courage to simply follow his gut feeling. Over the last few years, Canyon has become Germany's favorite cycling brand—and the brand design played a major part in that.

—
What about the logo lifecycle—does it differ from client to client?

A long-term business model tends to go hand in hand with a lasting logo design. Industries governed by trends, on the other hand, require relatively frequent adjustments to the brand appearance.

11

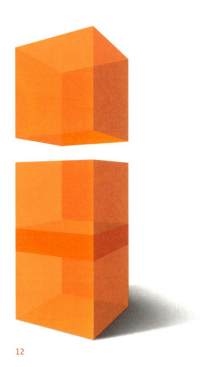

12

Media, technology, and software companies tend to be very dynamic, while the brand identities of banks, insurance companies, and nations enjoy a markedly longer "shelf-life."

Ideally, the brand itself will start a trend—instead of pandering to an existing one. As part of a brand's continual life we pay very close attention to any changes in the market, in society, and to the brand itself.

—

With this in mind, what is the average shelf-life of a logo?

A good logo will last forever. Nevertheless, significant changes in strategy need to go hand in hand with a commensurate logo refresh to communicate this process to the outside world.

As a rule of thumb, a logo should be reviewed and, if necessary, updated every 10 years or so.

13

14

03 / ZNÄK.

MONOGRAMS /
HEAVY METAL /
SPACIAL /
LABYRINTH /

01

LOVE OF LETTERS

(SANS) SERIF /
TYPOGRAPHIC /
ULTRA THINS /

Grip:

02

It is one of the oldest tricks in the book: spell out your name... with plenty of style.

The fall-back option for traditional corporations, institutions and broadcasters faced with financial volatility and a fickle future, type logos suggest a certain solidity, and double as a visual hope and anchor in uncertain times. Through the ages and over the ups and downs of the economic cycle, they have permeated absolutely every realm of the visual world—and they allow full-blooded typographers to come into their own.

In type logos, simple monogram designs pave the way for more elaborate solutions. Sans-serif variants emphasize solidity and forgo extravagance for pared-down beauty and perfection, while their embellished cousins, serif typefaces, epitomize understated elegance, yet also a subtle sense of fashion. With a strong nod to *Vogue*'s iconic logo, for example, Acme Industries ⁰¹ gave Bucharest lifestyle magazine *Zvak* this season's classy look.

03

Other designers try our optical nerves with more radical shapes and juxtapositions. Testing the limits of just how far their beloved letters can be twisted and tweaked, they sculpt experimental logos that verge on the cryptic. Strictly speaking, these visual identities are designs for designers, so we must interact with them further if we want to decipher the message. Company's ⁰³ logo for Live at your Local, for example, is a visual identity for an entertainment guide covering London's Islington and Hackney neighborhoods. Building on the notion of local community, the logo represents a series of interconnecting streets and offers plenty of scope for interesting excursions.

Nowhere are the limits to originality more apparent than in the realm of type-only logos. While every designer will invariably tell you they are aiming for something unique, timeless, and lasting, the latest slew of fashion fonts reveal just how trend-based this most basic and versatile of approaches has become.
This is most apparent in fashion, magazine, and music design, i.e. industries governed by trends themselves. Here, what comes around, goes around: just like shoulder pads or bell bottoms, type design is very much rooted in a certain stylistic movement, decade, or genre and highlights the cyclical nature of hype and fashion in our lives.

Take ATTAK's ⁰⁵ logo for Iron Maiden tribute band Up The Irons: faithful, yet updated, it is symptomatic of a much broader flock of designers who are reviving heavy metal fonts or their minimalist cousins from the New Wave movement. Edgy, angular, and masculine, they exude power, a touch of aggression, and provide a visual antithesis to all those happy, inoffensive bubble fonts.

01
Acme Industries

02
Heydays

03
Company

04
Daniel Carlsten

Oscar Properties
04

Yet while there is invariably a dash of irony and postmodern knowledge at play in appropriation, this particular rediscovery already feels a little bit contrived.

The progression, procession, and post-ironic resurrection of terminally unhip heavy metal fonts, hiphop styles, and New Wave references, right up to the current batch of part-time calligraphers, mirrors the changing trends in body adornments and tattoos. Whatever you wear on your skin or (record) sleeve firmly anchors you in a decade or genre.

05

05
ATTAK

06
Otto Dietrich

Next in line on the fashion front are super-fragile, ultra-thin, spindly shapes that cut to the quick and leave nothing but the bare bones of the letter. Right now, plenty of skeletal fonts are stretching their skinny lines across record covers, editorials, and topical products. Stripped of all superfluous markers, razor-skinny to the point of typographic anorexia, they require super-sizing to work at all. At first glance this might seem paradoxical—after all, visual identities should be scalable to work at any size—yet in their rejection of established logo conventions, they literally force us to take a closer look, and invariably claim plenty of space on the page. More minimalist illustration and marker than lettering, Otto Dietrich's 06 design for Galerie Desaga, for example, dispenses with any extraneous weight to transport an ethereal lightness, a slightly aloof out-of-this-world allusion that perfectly distils this ultra-thin trend.

Thus limited in their application, slender typefaces make ideal companions for editorial experiments, special editions, and intermittent identities. In these contexts, changing (type)faces is de rigueur and the cyclical nature of publications makes it easy enough to go with the times. That said, lasting brands would be ill-advised to opt for this latest logo flirtation: nothing looks as dated as yesterday's trend.

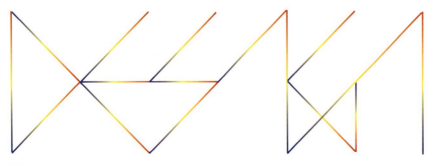

06

Love of Letters Ch. 03

01 **JAN EN RANDOALD**
    Kunsten Festival

Belgian design duo Jan en Randoald like to explore the ramifications of complex interactions, combinations, and repetitions.

This concept is exemplified in their logo design for the Kunstenfestivaldesarts, a Brussels-based event showcasing a wide range of different artistic endeavors. In order to reflect the variety of the festival program, Jan en Randoald created a visual identity that also branches out into various disciplines. It provides a formal decision tree and navigational superstructure that adds information with each repetition.

A clean-cut guide through a plethora of tempting exhibits and performances, this modular logo can be adjusted for each application (brochures, posters, website) and leads visitors through the fragmented world of art, from theatre and installations to readings, lectures, film, dance, and musicals.

Ch.03 Love of Letters

01 Fabian Bertschinger

02 Kokoro & Moi

03 LLdesign

04 Esther Rieser

05 TU SAIS QUI™

06 Akatre

01 BALDINGER·VU-HUU
École Estienne Paris

There are two sides to every story and many facets to education. With their logo and visual identity for École Estienne, a design school in Paris, Toan Vu-Huu and André Baldinger created a visible link between tradition and modernity, and a striking red line to tie the school's disciplines together.

The humble line has come a long way: as part of the design school's new identity, it traverses page borders and boundaries, yet always picks up where it leaves off, mirroring the lifelong continuation of education itself.

This principle also translates to the physical space of the old campus that is now a modern temple of education. Around the school, the logo boldly indicates the way from A to B or, in this case, from e(ntrance) to É(cole).

Ch.03 Love of Letters

Graphic Design Festival Breda

01 Rob van Hoesel

Erik Wåhlström / Fotograf

02 Martin Nicolausson

IL PARADISO DEI_CALZINI

03 LLdesign

C A
A •
—
CONTEMPORARY ART ARCHIPELAGO

04 Studio EMMI

Cie Greffe / Cindy Van Acker

05 Akatre

SVMMA SVMMARVM =

06 HelloMe

FUNDACJA
SZTUKWI
ZUAL
NYC
H

07 Edgar Bąk

DE QUEESTE
THEATERMAKERSHUIS

08 Brusatto

01 Autobahn

02 NODE Berlin Oslo

03 Matt W. Moore

04 Heydays

06 JUTOJO

05 Guillaume Peitrequin

07 Théo Gennitsakis

08 Floor 5

09 Yucca Studio

Ch.03   Love of Letters

01   Lorenzo Geiger

02   Frank Rocholl

03   Team Manila

04   e-Types

05   Emmanuel Rey

06   T. Gennitsakis & N. Rouyer

07   Bas van Vuurde

08   Form+Format

09   e-Types

Love of Letters   Ch. 03

01   Urbanskiworkshop

02   Lorenzo Geiger

03   Acme Industries

04   Emmanuel Rey

05   Avantbras

06   Dtam—TM

07   Mitchell Paone

08   Out Of Order

09   Annika Kaltenthaler

10   W://THEM

11   Dorota Wojcik

12   Irving & Co

71

Ch.03   Love of Letters

KAREN BY SIMONSEN

01 Scandinavian DesignLab

SATELLITE

02 FEED

COLLECTIF JEUNE CINEMA

03 Akatre

I Love Your Work

04 Raf Vancampenhoudt

THE BONSAI PROJECT

05 Rob van Hoesel

INDUSTRIAL EVOLUTION

06 Raf Vancampenhoudt

YURPS

07 De Jongens Ronner

CCSI SOS RACISME

08 Filippo Nugara

NYC

09 Wolff Olins

10 dancemade

 MIKKEL KESSLER THE VIKING WARRIOR

11 Mads Jakob Poulsen

72

Love of Letters Ch. 03

01 Identity

02 3deluxe

03 Edhv

04 Urbanskiworkshop

05 elRAiSE

06 GVA Studio

Ch.03   Love of Letters

voll

01   Huschang Pourian

Nederlands
Uitvaart Museum **tot zover**

02   KesselsKramer

TERROIR

03   Toko

kolle**kt**iv tokio

04   Gunnar Bauer

Smiley:Days

05   Mads Jakob Poulsen

06   Herr Metag

07   Bram Nijssen

kino.dk

08   e-Types

WILLAU™

09   eps51

Artwork.

10   Face.

01 adam gf

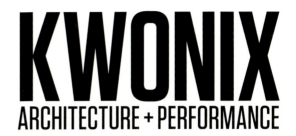

02 Ken Tanabe

03 Form+Format

04 General Projects

05 Landor Tokyo

06 COUP

07 Hörður Lárusson

08 Lifter Baron

09 Ji Lee

10 Base

Ch.03 Love of Letters

01 **LANDOR ASSOCIATES**
   Hertz

Rule no. 1: Don't mess with something that already works!

Paris-based brand consultancy Landor Associates knows how to preserve, cherish, and polish the essence of a brand. Its logo facelift for rental car specialists Hertz is a prime example of how to get it right and translate a mark to the new millennium without sacrificing any of its heritage or value.

Some careful, succinct polishing and a few subtle tweaks have ensured that the new logo retains its distinct black-and-yellow color scheme and italics, while gaining a modern, more rounded typeface to highlight the brand's progress and approachable nature.

02 Manifiesto Futura

03 Denny Backhaus

04 Markus Moström

05 e-Types

06 Lorenzo Geiger

07 Patrik Ferrarelli

76

Love of Letters   Ch. 03

01 Atelier télescopique

02 vonSüden   03 KismanVerhaak   04 Di-Da Komunikakzioa

05 Rob van Hoesel   06 Benjamin Metz   07 Base

GAVILLET & RUST

Geneva / Switzerland

Pages 78–80

Geneva-based graphic design studio Gavillet & Rust has become synonymous with uncluttered elegance, sometimes in the most unlikely of places.
With an incredibly diverse range of projects—editorial design for the Centre Pompidou in Paris, art direction for Marc Newson's watch label, and Hedi Slimane's Rock Diary, to name but a few—the team's logo and design work stretches from understated graphic bling to the simplest of character combinations.
Yet despite the contrasts, their love of letters and well-crafted typography always shines through—and finds a welcome outlet in Optimo, the studio's own digital type foundry.

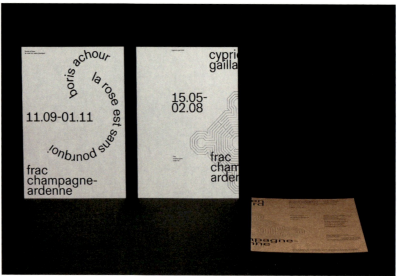
01

frac champagne- ardenne
02

03

You are well known for your type and book design—how important are logos in this context?

There are many parallels between the logo and typeface design process: just like a logo, a typeface should express an idea in a very concise and precise way. And our practical experience in editorial design with JRP|Ringier, whether text series or monographs, has taught us that book design also requires clearly defined typologies and codes that are not a million miles away from the creative process that governs a visual identity.

In this sense, we do not consider these categories separate fields of design—on the contrary, they are very much complementary. Obviously, being able to design a typeface helps us to draw more precisely and it also allows us to think of the logo as part of a more complex visual set.

In our work for SAKS [04] for example, we started out with some simple custom lettering that we later developed into a full-blown typeface to provide a more consistent and complete visual identity.

How did your collaboration with Jay-Z [05] come about? At first glance, you seem to have very different aesthetic styles.

This might surprise some, but Jay-Z has a strong interest in contemporary art, a field we have been active in for a while now, and we were introduced by the person who advises him on this matter.

The challenge was to design a logo that would bridge the gap between Jay-Z's extensive hip-hop background and his new company, Roc Nation, which aims to look beyond the boundaries of hip-hop and embrace other musical styles.

Our design picks up on his seminal visual signature, the diamond-shaped hand sign, to make the result more of a cultural icon than a straightforward company logo.

We aimed for a raw and robust design that would work on many future applications, from record covers to merchandising.

04

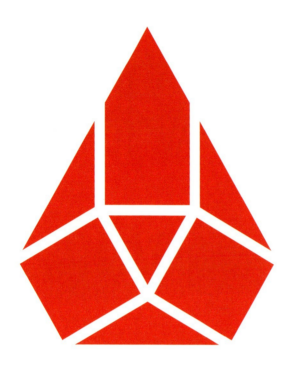

05

Was there anything unusual about this particular project?

All decisions were made by Jay-Z himself, no one else. That's rare for a company of this caliber—and good for us. When there is only one person making the decisions, you don't have to make compromises and it results in a very successful design process.

We had been fans of Jay-Z since his first album, so it was definitely great to be in the studio just after we had designed the logo and to hear him rap, "This is Roc Nation, pledge your allegiance!"

Could you single out another logo that works particularly well?

Well, all of them work in different ways, but we are very happy with the development of our visual identity for Frac Champagne-Ardenne [01–02], a center for contemporary art. The logo is based on a single typeface, which was designed by François Rappo.

Strictly typographic and black & white, it communicates the program in a very simple but disruptive way and this was something that the Frac public, both locally and internationally, recognized and accepted immediately.

And what about all-time favorites in the world at large?

To pick just one from a long list of favorites: the recycling symbol, designed by Gary Anderson in 1970. This public-domain graphic sign is well known around the world and continues to have many interesting reincarnations, like in the beautiful artworks by Kelley Walker.

On a different note, we are fascinated by transport information systems, so we would welcome the challenge to create a visual identity in this field. We could start with Geneva International Airport, which has what might be the worst airport logo in the world!

Love of Letters   Ch. 03

01 Wiyumi

02 Benoît Bodhuin

03 ASYL

04 TU SAIS QUI™

05 Guillaume Peitrequin

06 Kokoro & Moi

07 Jan en Randoald

08 Koehorst in 't Veld

09 The Action Designer

10 Koehorst in 't Veld

81

AKATRE

Paris/France

Pages
66, 68, 72,
82–85, 196

There is no standard Akatre style: the Paris-based art and design collective dabbles in a huge variety of media, from graphic design and photography to performance art.

Well-known for their carefully crafted typefaces and inventive installations, the three designers behind Akatre produce work that is invariably simple, stark, effective, and invested with plenty of attention to detail. This meticulous, yet light-hearted approach becomes especially apparent in the studio's logo and visual identity work: polished yet conceptual, Akatre logos are never just smooth and pretty; they always feature a distinctive twist, a hook to reel us in.

Édition 08

01

02

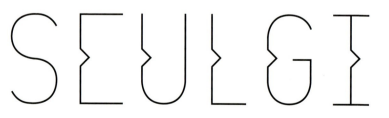 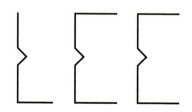

03

FUN
-
FE
STI
VAL

04

MOOD
ÉDITION
09

06

-TU
NAN
TES

05

—
Let's start with an easy one. What is your all-time favorite logo?

One of the best we have ever seen is the logo of the Centre Pompidou in Paris, which was designed by Jean Widmer. He played with the building's overall architecture and came up with a striking abstract shape that can be filled with meaning to express a lot of different things.

—
In more general terms, what makes a logo attractive to you?

To us, a logo should always strive to be the simplest possible symbol that defines a brand and enhances its recognition factor. In this spirit, we recommend sticking to just one color and aiming for an attractive composition. On the other hand, we are not huge fans of 3D logos (e.g. with drop shadows), especially when it comes to adaptation for the web.

—
So what do you look for when you are commissioned to design a logo or visual identity?

A logo arises from a melting pot of emotions and information. The trick is to create a graphic realm—a universe of sorts—that reflects the brand or project in a meaningful way. In order to get there, questions are all-important. During meetings we ask a lot to figure out the best way to communicate what our client is all about, to identify a specific detail that would define the brand in the best possible way, or to highlight a unique and interesting visual aspect.

07

What about the typefaces used in your logo design? Are they always your own?

Generally speaking, we prefer typograms to logotype, as we tend to craft our own typefaces from scratch with a logo in mind. A regular logo makes more sense for a commercial, well-known brand.

So is there a difference between creating visual identities for commercial clients and for those from the realm of art and culture?

When we tackle a project, we try not to distinguish between "commercial" clients and art or cultural assignments—this seems to be the best way to arrive at a beautiful result!

We also like to do the groundwork in advance—a lot of work goes into all our proposals. At the end of the day, this is still the best possible way to win your client's trust, no matter what their background.

How do you stop a logo from going stale? Does it need to be refreshed every year or so?

The simpler the signage, the more timeless the outcome. We don't usually create logos in isolation, but always propose a general underlying concept for every visual identity. Based on this concept, the overall look and logo can be re-evaluated, changed, and allowed to evolve over time. For example, a company might change its logo when a new partner joins the firm, or in times of economic hardship. In most cases, the logo is supposed to be something that lasts for a long time.

It doesn't really make a lot of sense to change it frequently, say, every year or so, as the logo is the face of the brand. It takes people time

LOUISE
08

09

10

to understand what the brand is all about and to really appreciate it. This means that a logo that doesn't change (like Apple or Nike) tends to get more recognition and has the chance to become iconic. Such a logo can even replace other means of communication.

Keeping the logo and its typography constant gives us leeway to adapt it for layouts, poster concepts, photography, etc. This way, we safeguard a coherent identity while always being a little bit different.

—
Finally, is there any particular client or project you would love to design a visual identity for?

There is still so much we'd like to do. We would love to do work for a museum, for stores, for other galleries, for theaters, and for movie posters. A music label (think covers and clips) would be great and, while we're at it, why not work for another magazine about art, design, or music? We already did it for *Mood*[01] magazine, but it would be great to make this a regular stint and to create the look and logo of a great magazine every month.

11

Ch.03   Love of Letters

01   John Beckers

02   Chragokyberneticks

03   Tobias Röttger

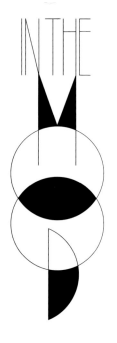

04   Faith

05   Designers United

06   Axel Peemöller

07   OPX

08   Siggeir Hafsteinsson

Love of Letters Ch. 03

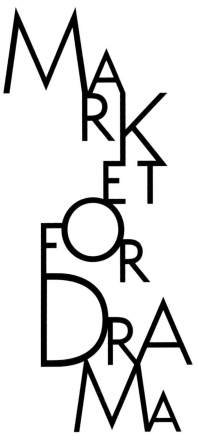

01 Grandpeople

02 Axel Peemöller

03 Grandpeople

04 Aldo Lugo

05 Axel Peemöller

Ch.03 Love of Letters

01 La Cáscara Amarga

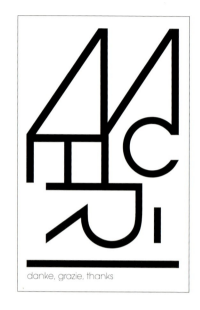
02 Esther Rieser

03 vonSüden

04 Handverk

05 Manifiesto Futura

06 Viola Schmieskors

07 KalleGraphics

08 Black-Marmalade

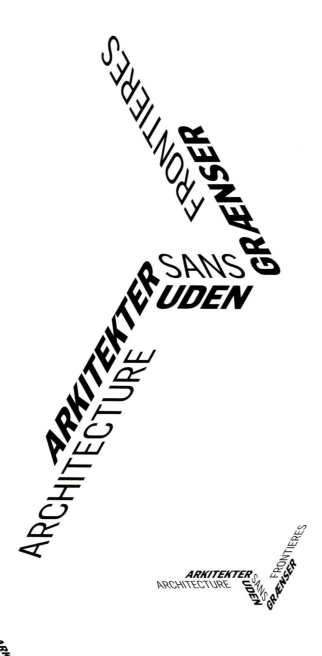

01 Emil Hartvig Studio

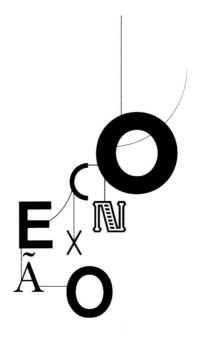

02 EMPK

03 OMOCHI

04 Bodara

Ch.03   Love of Letters

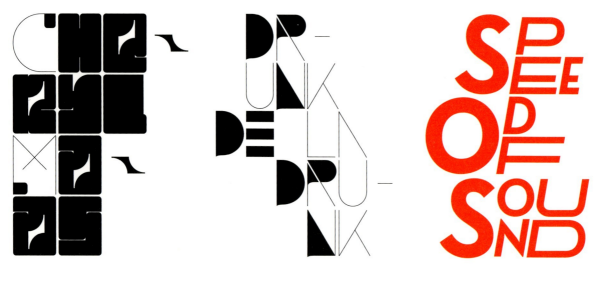

01   Marc van der Meer

02   Marc van der Meer

03   The KDU

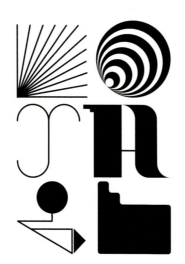

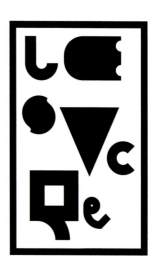

04   NODE Berlin Oslo

05   Nohemí Dicurú

06   Falko Ohlmer

01 pleaseletmedesign

03 Bram Nijssen & Marnix de Klerk

02 pleaseletmedesign

04 HelloMe

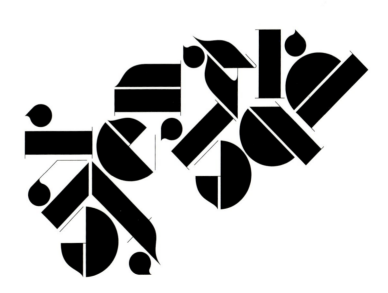

05 Non-Format

Ch.03 Love of Letters Ultra Thins

01 Monoblock

02 Coley Porter Bell

03 Fontan2

04 asmallpercent

05 Core60

06 Q2 Design

07 Mash

08 Mash

09 TNOP™

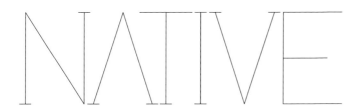

01 one8one7

02 Savas Ozay

03 Faith

04 Matteo Mastronardi

05 unfolded

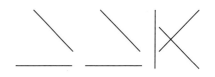

06 unfolded

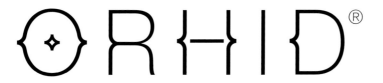

07 Zigmunds Lapsa

08 Graphical House

Ch.03 Love of Letters																											Ultra Thins

01   Jonathan Gurvit

02   Non-Format

03   Graphical House

04   KalleGraphics

05   Mads Burcharth

06   Siggeir Hafsteinsson

07   Heric Longe

08   BETA STUDIO

09   Sawdust

10   HoohaaDesign

02 Lundgren+Lindqvist

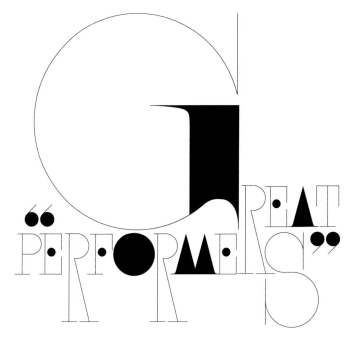

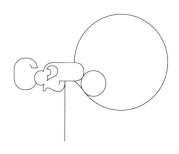

01 HelloMe

03 Out Of Order

04 one8one7

05 phospho

06 Chris Rubino

07 Manifiesto Futura

08 Chris Rubino

01 vonSüden

02 EMPK

03 Copenheroes

04 FEED

05 Fontan2

06 Manifiesto Futura

07 Otto Dietrich

08 Halvor Bodin

09 Projekttriangle Design Studio

Ultra Thins · Love of Letters · Ch. 03

01 Black-Marmalade

02 Mash

03 Non-Format

04 Jessica Walsh

05 Sawdust

06 The KDU

07 Digitaluv

Ch.03 Love of Letters　　　　　　　　　　　　　　　　　　　　　　　Monograms

01 modo

02 vonSüden

03 Analog.Systm

04 Alphabet Arm Design

05 EMPK

06 Ken

07 Creative Inc

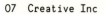
08 Transfer Studio

98

01 André Beato

02 Calango

03 modo

04 Grandpeople

05 typotherapy+design inc.

06 COUP

07 And Studio

08 Studio Output

09 HEYHEYHEY

10 Luke Williams

11 Gytz

12 Andrea Gustafson

Ch.03　Love of Letters　　　　　　　　　　　　　　　　　　　　　　　Monograms

01　Savas Ozay

02　Hörður Lárusson

03　Company

04　Monoblock

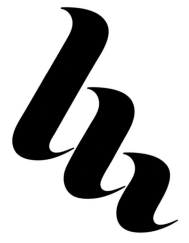
05　Sawdust

06　Indyvisuals　　　07　Just Smile And Wave

08　Christian Cervantes

09　Axel Peemöller

10　Axel Peemöller

01 Acme Industries

02 Acme Industries

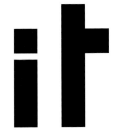
03 Face.

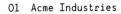
04 Savas Ozay

05 Hattomonkey

06 Designers United

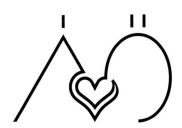
07 Analog.Systm

08 Demetrio Mancini

09 Clusta

Ch.03 Love of Letters				Monograms

01 Loic Sattler

02 The KDU

03 cerotreees

04 Benny Gold

05 C100 Purple Haze

06 Roy Smith

07 Aldo Lugo

08 superfried

09 chemicalbox

10 Mads Burcharth

11 Scandinavian DesignLab

12 Loic Sattler

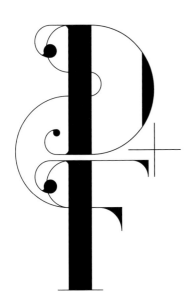

01 Face.

02 modo

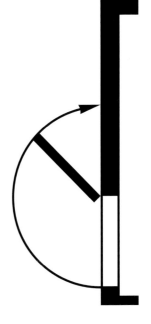

03 Andrea Gustafson

04 Áron Jancsó

05 Moxie Sozo

06 Moxie Sozo

07 Hattomonkey

01 Peter Sunna

02 ODD

03 Technicolor Grayscale

04 John Beckers

05 Peter Sunna

06 Floor Wesseling

Spacial Love of Letters Ch. 03

01 Chragokyberneticks

02 Perndl+Co

03 StudioSpass

04 Toko

05 Lab2

06 Tabas

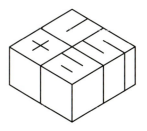

07 Julian Viera

08 Kate Moross

09 Jum & Cargo

105

Ch.03 Love of Letters Spacial

01 Edhv

02 Zigmunds Lapsa

03 Lifter Baron

04 Lifter Baron

01 formdusche

02 Accident Grotesk!

03 formdusche

04 Joshua Distler

05 CLAU.AS.KEE

06 visualism

07 illDesigns

08 EL MIRO

09 me studio

Ch.03   Love of Letters

01   Surface

02   Mind Design

03   Acme Industries

A/1
THE MEDLEY INSTITUTE
AW 2010

04   Studio Regular

05   Kokoro & Moi

06   Ken   07   Haus CPH   08   xy arts

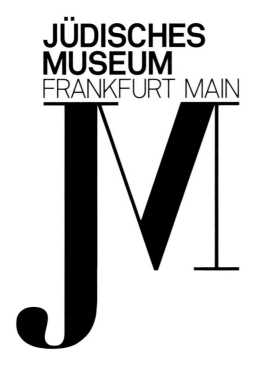

01 Surface

OPER / *Vorfreude* **\ KÖLN**

OPER / *Spielzeit 2010.2011* **\ KÖLN**

OPER / *Don Quichote* **\ KÖLN**

02 formdusche

Ch.03   Love of Letters

01 Sister Arrow & Hugh Frost   02 Red Design   03 cabina

04 Chris Bolton   05 Positron Co Ltd   06 Rocholl Selected Designs

07 La Cáscara Amarga   08 Struggle inc.   09 FromKeetra

10 FromKeetra

Love of Letters   Ch. 03

NOISETTES

01 Red Design

THE S|U|R|R|E|Y

02 Christian Cervantes

Tommila *Architects*

03 Kokoro & Moi   04 Face.

05 And Studio   06 Aldo Lugo

Ch.03 Love of Letters

01 Blake E. Marquis

02 The Pressure

03 LIMA-KILO-WHISKEY

Mistress

04 Blake E. Marquis

05 Bionic Systems

06 ilovedust

07 tomato

08 Like Minded Studio

09 Mads Burcharth

10 Mitchell Paone

11 TwoPoints.Net

01 A-Side Studio

02 Norwegian Ink

03 André Beato

ibn·nas pasta Montagna The FancyBaker

04 eps51   05 Demetrio Mancini   06 Studio Output

07 Autobahn   08 Kokoro & Moi   09 Mash & Peta Kruger

Ch.03 Love of Letters

01 Bo Lundberg

02 Celeste Prevost

03 Celeste Prevost

04 ruiz+company

05 Celeste Prevost

06 Cardamom

07 Chris Rubino

08 Filmgraphik

Love of Letters Ch. 03

TheOtherSideOfSerbia

01 Peter Gregson

EliasGunnarStudio

02 Mads Burcharth

PAMELA BÜTTNER   um[aʊt] junge kunst.
politische kunst.
mindestens.

03 Studio Regular   04 gebrauchsgrafikundso

05 John L. Nguyen   06 espluga+associates   07 FEED

Ch.03　Love of Letters　　　　　　　　　　　　　　　　　　　　　　　　　　　　　　　　Heavy Metal

01　ROMstudio

02　Hula+Hula

03　Siggeir Hafsteinsson

04　Negro™

05　TWhite design

06　Huschang Pourian

07　KalleGraphics

08　Pop Ovidiu Sebastian

FRANKMUSIK

01 Red Design

02 typism

03 X3 Studios

04 Matt Le Gallez

05 Aim Designstudio

06 Matt W. Moore

07 ALVA

08 Via Grafik

01 Fresh Estudio

02 Strukt

03 310k

04 Matt Le Gallez

05 Carsten Raffel

06 HandGun

07 modo

08 Masheen

09 Extraverage

10 Büro Destruct

01   The Pressure

02   UNIT

03   Vilaz

04   Atelier télescopique

05   DTM_INC

06   Negro™

07   Guapo

Ch.03 Love of Letters   Labyrinth

01 Matt W. Moore

02 Jewboy Corp™

03 The KDU

04 Matt W. Moore

05 C100 Purple Haze

06 Tim Bjørn

07 FEED

08 Face.

09 Gabe Ruane

01 Andrea Gustafson

02 Jet Black Tribal Ink

03 Moshik Nadav

04 Andrea Gustafson

05 weissraum.de(sign)°

06 Daniel Blik

07 Franz Falsch

08 3deluxe

Ch.04 Stroke of Luck

**ILLUSTRATION /
CHARACTERS /
LITHOGRAPHIC /**

04/

01

STROKE OF LUCK

**SCRIBBLE /
COMIC /
INK /
SCRAWLS /**

02

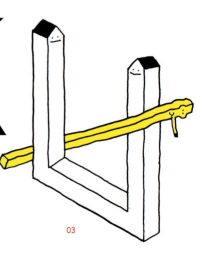

03

122

Anachronistic artistry, antagonistic anti-logos, cutesy figures, folklore-infused tribal drawings, classic silhouettes, pencil exercises, and clean-cut cartoon creations—the following logo examples are nothing if not character-istic.

01
THE SKULL DEZAIN

02
Anna Haas

03
The Lousy Livincompany/ Stefan Marx

04
Coley Porter Bell/ Adam Ellis

Among this colorful collection of illustrated identities, pretty much any style or means of expression rears its scribbled head. Some illustrators opt for tidy shapes—like Adam Ellis 04 and his farm-derived logos for It's That Organic Place—to serve as user-friendly previews of the associated product palette. Others produce examples that seem more icon or mascot than actual logo: like a complementary player to bolster the team, these sleek and slinky vectorized identities just want to be FriendsWithYou and lend their parent brand an approachable, professional face.

With its straightforward pre-school appeal, Max Kisman's p.124 logo for the fortieth anniversary of a Dutch cultural center in Indonesia combines all of the event's salient points—a Dutch windmill, a tropical palm tree, a building, the number 40—under one inviting roof. There is no need to decipher a code: everything is laid out in the open.

Dashed off, yet carefully considered, other illustration-based logos thrive on instant cheek and spontaneity, on crudely amateurish scrawls that tread the precarious line between naively fun and jarringly terrible. Take the makeshift and subversive faux-naive scrawls by German artist Stefan Marx 03, whose interpretation of a local bank mascot for T-shirt foundry The Lousy Livincompany copies a well-known toon character badly, but with unbridled panache.

Switzerland's idiosyncratic illustrators tend to go heavy on the ink and willful scratches. They explore the darker side of logo design, using pen, pencil, or ball-point to sketch out iconic images unwilling to fit a given mould. Thin lines meet the thick slashes of linocut and spilled ink, the noir of graphic novels, and the stuff of nightmares.

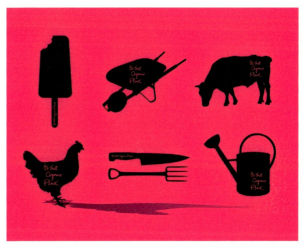

04

A proponent of this style, Anna Haas 02 & p.134, used strong slashes of luscious black to create a range of coarse logos for Swiss publishing giant Ringier. And this is by no means an isolated case: large corporations have come to love the appeal of rough strokes and the "unfinished" look of stark illustrations. Crude, basic, and in your face, these logos say, "Look! We dare! We improvise! We're on the level and not stuck in our ways!" By allowing, and even demanding, the artist's unmistakable signature style instead of a faithful CI rendition, multinationals buy themselves instant kudos and convey an image that is the exact opposite of a streamlined—and mainstream—corporate behemoth.

Incidentally, many of these "subversive" logo illustrations are far too complicated, fine-lined, color-drenched, or convoluted to work as a true, or truly versatile, logo. Yet as a gentle way of saying "enough already" to established styles and conventions, they accomplish exactly what they set out to do.

Ch.04   Stroke of Luck

01 Kismanstudio

02 Kismanstudio

03 Power Graphixx

04 Juntos otra vez

05 Juntos otra vez

06 Landor Associates

02 YOK

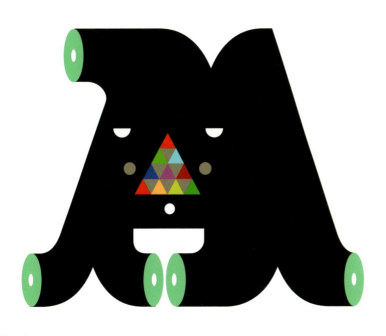

03 Sabina Keric

01 Juntos otra vez

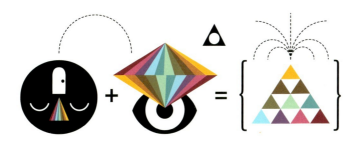

04 Juntos otra vez

05 Juntos otra vez

06 Juntos otra vez

Ch.04   Stroke of Luck

01   Juntos otra vez

02   Mitchell Paone

126

Stroke of Luck   Ch. 04

01   miniminiaturemouse

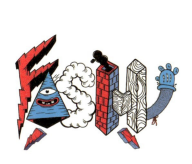

02   KOA

03   miniminiaturemouse

04   Juntos otra vez

05   Yuu Imokawa

06   Tstout

07   backyard10

127

Ch.04   Stroke of Luck

01   Andreina Bello

02   Eduardo Vidales

03   FriendsWithYou

04   backyard10

05   Jonathan Calugi

06   Wiyumi

07   Mikey Burton

01 Dtam—TM

02 Floor 5

04 Andreina Bello

05 Fons Hickmann m23

03 Matteo Mastronardi

06 Christian Rothenhagen

07 Moxie Sozo

TERRIER

02 Lapin Studio

03 Chragokyberneticks

01 HarrimanSteel

04 Mikey Burton

05 YOK

06 Fons Hickmann m23

07 Claus Gasque

Stroke of Luck   Ch. 04

01 MASA

02 44flavours

03 miniminiaturemouse

04 Mash

05 Bionic Systems

06 Sabina Keric

131

Ch.04   Stroke of Luck

01   Revivify Graphic Design

02   Struggle inc.

03   modo

04   Dudu Torres

05   modo

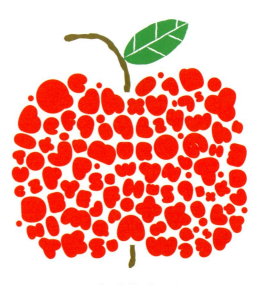

06   Jonathan Calugi

132

01 Hayes Image

02 milchhof : atelier

03 Celeste Prevost

04 Celeste Prevost

05 Denny Backhaus

06 Coolpuk

07 Designit

08 Designit

09 Coolpuk

01 Anna Haas

01 HAPPYPETS PRODUCTS
Pully For Noise Festival

Sticks and stones…

For Noise is an annual music festival held in the Swiss town of Pully, near Lausanne. At the height of summer, this three-day festival attracts a diverse crowd to a secluded forest setting—a site that has its own natural attractions.

Tasked with designing the festival logo and associated T-shirt motifs, the designers at Happypets decided to embark on a field trip to scout the site. The festival's setting reminded them of a medieval fort and, coupled with a shouty rock 'n' roll mouth, this association became their key visual. The T-shirts added a visual playground for the site's "regular" crowd—local scouts on a camping trip.

Inspired by traditional camping culture, Happypets collected and re-drew scout-related elements like branches and signposts to create an illustrated campground spread across the cotton-clad festival crowd.

01 Falko Ohlmer
02 Happypets products

03 designJune
04 designJune
05 The Lousy Livincompany

06 TU SAIS QUI™
07 Vivien Le Jeune Durhin
08 Just Smile And Wave

01 ATTAK

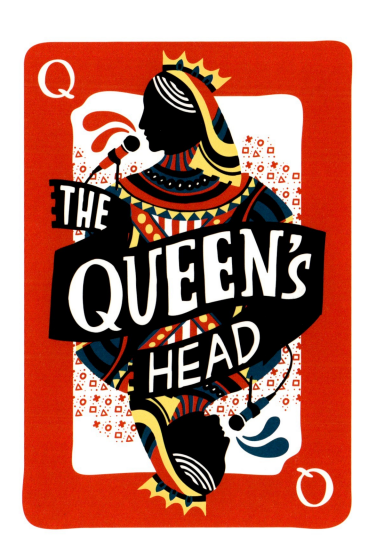

02 Kate Moross

03 OMOMMA™   04 Mash   05 Heric Longe

Ch.04   Stroke of Luck

01   TWhite design

02   TWhite design

03   Strukt

04   Ole Utikal

05   Masheen

06   Matthias Wagner

07   Via Grafik

08   TU SAIS QUI™

01 sellout-industries™

02 sellout-industries™

03 ZEK

04 Akinori Oishi

05 sellout-industries™

Ch.04 Stroke of Luck

01 44flavours

02 Kate Moross

03 REX

04 Mads Burcharth

05 Hexanine

06 Daniel Medeiros

Stroke of Luck   Ch. 04

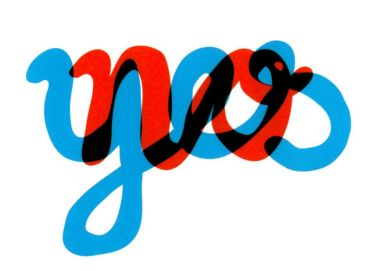

01 Christian Borstlap

02 Human Empire

03 Blake E. Marquis

04 Jürgen Frost

05 hintzegruppen

06 Kismanstudio

Ch.05 Signature

01

05/
SIG
NA
TURE

**ILLUSTRATIVE LETTERFORM /
SIGN PAINTING /
ORIENTAL /**

02

142

As part of the rekindled interest in hand-crafted fonts, illustrative lettering—from street art to high street—is enjoying a long-overdue comeback. Featuring bona-fide signature styles, handwriting samples, and ostentatious visual microcosms, these logos add a very personal slant and plenty of character to free-form lettering—and instant street cred to advertising and editorials.

Up until the early twentieth century, however, illustrated fonts played quite a different role. Back in medieval times, assiduous monks working in scriptoria around Europe might pour months of hunched-over dedication into a single introductory letter for an elaborate, visual hint of things to come. At the same time, the hand-painted, illustrative letterforms of early shop facades helped to attract customers with a less-than-perfect knowledge of the alphabet.

03

Fast-forward to the present, and modern-day designers might not slave away over their designs for months on end, but their sketched or drawn logos are equally charged with symbolism and heartfelt enthusiasm. Often a little rough around the edges, and all the better and more unique for it, their logos elevate amateurish touches to the rank of a deliberate, decisive, and prominent device. Carefully placed whims and mistakes broadcast the brand's appreciation for kinks and quirks, for that all-important human touch. This is no faceless corporation!

In this spirit, geeky street art, hand-drawn drop shadows, do-it-yourself fanzine styles, and insecure school-book scribbles recalling faded heartthrobs and favorite bands abound. In their almost intimate imperfection, these logos allow us to watch the flow and follow the illustrator's uncertainties and wiggles of the pen—like Ohara Daijiro's **p.147.01** logo for *Mozine*, which delights in going over the edges.

01
JMSV

02
ZEK

03
Weather Control/
Silvia Cordero
Vega

Always distinct and immediately expressive, illustrative letterforms are equally good at conjuring up era-specific connotations. JMSV's [01] psychedelic logo for Somos Una Triste Banda de Rock takes us back to the late 60s and early 70s, to the great unwashed, peace and love, harmony, and the joy of rocking out to your favorite band.

At the other end of the spectrum, logo designers are crafting incredibly intricate, letter-shaped ecosystems populated by myriads of tiny creatures, creepers, automata, and machinations, executed with breathtaking exactitude and mirroring natural structures. By exploring this colorful gray area between shape and significance, between flourish and information, they invest their objects and scenes with more obvious meaning and dissolve the boundaries between text and image.

And finally, we arrive at the most "authentic" incarnation of all: the signature logo or handwritten identity. Embellished with splodges and smears, Silvia Cordero Vega's [03] calligraphic icon for the 2009 annual report of School's Out Washington states nothing more—or less—than, "This is us!" Coming full circle, these signature styles and their implications of "standing up for quality with our good name" are starting to creep back into business—even in their (in)famous 1980s guise as permanent neon signage and a glowing example to the outside world.

Ch.05　Signature

Here comes Kis

01　Denny Backhaus

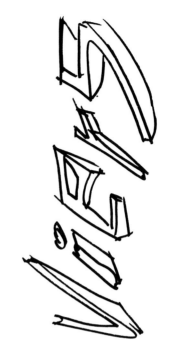

02　Vier5

The Mirror

03　Denny Backhaus

Florence + the machine

04　Sister Arrow

05　THE SKULL DEZAIN

144

Signature Ch. 05

01 THE SKULL DEZAIN

02 Eivind Nilsen

03 No-Domain

04 Ryan Massiah

05 COUP

06 Gustavo de Lacerda

07 No-Domain

Ch.05   Signature

01 **JUTOJO**
   <u>HOME clubnight</u>

Simple strokes for simple folks?

For HOME's monthly stint at seminal Berlin nightspot WMF, the club's principal logo—a take on a childhood drawing game—gets a welcome reshuffle in a series of limited-edition silk-screen poster illustrations.

In addition to the game, which requires the drawer to make a house without taking the pen off the paper, JUTOJO's design takes us "home" with several permutations of the word's four letters. For added visual impact in the club, the designers opted for UV colors to make the logo pop under black light.

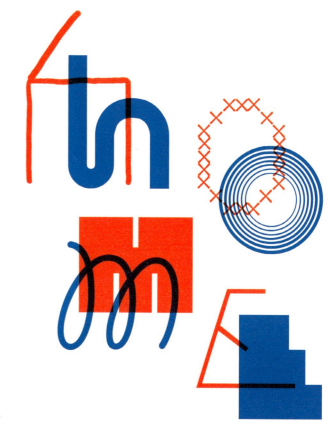

146

Signature   Ch. 05

01 OMOMMA™

02 JUTOJO

03 OMOMMA™

04 Buro Reng

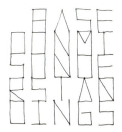

05 Jonathan Calugi

06 JUTOJO

07 Celeste Prevost

Ch.05 Signature

01 Heydays

02 FLAMMIER

03 Axel Peemöller

04 Via Grafik

05 Peter Gregson

06 Technicolor Grayscale

07 Face.

08 Hexanine

09 max-o-matic

10 max-o-matic

148

Signature   Ch. 05

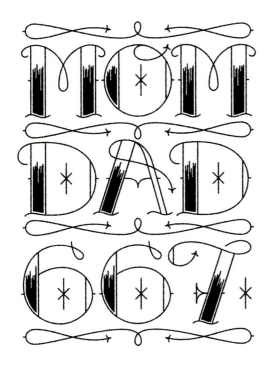

01   C100 Purple Haze

02   C100 Purple Haze

03   Chragokyberneticks

04   Penkin, Langenheim & Schultze

05   vonSüden

06   Jonathan Calugi

07   ujidesign

08   Fons Hickmann m23

149

Ch.05   Signature

01   Andrea Gustafson

02   DTM_INC

03   Revivify Graphic Design

04   Weather Control

05   Meatpack

06   Meatpack

07   Strohl

08   Manifiesto Futura

09   Boldº

10   44flavours

01 ellenberg-martinez

02 Typejockeys

03 Carlos Ribeiro

04 büro uebele visuelle kommunikation

05 General Projects

06 Typejockeys

07 Inventaire

08 Mr. Brown – creative boutique

09 The Luxury of Protest

Ch.05   Signature

01 ATTAK

02 Regina

03 ROMstudio

04 Axel Peemöller

05 Fresh Estudio

06 Axel Peemöller

07 Franz Falsch

08 Base

09 Anti/Anti

Signature Ch. 05

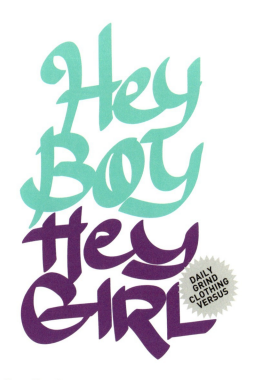

01 Team Manila

02 NODE Berlin Oslo

03 Estudio Soma

04 Goldjunge Grafik & Design

05 NODE Berlin Oslo

06 Boldº

07 Just Smile And Wave

08 Art Machine

153

44 FLAVOURS

Berlin/
Germany

Pages
131, 140, 150, 154—158,
161, 175, 179, 342, 349,
353, 368

Berlin-Kreuzberg's 44flavours adds a touch of spice to the local art and design scene with its expressive styles and illustrations.
Having grown up with graffiti and sampling culture, Sebastian Bagge and Julio Rölle encourage cross-fertilization of style snippets and ideas between their art and design work, between hand-crafted typography, graphic novel references, and slick corporate commissions.

01

02

03

04

—
How would you describe the prime objective of a logo?

A logo doesn't have to illustrate anything—it acquires functionality through use. The more people recognize a certain logo, the more its associations grow. To quote Paul Rand: "A logo becomes meaningful only after it is used. The illustration that represents the logo is the product and not the logo." The Swoosh is a perfect example. And the fact that it was designed by an intern makes it even better—I'd say it's a classic!

—
And what would be the biggest no-no in logo design?

A good logo has to be simple. It should work in black and be recognizable even when it is scaled down. So in my opinion the biggest no-no in logo design is to mistake an illustration for a logo. Considering my love for illustration, I still tend to make that mistake, but at the same time it is also what makes my style unique.

Using too many colors is another pitfall—just look at all the designs that came out in the 1990s. So keep it simple, but have fun with it! And don't create too many versions, just choose the one that you like best and show it to the client. Most clients can't handle too many options.

—
Speaking of clients, what kind of people approach you for logos? And what do they like about your style?

We work with a lot of musicians, fashion brands, extreme sport brands, and galleries, but we also do a lot of classic corporates. Fortunately, most of our clients are design literate, so they recognize that what we do is unique. We do everything by hand: design our own fonts, hand-paint them onto pieces of wood, and we only put them through the digital process right at the end.

We are big on breaking rules—be it Swiss design or graffiti. We destroy fonts, mix perspectives, and don't really care if something is hard to decipher, as long as we feel that it has that certain something. I think our clients know and respect this.

—
What about more "corporate" clients?

Well, 44flavours is a duo and Sebastian, my partner, is the one with the more traditionally corporate style. I am the experimentalist—I deal with all the handmade type. If the work requires that traditional corporate touch, then he will do the groundwork while I art-direct it. And vice versa: if the job requires something off-beat and wild, I will design it while he art-directs.

—
Okay, so how does this work in practice?

It all starts with research on who the client is and what their objectives are. If the briefing is really good, we can quickly move on to the creative work. I draw inspiration from the streets and sometimes go to the library to flip through some old books and magazines. Once I am charged up, I start to sketch. And when I have something that I like, it gets scanned and cleaned up. Even Sebastian, who prefers to work with digital tools, always has paper and pen at the ready—just to try things out.

05

06

07

Ch.05   Signature   44flavours

09

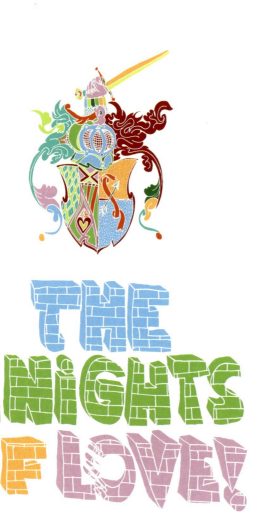

10

11

08

—
Several of your logos seem to be influenced by graffiti. Does this reflect your own background? Or how did this particular flavor slip into the final designs?

Those are definitely our roots. My whole creative career started with a spray can. I was about 13 years old when I got involved with the graffiti scene. After finishing school I tried to work within classic design parameters, but it didn't feel right—it simply wasn't me!

During my internships at Ecko and Zoo York I realized that the results got better when I just let the designs flow naturally, sticking to what I knew best. During this phase I got to work with a lot of great designers like Kimou Meyer, Christian Acker, Dan Funderberg, Max Vogel, and Will Carpio. Most of them have a graffiti, skateboard, or hip-hop background. Now the world has finally grown to accept post-graffiti design; it is practically a part of mainstream culture.

—
On that note—what is the story behind the cartoony series featuring a number of Berlin-based artists and musicians? p.161

This was part of a series for the cover of the Berlin magazine *Proud* and it is typical for 44flavours. Originally, I wanted to play with mixing different typefaces, but then I sketched out the first design and it was a real burner, so I decided to top it with every design that followed. I really believe that you get the best results from spontaneity. Your subconscious

156

is always processing information and you tap into it by just letting the pen flow. If you think too much, you might stifle the whole creative process.

—
Besides street art, there are quite a few references to letterpress and silk-screen printing, or at least to their aesthetics...

We love all of the more or less traditional techniques: woodcut, hot type, etching... But our favorite is definitely silk-screening. It is easy and great for instantly beautiful results. As we do a lot of free art projects, we feel privileged to have this space and scope for experimentation. The resulting insights and techniques often filter through to our design work in some form or other.

—
What draws you to this particular style? How does it capture what you are trying to portray?

I love handmade objects, old typefaces, and street signs. I take photos of them when I walk around and sometimes draw them, too. I love how time affects ordinary objects, how things age. For example, old layers of paint may resurface because some pieces of a sign were chipped away, or maybe the paint faded in one spot and then an older letter reappeared underneath. That's life's creative accident.

In my work, I try to emulate this ageing process. I usually work on wood and start off with layering different types of paint. While the last coat is drying, I pour coffee or tea over it, just to stain the result a bit. Then I might sand the whole thing down to expose the different layers. Afterwards, I paint the letters, sand them again, and repeat the whole process.

—
Sounds quite poetic. Is there always a narrative involved?

Actually, a lot of our logos have stories. The screen-print for the 44flavours beer label [p.349], for example, was a commission for an art exhibit. Instead of cash they "paid" us in vouchers for 1,000 beers at a nice bar in Berlin-Schöneberg. We are still working on clearing the tab, by the way!

Or take the 44flavours ice-cream truck [p.179]. Sebastian once came across such a truck in an old movie. It ended up inspiring our company name and the entire concept—'cause we got plenty of flavor(s)! When I was in Brooklyn I saw a similar truck with the same color scheme and finally created this design.

—
So is there anything you haven't done that you would like to?

I would love to design a stamp for the next football championship. Working with Michel Gondry would also be amazing: I could build giant letters out of wood for him. Redesigning the Berlin subway logo is up there as well! I know that Sebastian would flip out if he could work on a new MOMA corporate. And last, but not least, I'd love to make a business card for the rapper Mos Def!

13

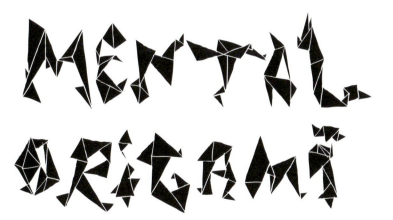

12

14

Ch.05   Signature

01   Wolff Olins

02   Chris Henley

03   Blake E. Marquis

04   Chragokyberneticks

05   Weather Control

06   Lab2

07   EyesCream

08   44flavours

09   Tstout

01 Juntos otra vez

02 Claus Gasque

03 Juntos otra vez

04 Luke Williams

05 Madhouse

06 Laleh Torabi

Ch.05   Signature

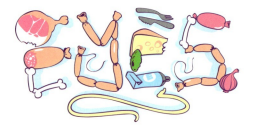

01   EyesCream

02   Coutworks

03   Julian Viera

04   HUSH

05   Struggle inc.

06   Struggle inc.

01 44flavours

Ch.05   Signature

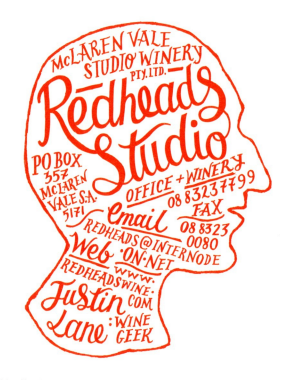

01 Like Minded Studio

02 Mash

03 EL MIRO

04 Indyvisuals

05 Indyvisuals

06 Young Jerks

07 Young Jerks

08 Young Jerks

Signature Ch. 05

01   John Vingoe

02   Project 1000

03   Acme Industries

04   elesefe

05   Braca Burazeri

06   Young Jerks

07   Haltenbanken

08   Benny Gold

09   sellout-industries™

10   Allan Deas

11   visualism

163

Ch.05   Signature

01 Taeko Isu

02 Fabian Bertschinger

03 Wissam Shawkat & Xandi

04 Wissam Shawkat

05 Wissam Shawkat

Signature   Ch. 05

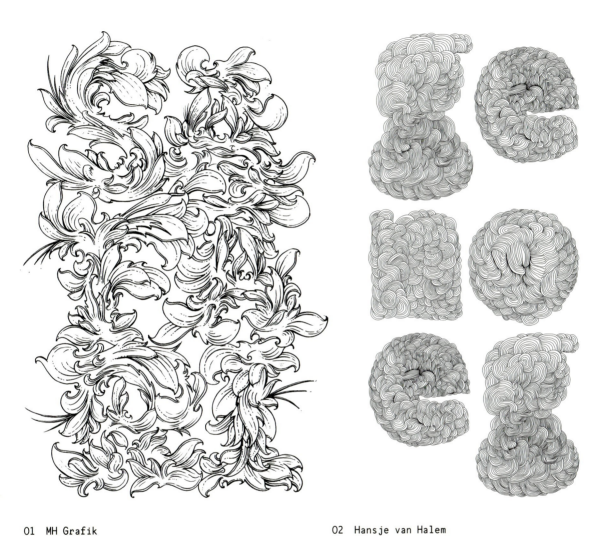

01 MH Grafik   02 Hansje van Halem

03 Chris Bolton   04 Hansje van Halem   05 Hansje van Halem

165

01　Taeko Isu

02　Taeko Isu

03　Taeko Isu

04　OMOMMA™

ア・ドラウニング
クロコダイル
ブック・サーヴィス

A DROWNING
CROCODILE
BOOK SERVICE

05　Maniackers Design

06　Taeko Isu

Oriental　　　　　　　　　　　　　　　　　　　　　　　　Signature　Ch. 05

01　ASYL

02　Felix Lobelius

03　ujidesign

04　ujidesign

05　COMMUNE

06　COMMUNE

07　COMMUNE

Ch.05   Signature   Oriental

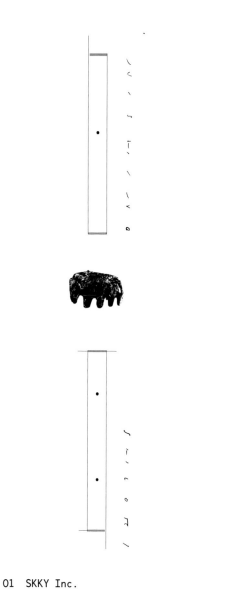

01   SKKY Inc.

02   SKKY Inc.

03   SKKY Inc.

04   SKKY Inc.

05   SKKY Inc.

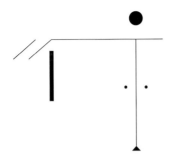

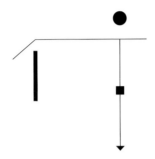

01 SKKY Inc.

02 SKKY Inc.

03 SKKY Inc.

06/ PRE-SCHOOL

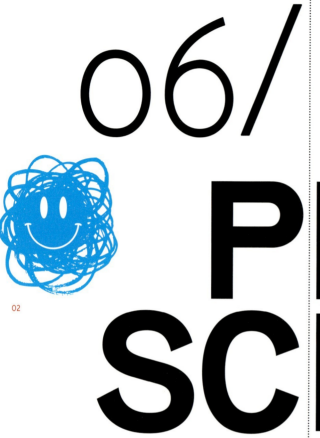

SIMPLE DELIGHTS /
BUILDING BLOCKS /
BACK TO SCHOOL /
PICK AND MIX /
CMYK /

Pre-School Ch. 06

04

We are hardwired to love and cherish childish features, to find them inviting, familiar, and worthy of protection. In our yearning for innocence and happiness, for the elusive happily-ever-after, for no gray areas or hidden deceit in uncertain times, we welcome playful and child-like images as a much-needed temporary respite.

In this spirit, the world is our playground and simple, CMYK-infused logos with a touch of childish innocence are starting to break out of the design niche previously reserved for obvious Toys "R" Us clones and childcare applications.

Stark, simple, and delightful, these visual identities are inspired by toddlers' sense of wonder as they try to work out how the world fits together. Block by block, step by step, this branch of logo design goes back to (pre-)school and, at times, to a world before letters and reading. The results are easy to grasp and rely on basic shapes, strong colors, and bold combinations.

01
Extraverage /
Karoly
Kiralyfalvi

02
Floor 5
(ArtSchoolVets)

From cutesy and well-rounded to angular anarchy, their image-infused typefaces have no time for fancy frills or gradients, but simply depict what they advertise—tools, animals, toys, building blocks—juxtaposed with basic, friendly, and universal icons otherwise found in early learning books.

With a gentle dose of Pippi Longstocking's trademark cheek, these logos love to go over the line, break with design rules, and reshape the world to their heart's delight. Deliberately topsy-turvy and colorful letters clamber over each other, and the designer's enthusiasm floods into the logos themselves. Some of the results, like `Acme Industries'` **03** logo for Kokolo, dip into the font box and come up with a beautifully jumbled typeface "mess", while others, like `Karoly Kiralyfalvi's` **01** design for the Hungarian National Gallery, take inspiration from a set of crayons.

With this simple sleight of hand, they conjure up a sense of friendly approachability, of being open and on the level. This style is well-suited to pop bands and festivals, but is also snapped up by universities and museums eager to throw off a stern or stuffy image.

03
Acme Industries

04
Jonathan Calugi

05
Tilt Design
Studio

Take `ArtSchoolVets'` **02** likeable icon: a charming, approachable ball of lines that mirrors our own creative chaos. By encouraging such direct associations, the creators of playful logos suggest that there is no hidden subtext and no strings attached. What you see is what you get.

Giving a brand a friendly face also helps to lower our defenses by appealing to our inner child. Even a serious message—or corporate whitewashing—can sneak past our radar when it looks this cute.

05

171

Ch.06 Pre-School

01 Rasmus Snabb

02 Rasmus Snabb

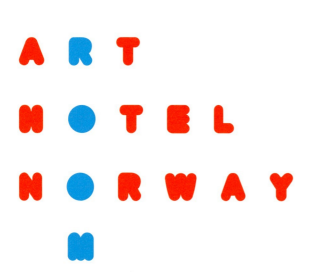 

03 UREDD   04 FoURPAcK ontwerpers

Pre-School   Ch. 06

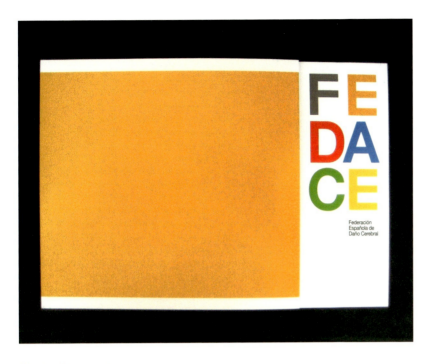

01 La Cáscara Amarga

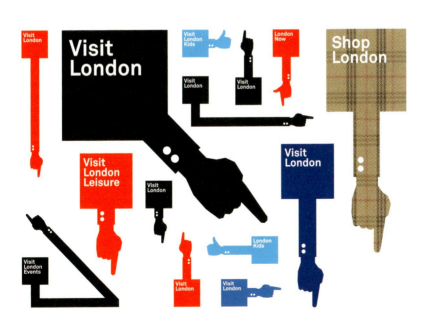

02 Joshua Distler

03 Base

173

Ch.06　Pre-School

01　Canefantasma Studio

02　Human Empire

03　Struggle inc.

04　Matt W. Moore

Pre-School   Ch. 06

01 urbn; interaction

02 FoURPAcK ontwerpers

03 Base

04 Falko Ohlmer

05 44flavours

06 Chragokyberneticks

07 Struggle inc.

08 Koehorst in 't Veld

09 A-Side Studio

175

KOKORO & MOI

Helsinki/
Finland

Pages
51, 66, 81, 108, 111, 113, 176–178, 293

Formerly known as Syrup Helsinki, Kokoro & Moi has been causing a creative stir on the Finnish design scene since 2001. A little irreverent and infinitely versatile, its visual identities for clients ranging from Artnet to Amnesty International and the Helsinki Regional Transport Authority rely on a mix of pared-down, playful approaches—and prove that practicality and fun are not mutually exclusive.

—

Your work for the Design Forum Finland [02 & p.66] mixes clean-cut type and hand-drawn scribbles. How did you translate the exhibition's concept of new Finnish design for a U.S. audience?

Besides having a reputation for being minimalist and sustainable, Finnish design loves to play with contrasts. This is something we picked up on in our work for the "Playful" exhibition and we took inspiration from the presented objects, comics, and examples of hobo culture.

We put all of these ideas together and they became part of a fresh visual mix that carries a hint of the new Nordic approach to design and culture.

—

So do you think there is something particularly Finnish about your style?

Sure, we have also been guilty of playing with contrasts! After all, this is a land of extreme contrasts, a place where long dark winters follow bright summer nights. By allowing different ideas, styles, methods, mindsets, and people to come together we create scope for discovery and invention.

—

How does this work in practice?

Every client has an inspiring story. It may be about their humble beginnings, a funny anecdote about their name, something on the birth of their business model, or a story about one of the company founders. These stories often provide a starting point that triggers our imagination and might resurface in some parts of the final identity.

On this note you should never start with the logo itself. The biggest mistake when asked to create a visual identity is to think that the logo is the focal point. While the logo plays an important part, it is just one of a wide mix of elements that includes other graphics, the overall color palette, typographical materials, copy, photography, etc. It is always the consistent entity that matters, not a single part of it, however significant that part may be.

01

02

K O K O

R O &

M O I

03

All of your designs show a strong love of typography. Do you design all of your own fonts?

Nope, but we try our best.

—
Did any of your ideas ever get rejected because they were considered too daring or risky?

Well, we have been asked to remove some genitalia from our proposals. I have to admit that we never saw them in the design, but some clients have a remarkable imagination. We should definitely consider hiring them.

—
Speaking of anatomy, *Renaissance Man* p. 293 appears to reference da Vinci's famous drawing. Is it just an apt metaphor or is there more to this story?

Renaissance Man is a Finnish house-music act. The duo originally met at an architecture office in Helsinki and immediately realized they were kindred spirits—they were both prime examples of cultural multitasking in work and play. So they decided to join forces and found a name that would reflect their interest in a wide range of fields, genres, and subjects.

Eventually, they decided to make the kind of house they really wanted and asked us to create a graphic identity inspired by polymaths, of which Leonardo da Vinci is perhaps the best known.

04

06

JIM & JILL®

05

Pre-School   Ch. 06

01   Chragokyberneticks

02   Chragokyberneticks

03   44flavours

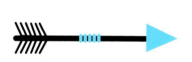

04   Jonathan Calugi

05   Human Empire

06   Huschang Pourian

07   The Lousy Livincompany

08   The Lousy Livincompany

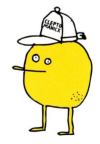

09   The Lousy Livincompany

Ch.06 Pre-School

01 Kismanstudio

02 Kismanstudio

03 Kismanstudio

04 Tabas

05 De Jongens Ronner

06 Coboi & Fageta

07 Axel Peemöller

08 OPX

Pre-School   Ch. 06

01   Coley Porter Bell

02   Büro4   03   Monoblock   04   Autobahn

181

Ch.06   Pre-School

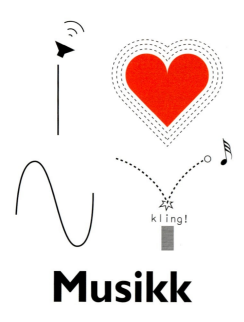

01 NODE Berlin Oslo

02 Chragokyberneticks

03 Designers United

04 miniminiaturemouse

05 HUSH

06 miniminiaturemouse

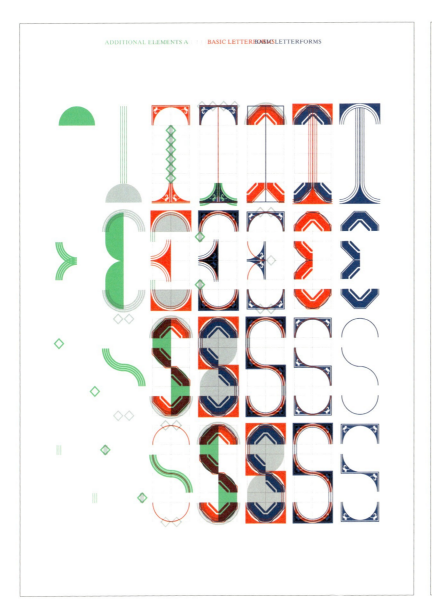

01 Mind Design

02 Mind Design

01 Jonathan Calugi

02 cabina

03 Fieldtrip

04 Jonathan Calugi

05 Grandpeople

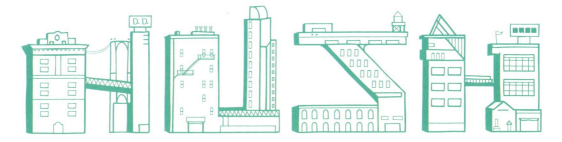

01 HUSH

02 Just Smile And Wave

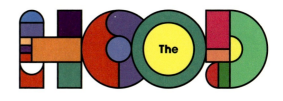

03 ALVA

04 FriendsWithYou

05 DTM_INC

06 FriendsWithYou

07 FriendsWithYou

08 FriendsWithYou

Ch.07   Mind the Gap

07/ THIS

01

DISTORTION /
GLITCH /
ERASURE /
SCRATCH /
DADA /
JUXTAPOSE /
REFUSAL /

MIND THE GAP

Safari CLOTHING

02

03

Life is the Smile with Decay

04

01
Blake E. Marquis

02
MH Grafik

03
Jet Black Tribal Ink

04
THE SKULL DEZAIN

05
typotherapy +design inc

This particular mental deception, an eminently useful trick of the mind, is something the logo designers in this chapter love to exploit to the max and beyond. Just how much can be taken out, erased, chipped away, perforated, alienated, twisted, and distorted without losing a word's inherent meaning? How much latent information do we really require to bridge the resulting associative gap? typotherapy+design inc 05, for example, ask us to fill in the blanks of PMA Landscape Architects' stationery—and then spin the tale a little bit further. In the end, it is up to us to plug in the semantic blanks and take that all-important leap of intellectual faith for a mental exercise that invariably prompts us to engage a little bit more with the logo in question. We cannot just scan, judge, and dismiss it; we have to give it an extra moment of our time and take a second look.

A logo that makes it harder to figure out what it's all about? It's not as absurd as you might think. The following works challenge the basic notion of a visual identity. Ranging from blatant denial and light-hearted visual put-downs to subtle mental darts that require a closer look and plenty of lateral thinking, these stubbornly recalcitrant designs entice us with the promise of revelation, with the satisfaction of "getting it" once we decrypt the logo's meaning or social and aesthetic context.

Exploring a wide variety of mental mechanisms, visual tricks, and distortive techniques, the resulting imagery takes us back down memory lane by forcing our brains to re-examine accepted reality. After all, we don't actually see what is all around us, but only our mind's translation of it, right side up and in full color. A similar trick comes into play when our little gray cells fill in the blanks between filmed frames or slurred syllables— we see or hear what isn't actually there. And when something in our sight diverges from the norm, from our expected framework of visual references, it simultaneously disturbs and delights us. Once we decode the hidden key it becomes truly satisfying.

05

While the technique itself has been around for a while, the latest batch of logo designers loves to expand it beyond its formal origins. Slash and shift, serrated edges, mixed-up fonts, wonky shading, fake 3D fuzz, negative space, and the removal of more than is strictly kosher... well, who said it has to be easy?

In their deliberate juxtaposition of styles and techniques not naturally destined to share the same page, these designers ramp up their logos' complexity levels—and associated visual complications—to the point that they become unreadable. They often collage three or more clashing codes and elements, from patterns and type to illustrations and photography. In doing so they create a welcome visual tension, a stylistic statement and call for attention, while at times bending the rules and definitions of logo design to near breaking point. Taken to the extreme, the resulting visual identities might dissolve into utter illegibility. Clarity agrees to take a back seat in these logos—after all, it's the thought that counts!

06 ZEK

For a touch of post-punk spirit, some designers might even conjure up a voluntary—and virtual—aesthetic censor. Zek's **06** logo for the You Are Dead To Me's, for example, plays on the notion of negation and creates something new by blacking out text and leaving only the pertinent parts of the letters visible. Three strikes and you are out!

In this spirited obstinacy, the current crop of constructive naysayers is not a million miles away from the grandfathers of doubt and rejection: the early twentieth century Dadaists. Ready to question absolutely everything, they found liberation in the complete rejection of established (aesthetic) rules and categorization. In their delight for nonsense and all things counterintuitive, they paved the way for contemporary cryptic logo designers.

Nevertheless, choosing such a radical approach inevitably whittles down the range of potential applications. Hailing mostly from the realms of music, design, and the arts, these logos require clients who are willing to skirt the cutting edge—and to risk being chopped up and devoured by the challenge. Yet with a target audience willing (and wishing) to go that decisive step further, they can afford to embark on this precarious balancing act and indulge in a spot of fearless experimentation.

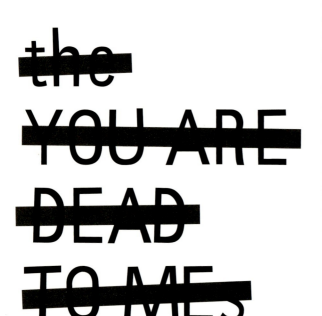

06

01 Team Manila

02 Loic Sattler

03 Guapo

04 Deanne Cheuk

05 Peter Sunna

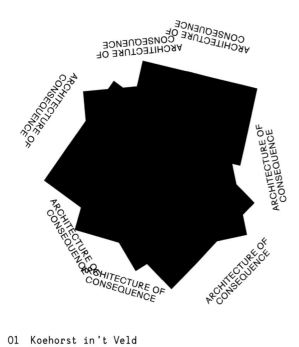

01 Koehorst in't Veld

02 büro uebele visuelle kommunikation

03 Zion Graphics

04 Dogma

05 Urbanskiworkshop

06 gebrauchsgrafikundso

01 **RICK KLOTZ**
Freshjive logo

Founded in 1989 by artist Rick Klotz, Freshjive is regarded as one of the originators and prime influencers of streetwear culture. In 2010, disillusioned by the scene's style, direction, and commercialization, Klotz decided to celebrate two decades of Freshjive with a radical relaunch and change of direction.

Like the phoenix from the flames, the company wanted to be reborn with a completely blank slate. And what could be more radical—and open—than no visible logo at all?

In its uncompromising renunciation of streetwear's current hero culture, of elaborate logos and graffiti-inspired tags, the bare rectangle champions radical understatement and leaves a gap to be filled by the wearer's own personality. Relieved of extraneous information, reduced to the max until the label itself disappears, the new non-logo is as uncompromising as the origins of street culture itself.

At the same time, it gives Freshjive the welcome freedom to fill this blank slate with a brand-new style and direction.

Ch.07 Mind the Gap   Erasure

02 Hattomonkey

01 Mads Freund Brunse

03 Indyvisuals

NATIONALITÄT
IDENTITÄT

BILDER
SCHLACHTEN

04 Fons Hickmann m23

05 Jürgen Frost

06 LogoOrange

07 Calango

THORBJÖRN ANDERSSON LANDSCAPING

01 Markus Moström

02 Scandinavian DesignLab

ORMOND CONTEMPORARY EDITIONS

03 Gavillet & Rust

04 Mads Jakob Poulsen

HEADLESSSHEEP

05 Marcelo Chelles

01 Pierre Jeanneret

02 Bleed

03 CLAU.AS.KEE

04 Q2 Design

05 Anthony Lane

07 EL MIRO

06 Philipp Pilz

01 Project 1000

02 Demetrio Mancini

03 Demetrio Mancini

04 0c/0m/0y/0k

01 Floor Wesseling

02 FLAMMIER

03 Matt W. Moore

04 The Action Designer

05 Akatre

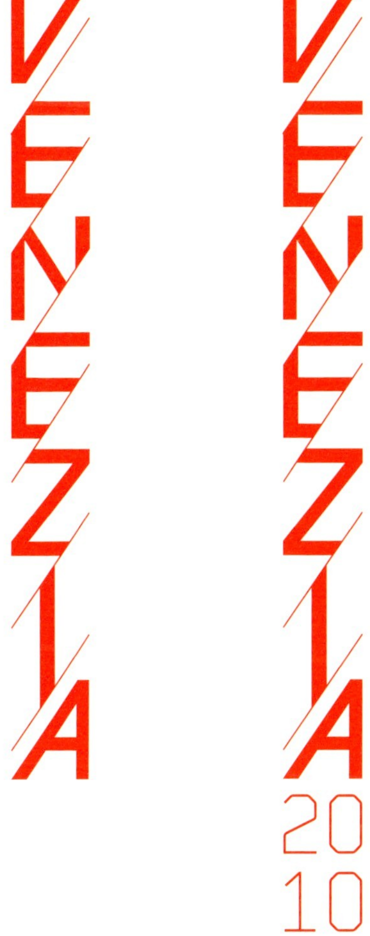

01 HelloMe

02 Magdalena Czarnecki

03 R. Vancampenhoudt & J. Van Aken   04 Edhv

05 Áron Jancsó

Ch.07 Mind the Gap

01 Fons Hickmann m23

02 Büro Ink

03 Felix Lobelius

04 Haus CPH

05 Buro Reng

06 büro uebele visuelle kommunikation

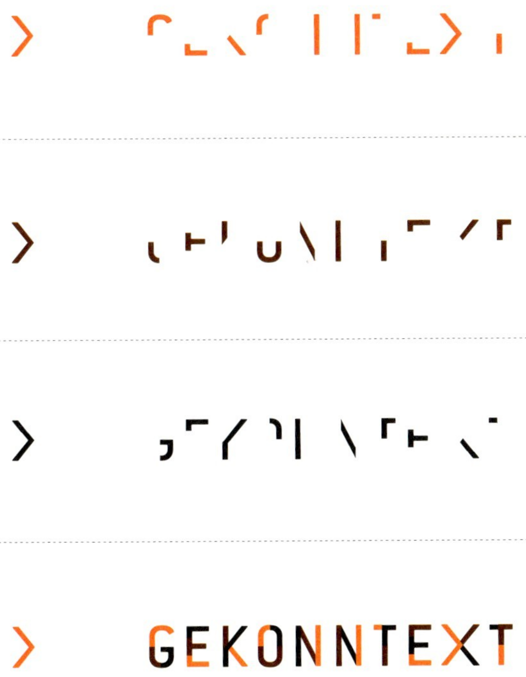

> CONTEXT

> KONTEXT

> GEKNACKT

> GEKONNTEXT

01 Wiyumi

PRO UKT
UND
V SION

02 minigram

HAM.LIT

03 milchhof : atelier

VREAU SĂ FAC
PUBLIC RELATIONS

VREAU SĂ FAC
MARKETING ONLINE

VREAU SĂ FAC
MARKETING ONLINE

VREAU SĂ FAC
PUBLIC RELATIONS

VREAU SĂ FAC
ADVERTISING

VREAU SĂ FAC
MARKETING

04 Project 1000

traces & empreintes

traces
et
empreintes

traces
et
empreintes

traces
et
empreintes

traces
et
empreintes

traces
et
empreintes

traces
et
empreintes

traces
et
empreintes

traces
et
empreintes

trac...s
...t
...mpr...int...s

traces
et
empreintes

01 atelier aquarium

02 Ryan Crouchman

03 No-Domain

01 COUP

02 Gustavo de Lacerda

03 FEED

04 Hexanine

05 Markus Moström

06 Foan82

07 Filmgraphik

08 Non-Format

01 Floor Wesseling

02 GWG inc.

03 Lab2

04 FoURPAcK ontwerpers

05 Daniel Medeiros

06 Out Of Order

01 3deluxe

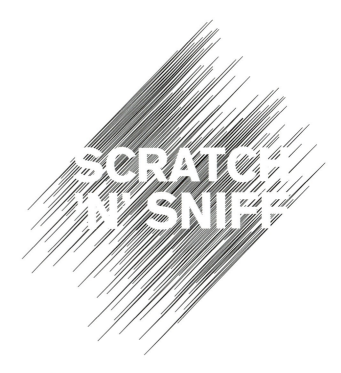

02 Bas van Vuurde

03 THE SKULL DEZAIN

04 Via Grafik

05 Philipp Pilz

06 REX

Ch.08 Liquid / Liquid

08/ LIQUID /LIQUID

EXPANSIVE /
EXTRA BOLD /
FOLD /
TAPE /
DRIPS AND DROPS /
BUBBLE /
HULA HOOPS /
TUBE /
TOOTHPASTE /

Go with the flow!
Firmly rooted in the here and now—and often bubbling with plenty of optimism—big, bold, and beautiful logos vie for space and our attention. Laid-back, unself-conscious, and self-assured, these chunky fonts and well-nourished signifiers stake their visual claim on the page.

While some of the following examples might appear sharp and angular, most display generous bulk and well-rounded curves, often exaggerated by forced overlays, with letters slipping and sliding all over each other in their scramble to be noticed.

01 Edhv
02 Chris Henley
03 nocturn.ro/ Alex Tass

Take `Alex Tass'` [03] luscious balloon bubbles: seemingly ready to burst, their blown-up, translucent ice cream shades epitomize the candy connotations triggered by many bubble logos. Other designs, like `Toko's` [05], design for ShopAround, are dripping to suggest freshness and creativity—look, the paint hasn't even dried yet!

Equally important and on display is a sense of continuity. Fashioned from one uninterrupted strand, tape, stroke of the pen, vapour trail, or trickle of cream, many logos retrace the passage of time in one confident, elegant stroke with more than a nod to La Linea.

05

20 JAHRE 周年 HAMBURG ハンブルク OSAKA 大阪

06

Folded and pleated, their ribbon-based cousins can reach origami-like qualitites. In the case of `Peter Schmidt Group's` [06] design to celebrating 20 years of town-twinning between Hamburg and Osaka, this metaphor is especially apt: the logo combines German austerity and Japanese craft in one meticulously folded two-tone design.

For an edgier iteration, look no further than the "no-go logo" fashioned from reshaped police tape or several references to DIY culture and jury-rigged imperfection, held together by copious reels of cassette or Gaffer tape.

04 Andy Mangold
05 Toko
06 Peter Schmidt Group

Last, but not least, these space-hungry logos also enter the third dimension in the guise of freshly squeezed paste, straight from the tube like `Andy Mangold's` [04] *Plush*. Luscious and thick, there is no getting around their sheer physicality and solid presence. A visual statement and then some, they shout: here we are!

With this intrinsic "attitude," bubble, drip, tube, and ribbon fonts have become a staple choice for music, fashion, and online use. Well-suited for headers and statements, they are often combined with generic typefaces—because these logos are the star of the show and claim the visual stage for themselves.

Ch.08   Liquid/Liquid   Extra Bold

01 Mash

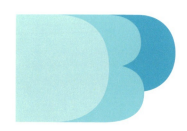
02 Mitchell Paone

03 Annika Kaltenthaler

04 Matt Carr

05 Serif

06 Vilaz

07 Base

08 Joseba Attard

09 Fontan2

10 SUNDAY VISION

11 Fontan2

12 Sawdust

01 Áron Jancsó

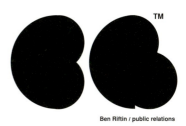

02 Jewboy Corp™

03 Sawdust

04 Áron Jancsó

05 Áron Jancsó

06 Haltenbanken

07 Haltenbanken

Ch.08 Liquid/Liquid Extra Bold

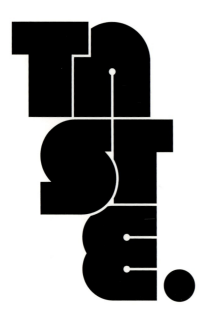

01 21bis

02 Luca Marchettoni

03 Faith

04 André Beato

05 V15

06 Acme Industries

07 Faith

208

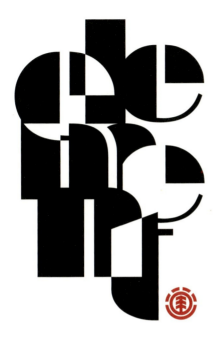

01 TWhite design

02 typism

03 Reaktor Lab

04 Martin Nicolausson

05 Julian Viera

01 The KDU

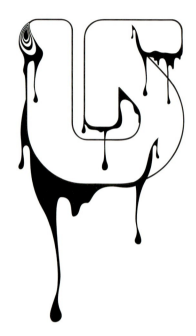

02 Tatiana Arocha

03 CLAU.AS.KEE

04 Siggeir Hafsteinsson

05 Juntos otra vez

06 Alex Trochut

07 Dudu Torres

08 max-o-matic

01 EyesCream

02 MH Grafik

03 Negro™

04 superfried

05 Serif

06 3deluxe

07 Aldo Lugo

Ch.08 Liquid/Liquid	Tube

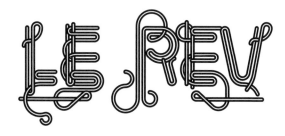

02 Blake E. Marquis

01 Chris Bolton	03 strange//attraktor:

04 Chris Bolton	05 Chris Bolton	06 Chris Bolton

 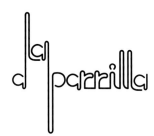 

07 Autobahn	08 Julian Viera	09 Julian Viera

212

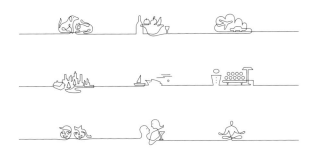

01 Felix Sockwell

02 Regina

03 Analog.Systm

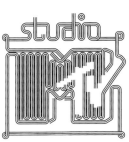

04 EyesCream

05 John Beckers

06 HoohaaDesign

07 Ekaterina Tiouleikina

08 HoohaaDesign

Ch.08 Liquid/Liquid   Tube

01 Buro Reng

02 Celeste Prevost

03 Foan82

04 Lifter Baron

05 Calango

06 Hype Type Studio

07 Fontan2

08 Via Grafik

09 Atelier télescopique

01 tomato

02 Young Jerks

03 Calango

04 Büro Destruct

05 Pierre Jeanneret

06 Büro Destruct

07 Foan82

08 Bo Lundberg & Jan Cafourek

09 903 Creative

10 Negro™

11 Foan82

12 Device

Ch.08 Liquid/Liquid

01 FoURPAcK ontwerpers

02 Felix Sockwell

03 Like Minded Studio

04 UNIT

05 UNIT

06 Benoit Lemoine

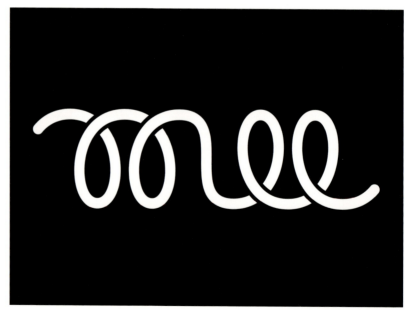

07 Calango

08 FEED

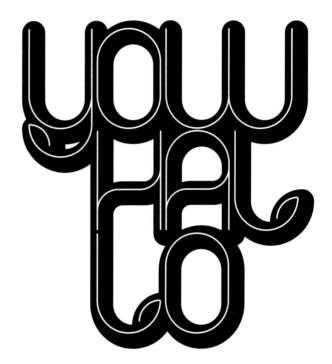

01 Jan en Randoald   02 Marc van der Meer

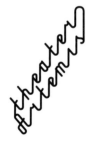

03 Jan en Randoald   04 Skin Designstudio   05 A-Side Studio

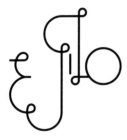

06 Ekaterina Tiouleikina   07 EMPK   08 Dtam-TM

Ch.08 Liquid/Liquid Toothpaste

01 GVA Studio

02 A-Side Studio

03 Anónimo Studio

04 ilovedust

05 Matt W. Moore

06 HelloMe

07 3deluxe

02 Negro™

03 Young Jerks

01 Foan82

04 LaMarca

05 modo

06 Mash

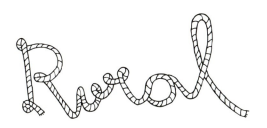

07 cabina

08 DTM_INC

01 Calango

02 Art Machine

03 Chris Henley

04 Regina

05 Dorota Wojcik

06 milchhof : atelier

07 Fabio Milito

08 Acme Industries

09 1508

10 Felix Lobelius

11 LogoOrange

01 Guapo

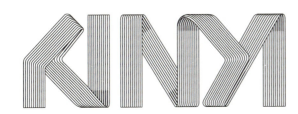
02 Leplancton

ANTE 20/10 UP

03 Lundgren+Lindqvist

04 Julian Viera

05 modo

06 Heloisa Dassie Genciauskas

07 Norwegian Ink

Ch.08 Liquid/Liquid Tape

01 THE SKULL DEZAIN

02 Autobahn

03 John Beckers

01 Felix Sockwell

02 NNSS

03 Julien Vallée

04 The KDU

05 Dogma

06 Julien Vallée

07 The KDU

08 Just Smile And Wave

09 CLAU.AS.KEE

Ch.08   Liquid/Liquid   Tape

01 Madhouse

02 Bas van Vuurde

03 atelier aquarium

04 John Beckers

05 TNOP™

06 modo

07 Jürgen Frost

08 Autobahn

09 Dogma

10 Insónia

224

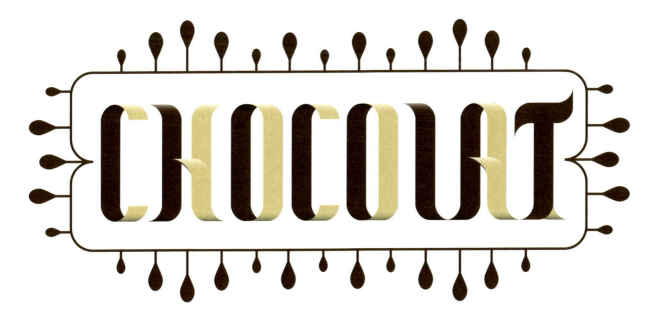

01 Dogma

Art4Hope

28. GRAFIČNI BIENALE
BIENNIAL OF GRAPHIC ARTS
ljubljana, 4. 9.–25. 10. 2009

02 Andy Mangold

03 ZEK

sustainable cities™

04 Yucca Studio

05 Designit

Ch.09   We Are Family

**LOGO-SETS /
REMIXES /**

09/
WE
ARE
FAM
ILY

01

02

226

03

While some brands prefer to stick to their tried and tested visual identity, others delight in controlled permutations. The following logo sets do not reflect fundamental alterations for changing tastes and times, but simply variations on a theme. Based on a single core visual or on pertinent logo elements, they always reference the brand's key identity.

Here, a little leeway goes a long way. In one school of thought, spin-off logos of the core identity help to advertise seasonal changes, limited editions, and topical events—from the obligatory snowflakes and Santa hats to cherry blossom festivals, charity appeals, and April Fool fun—or to differentiate between subsidiary companies and product families to showcase the breadth and flexibility available under the main brand. To target different customer segments, a clothing label, for example, might jazz up its logo to appeal to a younger or sports-oriented crowd, while soothing color schemes could indicate a maternity line without changing the brand's overall identity.

A different design approach treats logo sets as equal permutations of a pre-defined standard. Running through the gamut of possible variations, they retain a distinctive shape, color scheme, pattern, or layout, while allowing all other elements in the mix to run wild. In everyday use, these logo sets are not ruled by any obvious hierarchy or firm assignment of specific logos to certain applications. Often created by generative means, by an element of chance, or by a logo generator, they explore the idea of serialization and diversity made visible.

01
Matt W. Moore

02
Matt W. Moore

03
Landor Associates

True to the letter, the logo set designed for the 10th Biennale de Lyon **p.233**, for example, puts an X (the Roman numeral 10) through its paces to highlight the variety of styles and genres on show. In a similar vein, Landor Associates' **03** identity system for the City of Melbourne explores variations on a bold M to create a logo set as multifaceted as the city itself. It is a celebration of diversity and personal interpretation that is as future-proof as it is iconic.

That said, the key question remains as to which elements must stay unchanged to retain or convey a brand's core identity. After all, it is precisely the wealth of variation that pinpoints a great logo's fundamental visual qualities. A basic outline, a distinct color scheme, a certain curve: the more iconic and familiar, the more playful, weird, and abstract these logo experiments can afford to be without sacrificing the Pavlovian response to the parent brand.

04

04
Google
Creative Lab

05
Matt W. Moore

To this end, many sets are based on reinterpreting the original logo's underlying letters. For one of the most obvious and best known examples, look no further than our most popular search engine. Broken down to its fundamental characteristics—general proportions, colors, basic geometric shapes—the Google logo 01, 02, 04, 05 still says it all. Even a smattering of circles will do as clever placeholders for one of the world's most recognizable logotypes. Translated to bubbles, 3D shapes, or search pattern blobs, we can still decipher the encoded brand because it has infiltrated our everyday lives. The characteristic color scheme and general outline are always instantly recognizable.

At the same time, the recognition factor of an iconic logo also betrays how we are shaped by our surroundings, how easily we are swayed and prompted by our subconscious.

In *Super Size Me*, the documentary on the fast food industry, filmmaker Morgan Spurlock used a simple experiment to put our susceptibility for catchy hooks to the test. In front of the White House and other major Political landmarks, he asked U.S. citizens to recite their country's "Pledge of Allegiance," which they all learned in school from an early age, and the McDonalds Big Mac theme. While no participant made it all the way through the pledge, they all managed to rattle off the more complex burger jingle without a hitch.

Branding that is clever, iconic, and comprehensive— aural, visual, or otherwise—leaves its mark on our collective consciousness. Think German Telecom's distinct use of magenta across a wide range of media, sub-brands, and campaigns. Love it or hate it, the mental connection is here to stay, across all logo sets and variations.

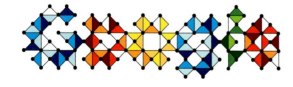

05

01 **FROMKEETRA**
Time and Place Workshop

There's a time and place for everything—and Keetra Dean Dixon has anchored both in her ever-changing logo design for the eponymous Time and Place Workshop.

A collective of experimental makers in the realm of new media and experiential design, the Time and Place Workshop deserved an equally challenging visual identity. Centered around a fixed framework defined by several axes (or tiny arrows) that reflect the collective's computational tools, the logo itself evolves over time: each iteration is generated from a visual library of handmade and digital brand elements.

To allow for further embellishment, the printed version of the logo can be reduced to little more than its defining arrows, filled with a minimum of basic elements. This enables the Workshop's participants to enrich the design by hand or other experimental techniques.

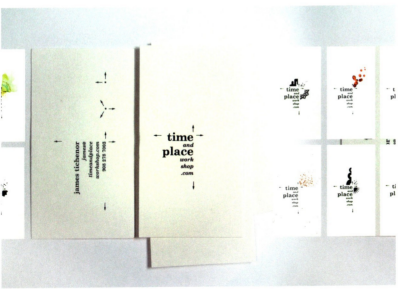

01   CÔME DE BOUCHONY
La Surprise

How do you surprise a client called La Surprise? With a clever ID generator, of course!

In order to distil the agency's essence, Paris-based graphic designer Côme de Bouchony created a toolkit that delivers infinite variety and gives the client the final say and scope for making spontaneous changes.

Whittled down from a huge selection of monochrome shapes, from delicate to bold, from empty to solid, de Bouchony picked the best from three groups: simple rasterized shapes, abstract bolds, and complex light forms.

With the basic framework fixed in place, the client is free to pick shapes from each group and reassemble them to create a specific mood. This allows for almost unending and infinitely complex permutations of elements, overlays, and compositions for a wide range of corporate identity applications and stationery.

Couched within these aesthetic rules, each variation is a surprise and a celebration of the constant spontaneity, flexibility, and creativity at play within La Surprise itself.

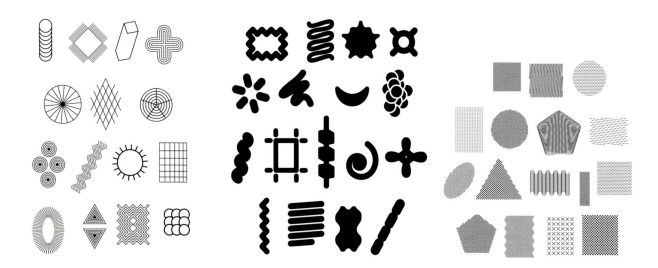

 La surprise
 La surprise
 La surprise
 La surprise
 La surprise

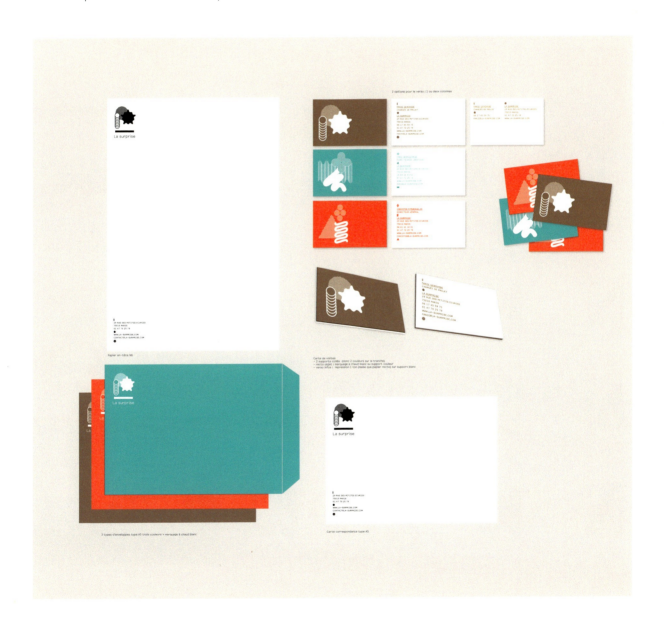

Ch.09 We Are Family

01 Toko

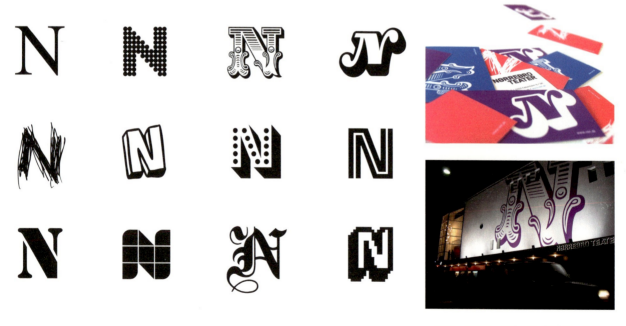

02 Scandinavian DesignLab

01 Donuts

02 Landor Associates

03 Felix Sockwell & Thomas Fuchs

Ch.09　We Are Family

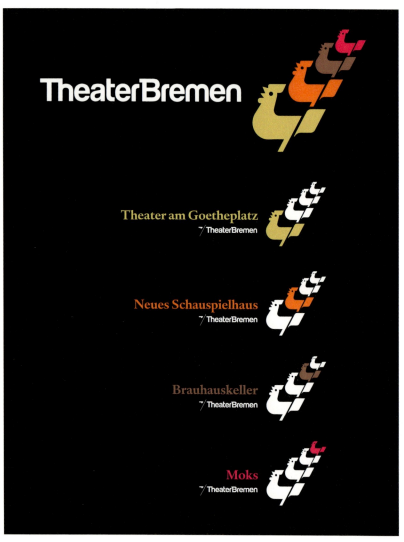

01　Mutabor

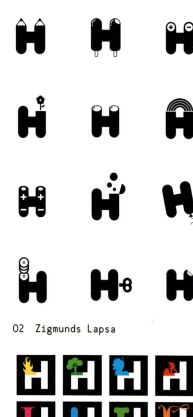

02　Zigmunds Lapsa

03　Floor Wesseling

04　Felix Sockwell, Thomas Fuchs & Steven Heller

We Are Family   Ch. 09

01   milchhof : atelier

235

Ch.09 We Are Family

01 REX

02 REX

03 Zeroipocrisia

04 Hattomonkey

01 **WOLFF OLINS**
AOL

In early 2009, AOL announced its departure from parent company Time Warner. Looking for a complete brand overhaul and a fresh start, AOL decided to retain its name, but to change its approach and overall image.

The newly independent company was keen to shake the persistent 1990s connotations of being a staid and fairly restrictive internet and content provider. It turned to NYC brand consultancy Wolff Olins for a radical redesign that would embrace and reflect its position in the fragmented, non-linear online world.

In AOL's new fluid and flexible identity, only the trademark typeface remains, while a slew of changing images place the three letters against a background of bright, playful, and modern elements that make it clear that AOL is very much alive!

Expressed in optimism, youth, splashes, and splurges, the design features a modern look that runs over the edges—and finally leaves the walled garden behind.

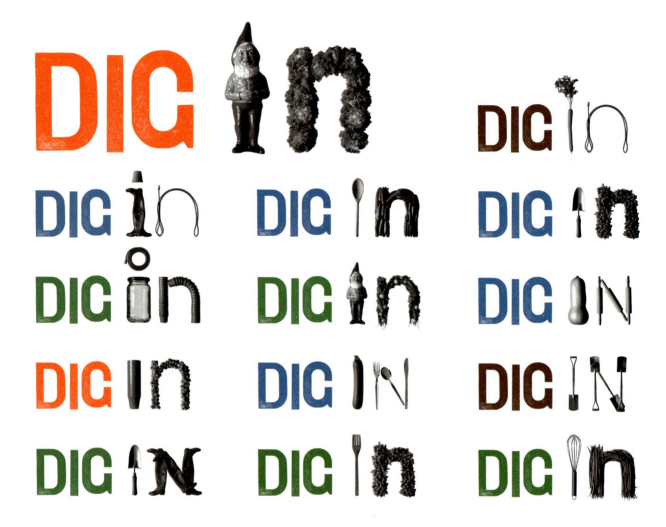

01 **HARRIMANSTEEL**
    BBC Dig In Campain

Lost the plot? Don't fret—HarrimanSteel have come up with a range of tasty reminders to encourage culinary self-sufficiency.

As part of a UK-wide BBC campaign to promote growing and cooking our own food, Dig In attempts to chip away at any ingrained laziness and motivate people to get involved and into the great outdoors. Why fork over your hard-earned cash for expensive pre-packed supermarket food when you can make your own?

For Dig In's multi-part and multi-platform brand identity, HarrimanSteel came up with a basket of logos that match do-it-yourself wood-block prints and gardening and kitchen implements with their delicious results—plucked straight from life or the nearest shelf.

The result combines cause and effect in a single, easy-to-grasp image that conveys the immediacy and satisfaction of knowing what's on your plate.

We Are Family   Ch. 09

01 Landor Associates

02 Trademark™

03 superfried

239

Ch.09 We Are Family

01 Rinzen

02 milchhof : atelier

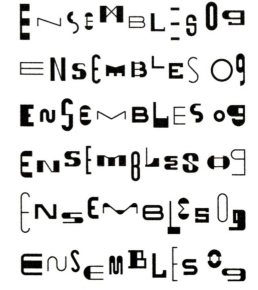

03 Coley Porter Bell   04 ASYL

240

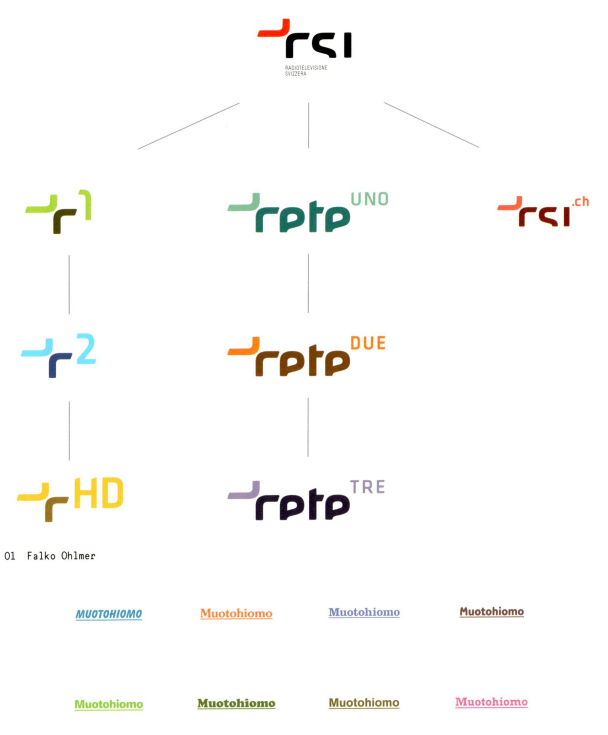

01 Falko Ohlmer

02 Rasmus Snabb

Ch.09 We Are Family

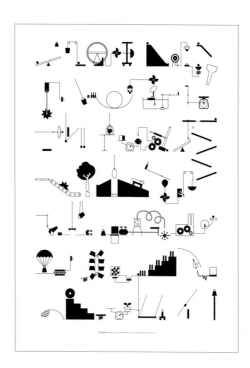

Touchpoint.

01 HarrimanSteel

02 Project 1000

03 Dtam-TM

242

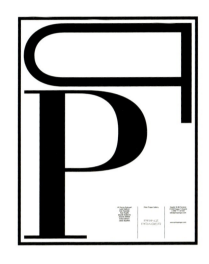
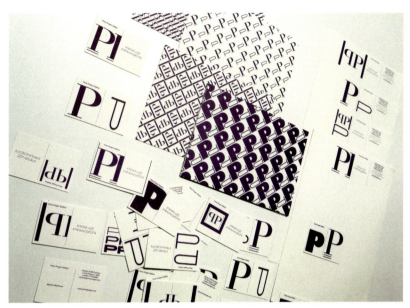

01 Advancedesign

02 Barnbrook

03 Barnbrook

Ch.10   Data

NEO-GEO /
ZEBRA /
ZIG-ZAG /
DOTS /
OP-ART /
GRADIENT /
INFORMATION
GRAPHICS /

01

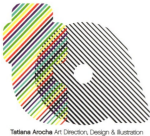
Tatiana Arocha Art Direction, Design & Illustration
02

10/
DATA

PARALLEL LINES /
PATTERNS /
MANDALA /

03

04

244

The following examples draw on information graphics and "misuse" statistical or analytical tools to create a visual representation of a brand's or project's intrinsic essence.

The resulting designs invariably start from basic shapes or scripts and then develop a life of their own. Think processing, 3D modeling, isolines, wireframes, but also the simple joys of geometry, of harmonic lines and shapes, of symmetry and building blocks, of seismic waves and sound patterns. The results are logo templates that range from clear understatement to dizzyingly complex multiverse models.

The associated projects and clients often hail from the realms of design, architecture, and education because generative logos underscore the rigor as well as the creative ramifications, facets, and meanderings of these particular disciplines.

01
EBSL /
Erik Kiesewetter

02
Tatiana Arocha

03
ZEK

04
Extraverage Productions

05
P.Valls &
G. de Lacerda

While scientific principles or connection patterns, tamed and transformed for the occasion, reference an institute of learning or the network behind it, other designs might mimic the visual-memory triggers of circuit-board layouts, pixilated retro computer games, refractive kaleidoscopes, enlarged newsprint dots, graphic design in-jokes like color pickers, or—in the case of Zek's **03** Jackson wireframe logo for K4—3D modeling software.

Others go back to school with basic lessons in geometry that showcase colorful diversity, yet remain abstract enough to serve as a vessel for almost any variable content. More ambitious souls trade up to head-spinningly intricate fractal surfaces that seem to break more than a few rules of visual perception. Very much driven by concept and principle, these logos might actually let legibility or visual "decryption"—a must in logo design 101—fall by the wayside.

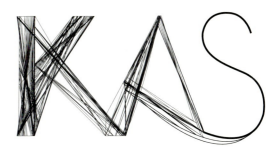

05

A great example of these dos and don'ts is the current resurgence of monochrome patterns. Parallel lines in particular can be incredibly hard on the eyes.
A substantial number of contemporary logo designers play with the notion of contrast and irritation, with repeated monotony and slight variations, to force us to unravel the code hidden in the little disturbances, eddies, and swirls. Shapes might emerge from a clear-cut grid or from seemingly random chaos. Alternatively, logos and lines may morph into a pattern until the original brand disappears. As a result, we become first-hand witnesses of beautiful chaos and symmetry—this is artificial creation at its best.

And while this particular strand of logo design is not exactly rocket science, a basic understanding of the underlying mathematical principles surely helps.
Those with a few scripting skills, for example, can stage controlled generative experiments with a range of surprising outcomes. Based on specific rules or algorithms, these logos might retrace the path of light dots, grow fantasy molecules out of bubbles, or explore the winding ramifications of natural growth and decision trees.

When this concept translates into real-time applications, we are rewarded with (r)evolutionary logo animations. Moving from single-frequency spectrum to full-blown cloud, onlab's **p.286** identity for the online music service SoundCloud encapsulates the platform's distribution of sound over time and on the web in a succinct digital identity and a great visual metaphor for information brought to life.

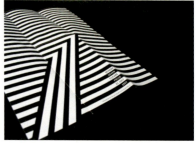

02 Landor Associates

ICONS OF ECO

01 Nicklas Hultman

03 Urbanskiworkshop

Op-Art Data Ch. 10

01 Serif

02 Luke Williams

03 superfried

04 Luca Marchettoni

05 atelier aquarium

247

Ch.10   Data

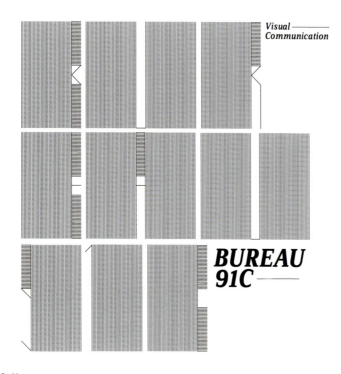

01 HelloMe

02 Luca Barcellona

03 Grandpeople

04 Luke Williams

05 xy arts

06 General Projects

07 Via Grafik

08 Nohemí Dicurú

01 one8one7

02 Mash

03 La Cáscara Amarga

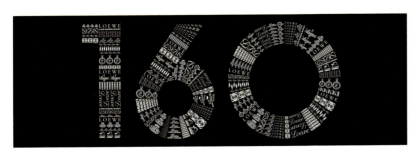

04 Base

Ch.10   Data   Dots

01   Donuts

02   Boldº

03   Fons Hickmann m23

04   Matt W. Moore

05   Siggeir Hafsteinsson

06   MetaDesign

07   Floris Voorveld

08   Designers United

250

01 Fontan2

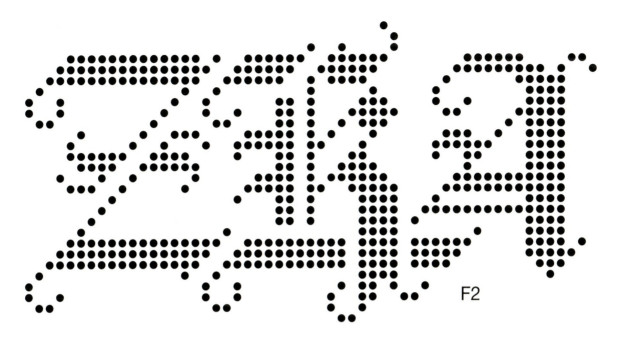

02 Red Box Inc.

03 The Luxury of Protest

Ch.10 Data

Kulturhauptstadt Europas RUHR.2010

01 Edgar Bąk

02 Fons Hickmann m23

03 Lorenzo Geiger

04 The KDU

05 FromKeetra

07 Fons Hickmann m23

08 Monoblock

06 W://THEM

09 nocturn.ro

10 Guapo

252

01 Urbanskiworkshop

02 AND

03 Büro Destruct

04 Bleed

05 Power Graphixx

06 The KDU

07 X3 Studios

08 FriendsWithYou

09 John Beckers

Ch.10 Data

01 1508

02 Robi Jõeleht

03 Fons Hickmann m23

04 sellout-industries™

05 OMOMMA™

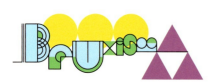

06 Tsuyoshi Hirooka

07 C100 Purple Haze

08 ZEK

01 **TWOPOINTS.NET**
    Bango Music

Variations on a theme: the most basic of colors and geometric forms, recombined and overlaid in a plethora of different shapes. A framework and premise that lend themselves to serialization and label work.

Banjo Music composes soundtracks and jingles for commercials, movies, and television. Their huge variety of on-spec work requires an equally wide range of musical styles. To this end, TwoPoints.Net's visual system for Banjo Music's corporate identity reflects both the tension and variety between the overall label and each project or application.

Two distinct, gentle tones and one typeface in different cuts make the resulting logo distinct, while leaving plenty of leeway for individual variation. "We played with a design synonymous with musical notation: a system that can be as simple as a single note, or as complex as a symphony with both harmony and disharmony."

01 Grandpeople

02 yippieyeah cooperative

03 General Projects

04 eps51

05 NR2154

06 Büro4

07 milchhof : atelier

08 Mammal

09 one8one7

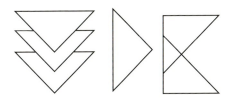
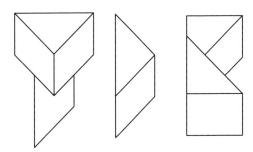

01 Escobas

02 unfolded

03 Negro™

04 Kismanstudio

05 Taeko Isu

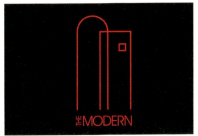

06 Mammal

07 HelloComputer

08 Jürgen Frost

Ch.10   Data

YA ES 215?.

01   No-Domain

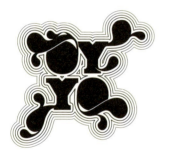

02   Dogma

03   Donuts

04   ALVA

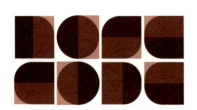

05   Anónimo Studio

06   Black-Marmalade

07   Extraverage

Data   Ch. 10

01   The KDU

02   UREDD

03   Hula+Hula

04   milchhof : atelier

05   ALVA

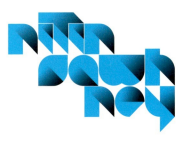

06   Fabio Lattanzi Antinori

07   Negro™

08   OMOCHI

09   Strukt

Ch.10   Data

02 Face.

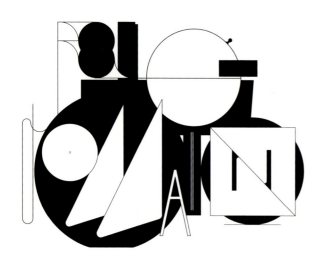

01 No-Domain

03 Fontan2

04 Non-Format

05 No-Domain

06 Ken

07 Manifiesto Futura

08 UNIT

09 Fontan2

260

01   No-Domain

02   No-Domain

03   No-Domain

04   Mr. Magenta

05   Positron Co Ltd

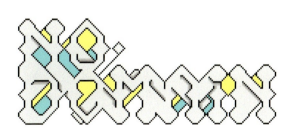

06   Gustavo de Lacerda

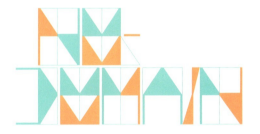

07   Mads Burcharth

08   No-Domain

09   No-Domain

Ch.10   Data

01   Peter Sunna   02   Matteo Mastronardi   03   cerotreees

04   10 Associates   05   Stefan Hornof   06   Acme Industries

07   Sawdust   08   Sawdust   09   Brusatto

10   Søren Severin   11   Scandinavian DesignLab   12   A-Side Studio

01 Fabio Santoro

02 Sawdust

03 Positron Co Ltd

04 Company

05 Lundgren+Lindqvist

06 Haltenbanken

07 Gustavo de Lacerda

08 Heric Longe

09 Heric Longe

10 No-Domain

Ch.10   Data

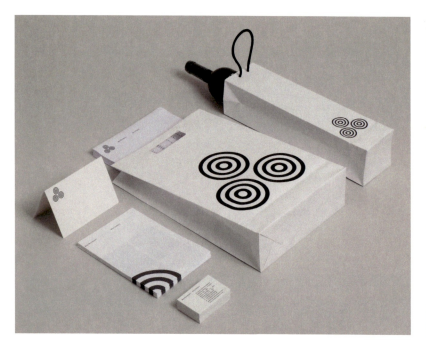

01   Hey Ho

02   Company

01 **FEED**
Mobile Media Lab

It's all in the process: Canada's Mobile Media Lab asked graphics wizards FEED to approach their new brand identity as an experiment that would reflect the lab's own R&D process, as well as the technological and creative aspects of their working styles.

Elegantly skirting all clichés of bitmap typefaces and pixel graphics, FEED conjured up a generative system (using Fontstruct and Scriptographer) that allows users to make subtle changes to the symbol while preserving its recognition value. The result: three series of symbols, each designed on a grid with a different number of units and assigned a specific color.

Suited to a wide variety of applications, from stationery to changing promotional items, the logo even retains its evolutionary aspect over time: eventually, the graphics on Mobile Media Lab's website will change according to user comments posted on the website.

MIND DESIGN

London/
United Kingdom

Pages
108, 183, 266–268

Mind Design is a London-based independent graphic design studio founded by Holger Jacobs in 1999.
With a strong focus on craftsmanship and typography, the studio pursues a fresh and refreshingly oblique approach to developing visual identities and integrated design for print, web, interior design, and architecture.

What is the first thing you do—or find yourself inspired by—when commissioned to design a logo or visual identity?

A good logo should always be unpretentious and truly reflect the company or organization it represents, ideally in an original way. To this end, don't look at too many logos; trust your instincts, look around you, and start to see things as shapes. Everything can be an inspiration.

I usually wait a little and just walk around with the brief in my head. Often enough, there is suddenly a connection with things I notice by coincidence. After a week or so, I tend to have more ideas than I really need and we put them on the computer to see what they could actually look like. This is followed by a long period of tweaking and fine-tuning. We often design countless variations until we feel that there is nothing left to be added or taken away.

To what extent is the client involved?

It is a step-by-step process. We tend to show the client all of our initial thoughts, so they become quite involved in the development. Just remember, this is not always advisable—you need to know who can handle it and who can't. Clients frequently want to make changes that wouldn't work visually, or try to squeeze too much into one logo. When this happens, you obviously have to argue your case. Once we have narrowed it down to one logo idea, we broaden our scope again and explore its possibilities.

By the way, I think it is a myth that designers always want something radical and clients something safe and conventional. Often it's the other way around!

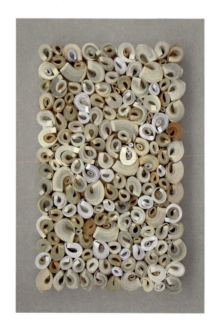

01

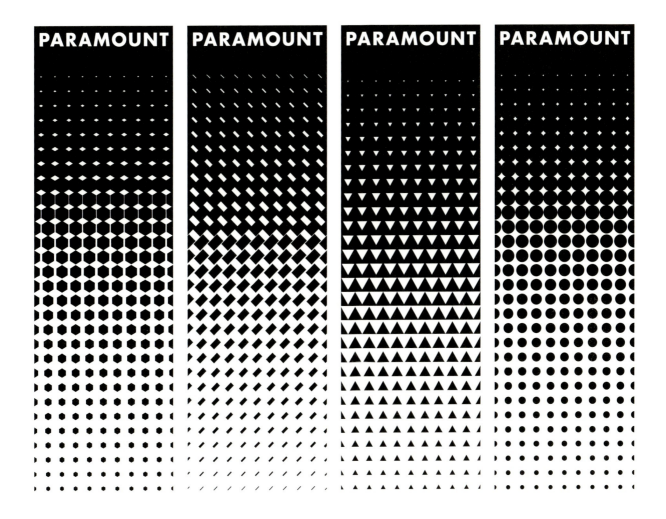

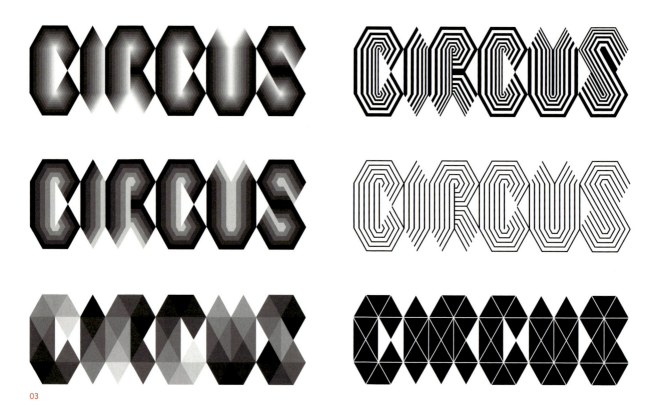

03

So what kind of clients does your studio attract?

Many of our clients are entrepreneurs or start-ups and they like to work with designers that are very hands-on. We don't waste their time with lengthy brand-strategy or positioning presentations; we try to get to the real work as quickly as possible. Form and content go hand in hand.

How does this translate to the Paramount[02] logo and visual identity? Can the resulting patterns be varied or altered by the client?

Paramount is a club and event space situated on the top three floors of the Centre Point building, one of London's first skyscrapers. Our design concept is simple and based on two aspects: the building's architecture and the notion of height. We created a set of four graduation patterns that reflect an upward movement. Each pattern is based on one of four simple shapes (hexagon, triangle, circle, or stripe) found on the building or in its interior, and then repeated it 33 times (for 33 floors). We also made a shorter version of the logo and a word mark but those should only be used when there is not enough space for the tall version.

Sections of the pattern were used for different applications. Variation was important, considering the wide range of media and applications the patterns would be used for (brochures, stationery, menus, tapestry, signage, sliding glass screens, etc). As long as the patterns are cropped in the right way (always across the centre), they are suitable for an almost infinite number of uses.

And what does the Znips[01] logo represent? How does it tie in with the book installation?

Znips was a small project for a hair and beauty salon in southwest London, inspired

07

04

by cut-and-paste punk graphics and — quite obviously — strands of hair. At first the logo felt a bit unrelated to the overall shop environment, so the owner asked us to come up with an idea for a wall she wanted to cover. We cut a lot of old books into small strips and rolled them up like locks of hair. It was a simple and cost-effective way to connect the logo with elements of the interior.

—
In terms of typography, your designs for Gumbo and Tess[p.183] are faintly reminiscent of ransom notes.

The Gumbo logo was designed for a children's animator and cartoonist. It is a simple interpretation of the word "gumbo." On the website the font of each letter changes randomly to reflect the different styles of his work.

Tess, on the other hand, was a little more complicated and a collaboration with Swiss designer Simon Egli. The resulting identity for this modeling agency draws on several logo variations based on a modular system of art-deco–inspired elements. The same elements are then used to frame images of the models on various printed applications. In theory, the system allows for many logo variations, but we limited it to six color and six black-and-white versions for general use.

—
Apart from your own work, what is your all-time favorite logo?

The 1968 Mexico Olympics design by Lance Wyman. It not only connects elements of traditional Mexican culture with op-art, but it is also part of a simply beautiful multi-faceted system. It is an example of true craftsmanship that seems to have inspired its era's marketing ideas rather than being controlled by them.

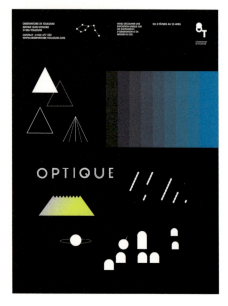

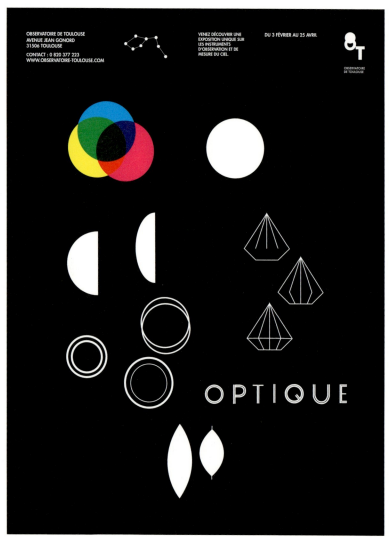

01 **AVALANCHE**
Toulouse Observatory

Parisian-based design duo Avalanche often start from a word or image that inspires them at a particular point in time. Encompassing a complete rethink of both basic logo and visual identity, their work for Toulouse Observatory is the result of a happy coincidence: as chance would have it, a rayograph (more commonly known as "frame" or "photogram") by Man Ray was lying on their office desk and became the design's natural starting point.

Exploring and exploiting the simplicity of color mixing by overlay, prismatic effects and optical illusions, Typography Optics was created from pieces of cut cardboard to reference the observatory's inherent focus on light, prisms, lenses, and geometric optics. In a final twist of design sleight of hand, the broad field of optics was then linked to its counterpart in the sky (e.g. via planets, constellations, and the Milky Way).

The subsequent identity incorporates two initials: O for "observatory" and T for "Toulouse," and the first letter's shape serves as a reminder of the location's singular—and staggeringly huge—lens. In the interpretation of the observatory's various optical devices, and in the reliance on black and white interspersed with the three primary colors of the prism, the resulting logo and visual identity achieve a remarkable coherence in shape and color with a clever touch of science appeal.

Data   Ch. 10

01 ADVANCEDESIGN
The Brno House of Arts

Let's get critical! In their work for the Brno House of Arts, Advancedesign decided to test — and overstep — the limits of their initial assignment. The resulting design is no run-of-the-mill corporate identity, but an ever-shifting "corporate alterity." Instead of a lasting and solid trademark (as prevalent in the realm of business), the designers opted for a constantly changing logotype that would replace uniformity with infinite variety.

Reminiscent of a color picker, the basic design consists of three layers of concentric circular surfaces. While the first stratum contains 24 color variants, each representing one hour of the day, the second layer features 60 differently colored circles to represent the minutes contained in this hour. Finally, there is a third tier for the 60 seconds of every minute.

According to the time of observance or generation, the logo shape and color scheme will display a combination and overlay of the specific colors assigned to the hour, minute and second hands of a clock-face. As a result, the museum's logo becomes as individual and unique as the encounter of an artist with the House of Arts. And while the circular shape pays homage to an institutionalized ideal of art, its deformation denotes the artist's perpetual effort to transgress or enlarge this framework.

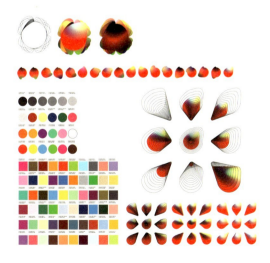

271

Ch.10 Data   Edhv

EDHV

Eindhoven/
The Netherlands

Pages
37, 73, 106, 197,
204, 272–275, 365

Extremely versatile and always surprising, the designs and logos crafted by Dutch studio Edhv like to toy with our sense of perception.
Whether kaleidoscopic refractions, time-based logos, or even insect-generated identities, the resulting works reveal the process of generation—and a pure delight in experimentation.

What do you look for in a great logo?

A good logo should look like it has been around for a while. It should never force itself into your visual cortex, but slide straight into your long-term memory.

At the same time, a logo can hide a lot of details specifically crafted into it by the designer. These details often remain unnoticed—which means the designer did a good job. More often than not, the devil is in these details and a good logo can convey a complex message.

The FedEx logo, for example, has everything a logo should have: robust typography, simplicity in form and color, and a very recognizable and timeless design. Last but not least, there is the clever arrow hidden inside. A classic! It always attracts my attention.

So is that the magic formula?

For me, there is also another side to the equation. A successful logo does not always have to look nice, be well executed, or even communicate successfully. When I think about it, there is much more to a good identity.

During a holiday on a Mediterranean island, for example, I passed by a market where there were a lot of trucks parked, all belonging to local butchers. All of their logos showed a happy pig. Some of them were chopped in half, but that didn't stop them from smiling. I found this really interesting because it seemed to indicate that the logos of this particular microcosm influenced each other. The smiling pig had become a de facto standard. Is this good or bad? I guess, for the local butchers, it worked. And it taught me that logos are also subject to deeply embedded, hard-to-break traditions.

01

272

02

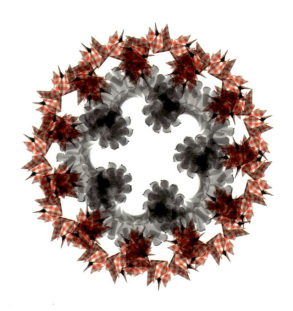

03

Sounds like conflicting evidence. How do you navigate these contradictions?

To innovate in design, you have to leave the safe path, which is probably the hardest thing to do as a designer. See how far you can push your clients but do not push them over the edge! Use reason instead of opinion: don't let your personal designer needs and pleasures get in the way of the message that the logo is supposed to convey. Peel off as many layers as you can to get to the absolute DNA of the identity. Freak out every once in a while.

And do not underestimate the effect of third-party criticism after your job is done. People tend to be suspicious of anything new. It can make a client very insecure, even if you did a really good job.

There seems to be a strong conceptual slant to your work—visual identities and otherwise.

If you work with us, you never know what you are in for. Even we don't know what we are in for. Our research tends to be intense and ambitious. Clients who recognize and understand the added value of this are rare. But those who give us the freedom to wander off and explore these unconventional paths are sure to get something unique and lasting.

It takes a lot of guts to break with traditions in Logoland. Not just for the designer, but also for the clients because, in the end, they are the ones sticking their necks out. Designers and clients really need to trust each other, otherwise it simply will not work. So we take our clients along for the ride and slay the dragons together. With more corporate clients, we have to take their whole organization along—otherwise they can become the dragons you are out to slay! Now that would be a mess.

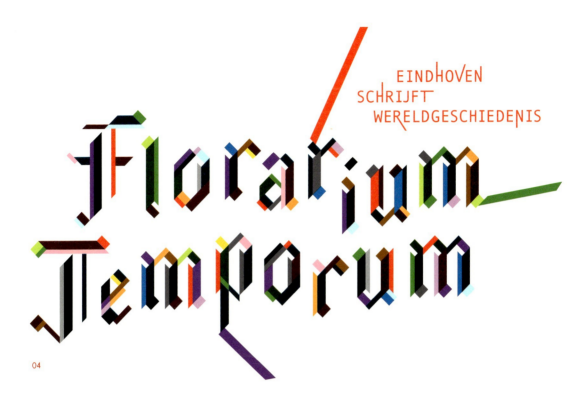

04

Moving on to your featured logos: could you explain the background to your Florarium Temporum design? [04]

This was an identity for an exhibition on a book written in 1472. The original cover had been lost, so we designed a new logo inspired by calligraphy and stained glass windows.

And how about the "growing" project for De Buitenwereld? [p.365] **How did it work in practice?**

De Buitenwereld (Dutch for "the middle of nowhere") is a restaurant on a traditional Dutch farm in—you guessed it—the middle of nowhere. During our research we came across some old graphics inspired by nature. So we asked ourselves how we could translate this aspect into contemporary, naturalistic imagery, and whether it could actually work as an identity.

We wanted to capture the notion of growth, so we made stop-motion movies of tiny plants growing out of pre-cut paper. The result worked really well, because the logo grows from invisible to readable to overgrown to unreadable, before finally going of control. In this way, we managed to integrate the fourth dimension of time into the identity.

Bits 'n Pieces [01, 02] **also explores our ties to nature.**

"Bits 'n Pieces" was the name of an exhibition in New York on post-digitalism. During the brainstorming phase for our own exhibition piece, we discovered millions of tiny creatures crawling around in the soil of our banana plant. It was absolutely fascinating. At the same time, we had also really enjoyed the "out of control" aspect of De Buitenwereld. So we decided to work with insects to see if we could generate and isolate specific identities by tracking their movements and behavior. Every insect species has its own unique way of moving around. Soon, we started to do posters, logos, and even three-dimensional furniture and jewelry based on these movements. Next step: architecture?

NR2154

Copenhagen / Denmark

Pages 256, 276–281

NR2154 is a multidisciplinary design team based in Copenhagen and New York. Besides logos and visual identities, the studio also creates typography, exhibitions, books, magazines, websites, films, and campaign material.
A framework for loose collaboration, the design studio evolved from the two founders' cooperation on several magazine launches. Today they work independently and together on various projects in the framework of NR2154.

Despite living and working in different cities, their original motto, "the project always comes first", still stands and is reflected in the project number that gives the studio its name.

01

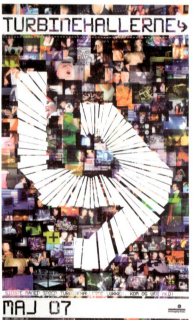

02

03

04

Could you run us through the NR2154 logo creation process?

It all starts with research—and with suppressing your instinct to just go ahead with the design. After this initial step, we jot down and sketch out our thoughts and ideas. This is a very important phase because, at this point, you are still able to look at the task and design with fresh eyes. The next step involves testing typefaces, symbols, colors, etc. Once all of this has been done, we can start to assemble the different elements and distil our ideas into logo proposals to be tested in context.

Do you instinctively "know" what is right for a particular client?

Method is the key, but intuition is also very important, even though sometimes you have to go against your instinct and kill your darlings. For example, we once did a logotype for a magazine called *F100*. It was extremely simple, but unfortunately it could also be read as FIDO. When readers made fun of this, the editors got very unhappy and we had to change the logotype.
Looking back, changing it was probably a big mistake, considering all the attention the original logo generated—and because perfect is not always best!

Your own logo and business cards are based on a grid system [05, 06]. How does that work in practice?

We created a simple grid to be filled with a generated typeface. While we have a set font for digital use, there are absolutely no rules for the handwritten version; everyone can use their own signature style. This way, the visual identity reflects the overall structure and set-up of our company: a multidisciplinary design network that gives designers their own space and freedom.

05

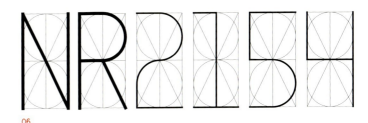

06

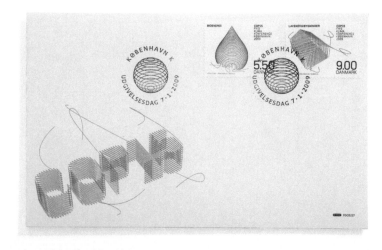

07

08

We were also intrigued by your work for the Royal Theatre's Turbinehallerne [01, 02] in Copenhagen. The defining elements (arrows and letters) seem to be deliberately cut up and overlaid. Does this reflect the theater's direction or intent?

In its former state, the Turbinehallerne was used to produce huge electrical turbines, so when we designed the theater's visual identity, we imagined these big turbine blades cutting through the typeface, photos, etc. At the same time, the dissection and reassembly also symbolizes the mix of performance, music, art, and social interactions in a theater that is trying to do everything differently.

A similar aesthetic comes into play in your designs for LiveWired Music [03]. What is the idea behind this particular visual identity?

The idea was to communicate the notion of "connecting, combining, and sharing," which is LiveWired's goal on an artistic and community level. This is illustrated by the logo's unbroken line and connecting letters.

And what about the UN Climate Change Conference in Copenhagen [07–11]?

When we started to work on our initial logo proposal, we had just read *An Inconvenient Truth* by Al Gore and found ourselves shocked but also inspired by it. The book's famous graph, depicting the simultaneous—and speedy—rise of temperature and CO_2 levels, gave us the idea to use a "temperature line" in the conference logo to represent each of the UN's 192 member countries.

We started out with a visual that referenced the atmosphere, but the globe—the blue planet—turned out to be a far stronger image. After all, the Climate Change Conference was not just about CO_2 emissions. We later realized that the symbol transcended its scientific meaning: different people saw different aspects related to the world, communication, cohesion, and climate. When that happens, you know that you have found an interesting solution.

Finally, are there any other logos out there that you love and admire?

The WWF logo: despite its serious message, it is so simple, clear, and positive. And it would be great to design a logo for the Olympics!

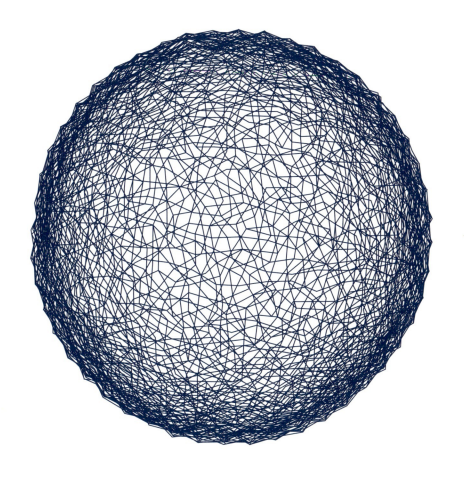

COP15
COPENHAGEN
UNITED NATIONS CLIMATE CHANGE CONFERENCE 2009

Ch.10   Data

NR2154

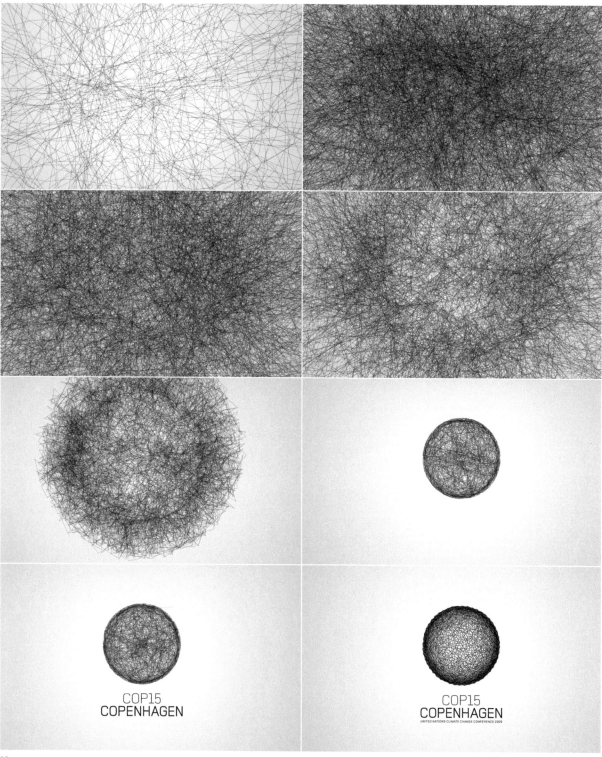

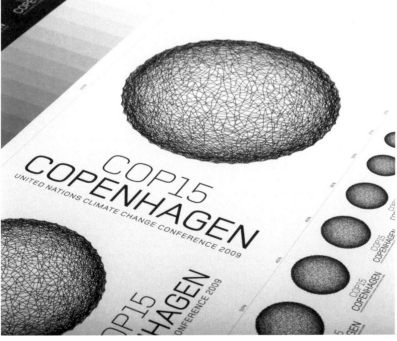

/

Selected from 268 proposals, NR2154's logo and visual identity for the 2009 United Nations Climate Change Conference underscores the dichotomy inherent in nature and in our own relationship with the world.

Based on just two colors (white to signify a new beginning and the UN's peace missions, blue for our blue planet) and a network of lines representing each UN nation, the logo presents us with a complex structure that could be heading towards unrest or balance, just like Planet Earth.

In this sense, the logo, and its animation, signifies challenge and chance, pitfalls and potential, and confusion, chaos, and coherence. It reinforces the conference's import and urgency: the fact that, from this moment on, things could go either way.

Incidentally, the corporate identity package also included postage stamps to carry the message around the world.

01 SAGMEISTER INC.
Casa Música p.282–285

Built to celebrate Porto's year as the European Capital of Culture in 2001, Rem Koolhaas & Ellen van Loon's striking Casa da Música plays host to a huge variety of different sounds and events, from high-brow symphonies to exuberant club nights.

This massive geometric structure has added a new landmark to the region and is truly unique, featuring solid walls, odd angles, uneven sides, and sharp corners. This is reflected in Stefan Sagmeister's bold and versatile visual identity: from orchestra to minimalist beat, from rough paper models to Perspex crystals, Sagmeister's approach reinvents the structure as a musical gem and takes it out into the world.

 casa da música    casa da música

 casa da música    casa da música

 casa da música    casa da música

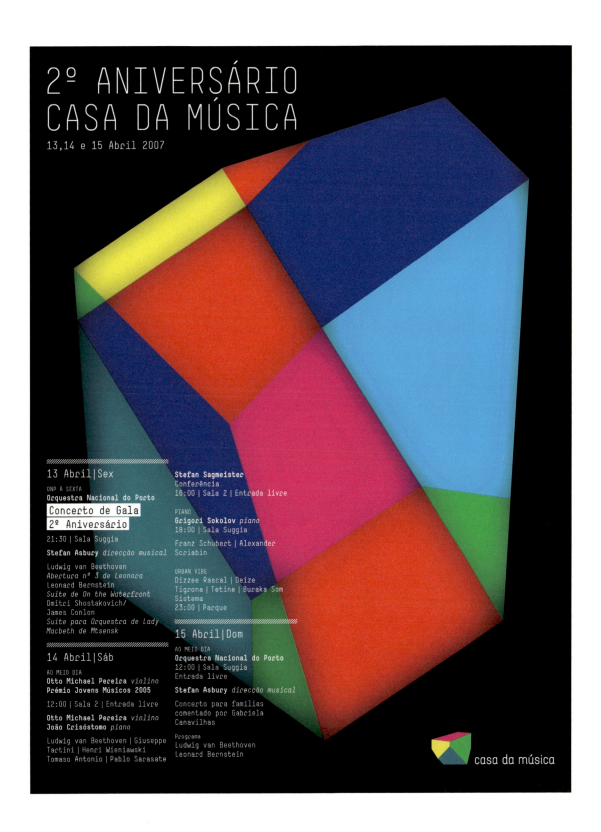

Ch.10 Data   Sagmeister Inc./Casa Música

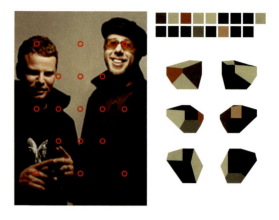
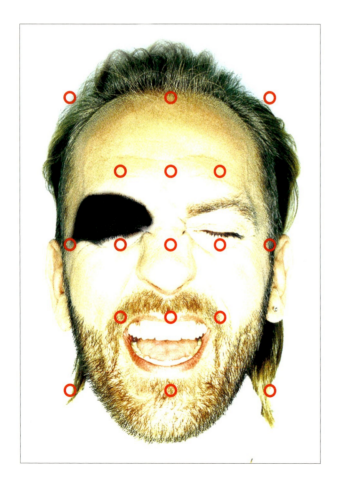
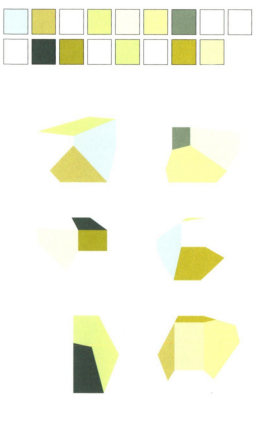

/

As an added extra, a logo generator provides bespoke identities for each event. Simply upload the artist's promo picture, and a color picker will do the rest. The resulting, multi-faceted logo might feature Mozart's earthy patina, pop-infused acid lemon tones, or a range of cool clubbing grays.

As such, Sagmeister's logo permutations and 3D studies highlight the different sides of this unpolished gem—and reveal the breadth of glistening facets hidden within.

Ch.10 Data

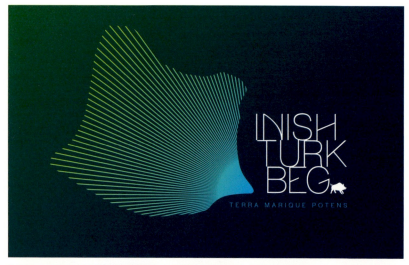

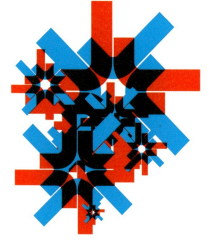

01 Coley Porter Bell

02 Faith

03 ODD

04 onlab

286

01 **KURSIV**
   Copenhagen Natureschools

Peter Graabaek's logo for Copenhagen Natureschools encourages future students and their parents to find their own branch of learning and education.

A perfect replica of itself on increasingly smaller scales, the logo mimics the structures and geometry of the natural world. Strict and strictly governed, yet organic and playful at the same time, the fractal-like pattern allows the logo to invade its surroundings, endlessly growing and replicating itself.

Like a benign version of the ancient Greek Hydra, each continuation opens up three new branches and thus a new path. In doing so, the logo reflects the wealth of ramifications and new opportunities present in nature, school, and our lives.

Ch.10   Data   Mandala

01 nocturn.ro

02 strange//attraktor:

03 The KDU

04 REX

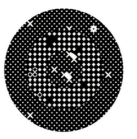 
05 Toko   06 Hold   07 Masheen

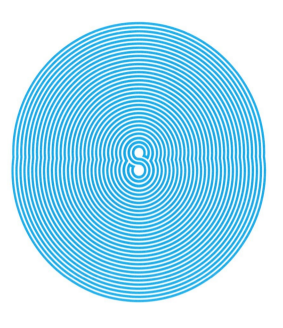

01 The KDU

02 The Action Designer

03 cypher13

04 1508

01 Manifiesto Futura

02 Team Manila

03 Floor 5

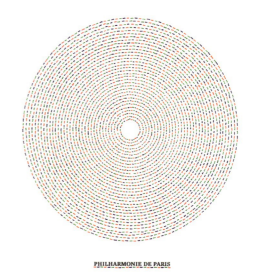

04 Xavier Barrade & Mathieu Laroussinie

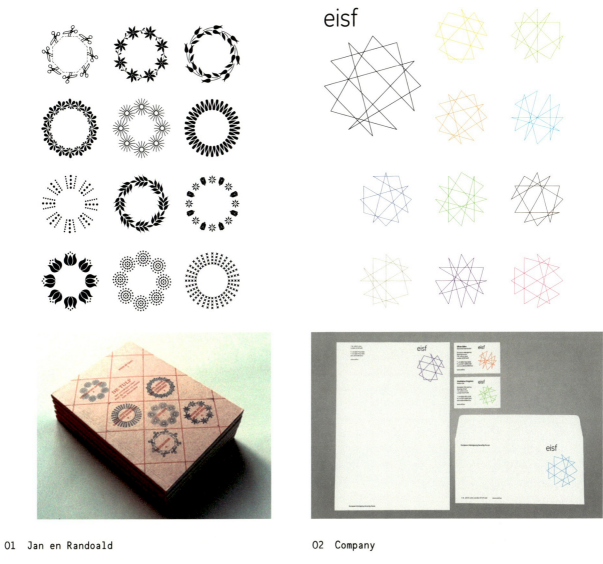

01 Jan en Randoald
02 Company

03 Hattomonkey

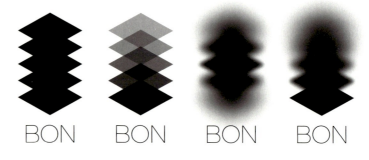

02 Accident Grotesk!

01 Mash

03 Accident Grotesk!

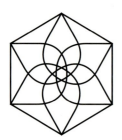

04 Accident Grotesk!

05 Accident Grotesk!

 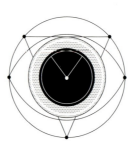 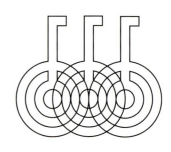

06 Anthony Lane

07 Dtam-TM

08 La Cáscara Amarga

  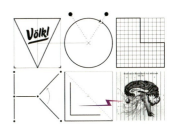

01 Kokoro & Moi   02 KOA   03 backyard10

04 Büro Destruct   05 Brusatto

06 Analog.Systm   07 Gabe Ruane   08 T. Hirter & A. Stebler

09 Fons Hickmann m23   10 Peter Schmidt Group   11 REX

01 Søren Severin
02 Identity
03 Estudio Soma

04 Benoît Bodhuin
05 Meatpack
06 Heric Longe

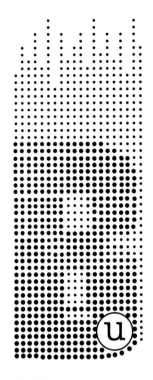

01 elRAiSE

02 HORT

03 The KDU

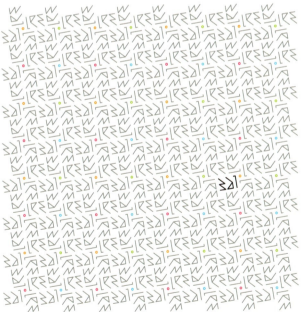

04 The KDU

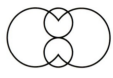

01 **HORT**
Booka Shade

Two peas in a pod, yet both one of a kind: Walter Merziger and Arno Kammermeier of DJ and production duo Booka Shade have been collaborating for more than a decade, while also pursuing their own separate projects.

To reflect these variations on a theme, HORT came up with a modular set-up for the duo's DJ performances. Based on the design agency's unique Booka Shade typeface, which is constructed of simple geometric shapes, the resulting logo variations tweak a signature triangle and figure eight into a pared-down tree, a bespectacled face, a broad-beaked bird (for solo performances), or a stylized pair of decks when both DJs play together.

Instantly recognizable despite these variations, HORT's design underscores the fact that this is a matter of small differences. After all, both members of Booka Shade are on the same page—musically and otherwise.

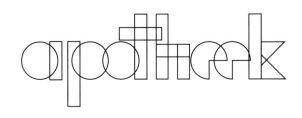

02 GVA Studio

03 LLdesign

01 TWhite design

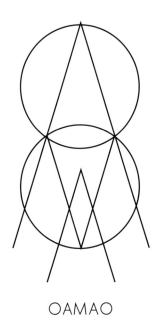

05 Mads Burcharth

06 ALVA

04 HelloMe

07 Calango

Ch.10 Data

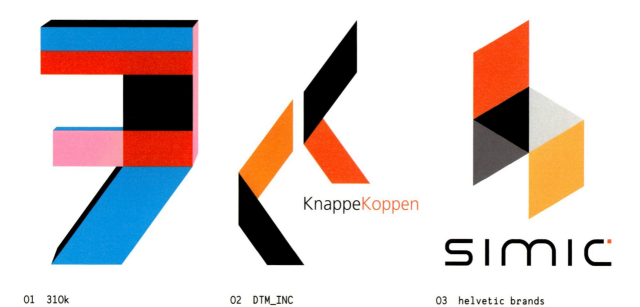

01 310k

02 DTM_INC

03 helvetic brands

05 modo

04 Identity

06 Toko

01 **HEYDAYS**
   ITI identity

Software company ITI is considered a pioneer in automation technology, solving everyday challenges in all parts of life. Picking up on this business philosophy, Oslo-based design studio Heydays decided to go for an equally out-of-the-box solution that would reflect ITI's functional, yet flexible approach.

Based on the six-sided blueprint of a standard cube, the resulting visual identity hints at countless possible permutations. As such, it illustrates the wealth of ITI options on offer across a wide range of company communication measures, from stationery and manuals to pens, business cards, and digital storage media.

02 cabina

03 Madhouse

04 Leplancton

05 Wolff Olins

Ch.10 Data

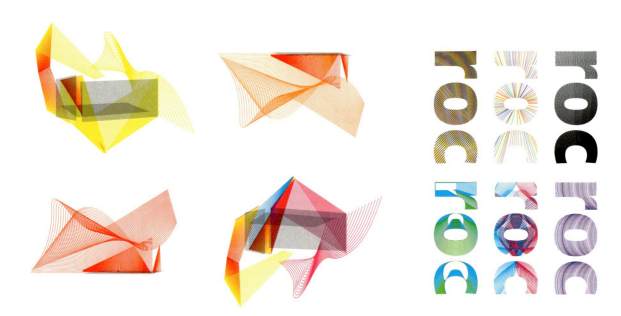

01 Fons Hickmann m23

02 Fons Hickmann m23

03 Hansje van Halem

04 Hansje van Halem

05 Falko Ohlmer

300

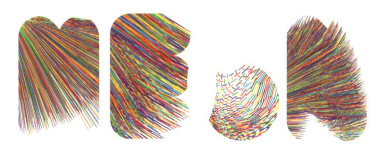
01 Acme Industries

02 Christian Rothenhagen

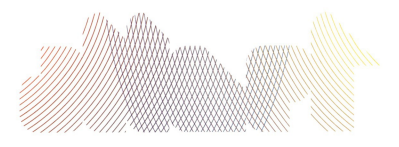
03 Stefan Romanu

04 Matt W. Moore

05 Bodara

06 The KDU

07 Autobahn

08 M.F. Brunse, M. Clottu & A. Zouari

Ch.10　Data

01　Théo Gennitsakis

02　Stylism

03　Théo Gennitsakis

04　Slang

05　Dennis Herzog

06　HelloMe

07　Rocholl Selected Designs

08　cabina

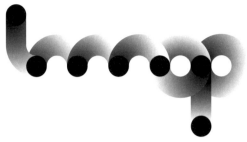

01 cerotreees

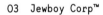

02 The KDU

03 Jewboy Corp™

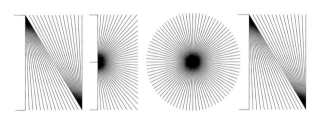

04 Manifiesto Futura

05 Faith

06 Tsuyoshi Hirooka

Ch.10 Data

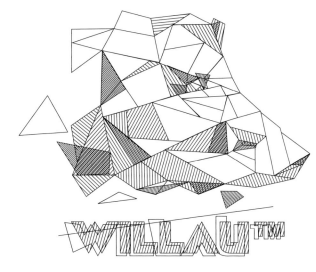

01 Koehorst in't Veld

02 eps51

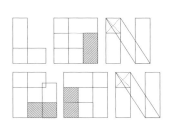

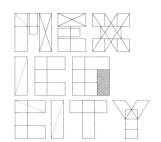

03 John Beckers

04 John Beckers

05 John Beckers

06 Stefan Romanu

07 Staynice

08 Franz Falsch

Data   Ch. 10

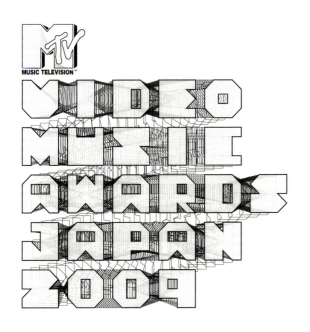

01   Tsuyoshi Hirooka

02   Just Smile And Wave

03   Moshik Nadav

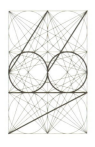

04   C100 Purple Haze

05   Raf Vancampenhoudt

06   ZEK

07   Emmanuel Rey

305

11/ ORNAMENTAL

CRESTS /
CALLIGRAPHY /
VICTORIAN /
FLOURISHES /
GOTHIC /
RAMIFICATIONS /

01

02

03

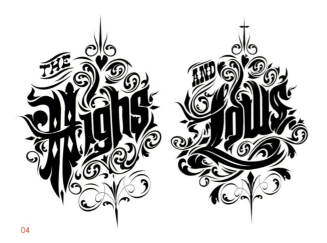

04

These logos appear intrigued by calligraphy and gothic cuts, and chart the journey from medieval church pews to street culture, from abstract typographical riddles to elaborate, richly populated flourishes.

04
Like Minded Studio / Luca Ionescu

05
We love moules frites

Like modern badges of honor, contemporary coats of arms herald a change in logo design and a cautious return to traditional skills. A prime example is Luca Ionescu's 04 *Highs and Lows*, an elegant solution that firmly transports crested, ornamented symbolism to the present and bridges the gap to underground heraldic references prevalent in graffiti and hip-hop culture.

Purists, look away now. With plenty of superfluous style and flourish, ornamental logos give tradition and craft a welcome typeface-lift. Conveying a sense of lush extravagance, of weighty hauteur of haute couture, they pay homage to the finer things in life by infusing logos with a hint of nostalgia and old-fashioned elegance.

Other designers encourage their letters to sprawl and spawn new life, conjuring up carefully pruned flora and fauna that seems ready to escape the restrictions of the alphabet.

01
Wissam Shawkat

02
THE SKULL DEZAIN

03
Áron Jancsó

Following the flow of the pen and giving it freedom to roam and embellish, these unnecessary, yet delightful swirls refresh established—and possibly staid—brand identities. Chic, classic, and up-to-date, ornamental logos promise instant rejuvenation with a retro twist, and range from straightforward beautification measures to deliberate games of information hide-and-seek among their delicate whorls, lines, and filigrees.

In this tricky realm between hand-sketched indulgence and almost rigid, computer-generated structures and offshoots, the ornamental balance is shifting slightly from borrowed life-forms and forays into Wonderland towards formal typographical exercises and calligraphy encoded with extra lines and patterns. And in their nod to Far Eastern penmanship, these visual identities also reflect the global nature of logo design. Naturally, ornamental exercises are not confined to our own Roman alphabet, but lend themselves equally well to Arabic, Hebrew, Thai, or Chinese, to name just a few non-Western alternatives.

05

Ch.11 Ornamental

01 Tim Bjørn

02 Hype Type Studio   03 Tatiana Arocha   04 Mash

308

Ornamental Ch. 11

01 miniminiaturemouse

02 Loic Sattler

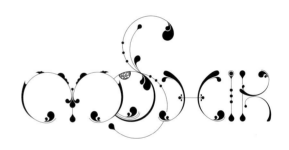

03 Moshik Nadav

04 phospho

05 Deanne Cheuk

06 THE SKULL DEZAIN

07 Mammal

309

Ch.11   Ornamental

01   Jared Mirabile

02   Zion Graphics

03   Faith

04   Burro Design

05   Dog and Pony

06   DTM_INC

07   NALINDESIGN™

08   Benny Gold

09   THE SKULL DEZAIN

10   DTM_INC

11   Filmgraphik

Ornamental Ch. 11

01 Federico Landini

02 Chris Rubino

03 ATTAK

04 Black-Marmalade

05 Philipp Pilz

06 Autobahn

Ch.11   Ornamental

01   Derek A. Friday

02   Rasmus Snabb

03   ellenberg-martinez

04   Joshua Distler

312

01 Luca Barcellona

02 Hula+Hula

03 ellenberg-martinez

04 NNSS

05 Reaktor Lab

06 Stefan Romanu

07 Moxie Sozo

08 Allan Deas

09 Allan Deas

10 Leplancton

11 Project 1000

12 Philipp Pilz

Ch.11   Ornamental

01 Wissam Shawkat

02 Wissam Shawkat

03 Wissam Shawkat

04 Wissam Shawkat

05 Wissam Shawkat

Ornamental Ch. 11

Edmonton Azure   Mashal Al Abdool

01 Wissam Shawkat   02 Wissam Shawkat

03 Wissam Shawkat   04 Wissam Shawkat   05 Wissam Shawkat

06 Alen 'Type08' Pavlovic   07 Wissam Shawkat   08 Wissam Shawkat

Ch.11   Ornamental

01   The KDU

02   Like Minded Studio

03   Tatiana Arocha

04   Tatiana Arocha

05   The KDU

01 Base

02 Studio Baum

03 The KDU

04 Toko

05 X3 Studios

Ch.11   Ornamental

01 ATTAK

02 The KDU

03 OMOMMA™

04 Mehdi Saeedi

05 Wissam Shawkat

Ornamental Ch. 11

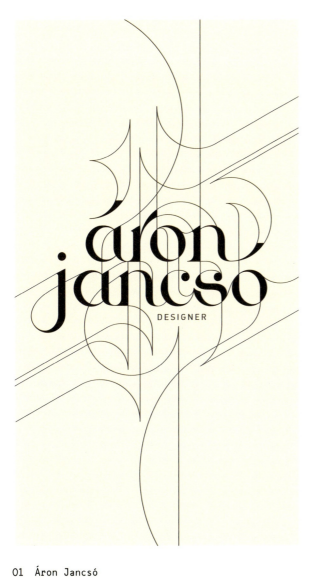

01 Áron Jancsó

02 TWhite design

03 Ali Khorshidpour

04 xy arts

05 Mehdi Saeedi

06 Mehdi Saeedi

Ch.11   Ornamental

01   Mitchell Paone

02   Madhouse

03   Zion Graphics

04   Studio Output

05   Andrea Gustafson

06   Mitchell Paone

07   Faith

01 KalleGraphics

02 Lab2

03 Base

04 The Action Designer

05 Markus Moström

06 Daniel Blik

07 Accident Grotesk!

08 Blake E. Marquis

Ch.11 Ornamental   Gothic

01 Matthew Manos

02 Aldo Lugo

03 Jared Mirabile

04 Fresh Estudio

05 Face.

06 No-Domain

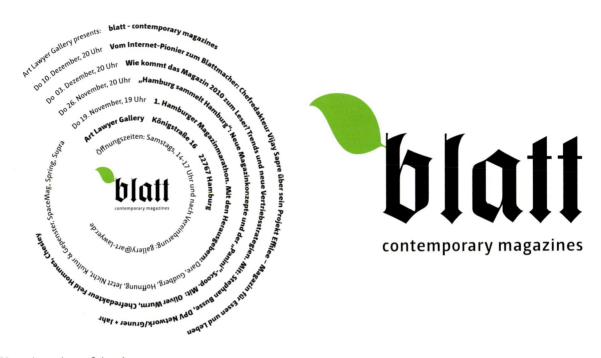

01 gebrauchsgrafikundso

02 A-Side Studio

03 Bleed

04 Áron Jancsó

05 LaMarca

06 The KDU

Ch.11　Ornamental　　　　　　　　　　　　　　　　　　　　　　　　　　　　　　　　Gothic

01　Floor Wesseling

02　THE SKULL DEZAIN

03　Áron Jancsó

04　Zion Graphics　　　　05　Like Minded Studio　　　06　Benny Gold

07　Jared Mirabile　　　　08　Hype Type Studio　　　　09　ATTAK

01 cerotreees

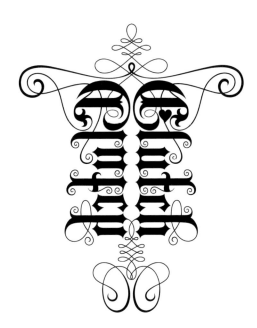

02 Andrea Gustafson

03 Inksurge

04 The KDU

05 Working Format

06 Jared Mirabile

07 Jared Mirabile

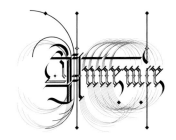

08 cerotreees

THE KDU

New York / USA

Pages
38, 42, 90, 97, 102, 120, 210, 223, 252–253, 259, 288–289, 295, 301, 303, 316–318, 323, 325–329, 341

01

Brooklyn-based The Keystone Design Union (The KDU) is a global creative collective with over 700 members from disciplines as diverse as magazine publishing, medicine, photography, fashion, and architecture.
Despite several prestige clients on its consultancy roster, The KDU frequently explores logo options that can, at first glance, appear daring or left-field.
While preserving the spirit of the core brand, The KDU might surprise a snowboard manufacturer with a rather sober, conservative look, or add a touch of street to an old-fashioned mark.

02

03

04

05

—
A lot of The KDU's output is not necessarily "mainstream," yet you enjoy a high-profile client base. What do you think attracts big-name companies to The KDU?

Ha! I don't know how to answer that. Everything we show has been approved by our clients, so hopefully that makes it mainstream to some extent.

I think big clients are attracted to us because we put strategy and business first. We see design as a lubricant of the overall business system. When we create a visual identity, we don't make art, but design solutions that help our clients grow. What some might see as radical, we see as necessary. So even if the solution seems a bit out of the box, it is ultimately driven by a desire to help our clients.

—
So what tends to be the first step in designing a logo or visual identity?

We try to figure out what the passion is behind the company. What is its history? Who started the brand and why? Is there a natural narrative we can tap into? We love to work with passionate people who speak about their business with love—not managers forced to adopt their current brand's rhetoric. I find that using the truth in identities is always more effective than creating something from your imagination.

Generally speaking, you should always try to avoid trends and look to icons developed 50 or more years ago that are still alive and well today. However, while a main brand mark should be timeless, classic, and simple, beyond that it is okay to explore various treatments and styles to communicate more effectively with certain consumer groups—but you always need a strong core icon.

—
How do you know which designer from your pool is "right" for which project? Do you pit their talents—and designs—against each other?

We never pit people against each other, but there is a healthy amount of competition in the network. I usually pick which members create solutions for which client. It all boils down to understanding who has the right perspective and experience, which means I have to understand literally hundreds of different personalities, working methodologies, styles, and tones!

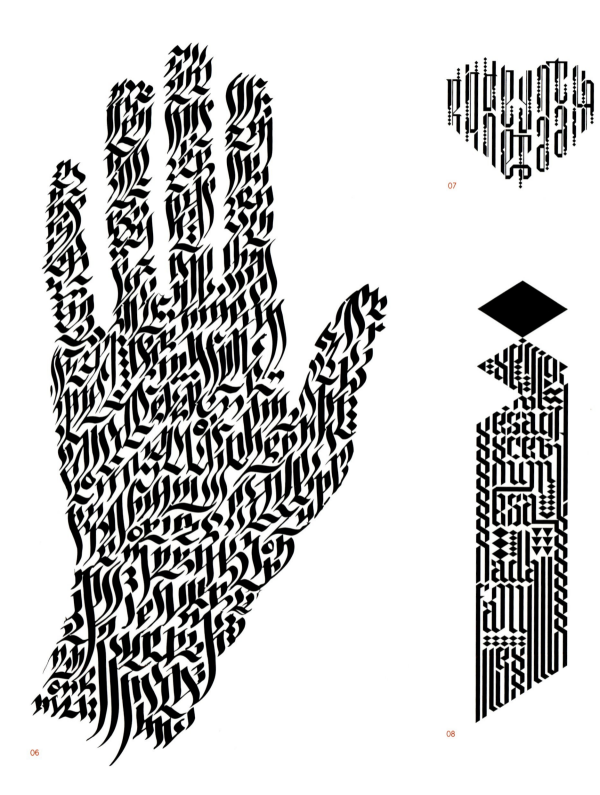

06

07

08

09

10

11

12

And how do you know when you are finished?

We don't really have a process—it is very organic and can go fast or very slow. Ultimately, it's a gut feeling. You just know when it's right. You can feel when something is not refined enough, just like you can tell when it is being overworked. I think the designer's instinct plays the largest role in determining when the mark is ready.

Several of your submissions flirt with calligraphy or graffiti references.

Not graffiti, but calligraphy has always been a strong influence. While I respect graffiti, it is a culture that my partners and I have not directly contributed to. At the same time, I think that the lines between calligraphic and graffiti styles are becoming more and more blurred in the modern world.

Are there any secret favorites in the mix?
It would be impossible to select just one logo, but personally, I prefer the more organic logos that are hand-drawn and heavily reliant on word marks. One that stands out is the work we did for LVMH. It gave us the chance to explore new takes on icons that have been in use since 1765. You have to be extremely careful and considerate when you are reworking a large brand with such a rich history.

What about seminal brands outside of the KDU universe that got it right?

I love Mercedes-Benz, with Apple's timeless icon a close second. The Mercedes form is elegant and simple and it works well within the context of automobiles. Actually, I would love to work with automobile identities more—from both a naming and overall visual identity standpoint. I think so many car companies could improve on their models' ID and turn each into a powerful sub-brand within the company.

Ch.11   Ornamental

01   Jared Mirabile

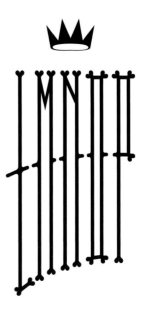

02   cerotreees

03   Ben Whitla

04   Raf Vancampenhoudt

05   Guapo

06   cerotreees

01 Designers United

Ch.11　Ornamental

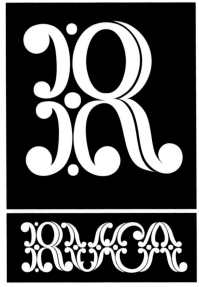

01　Like Minded Studio

02　Yucca Studio

03　Like Minded Studio

04　Jet Black Tribal Ink

05　TWhite design

06　Jared Mirabile

07　Xavier Barrade

08　Jet Black Tribal Ink

09　THE SKULL DEZAIN

Ornamental   Ch. 11

01   KOA

02   Luca Barcellona

03   DTM_INC

04   310k

05   Aldo Lugo

Ch.12 Retro/Naïve

12/ RETRO/NAÏVE

01

02

NOSTALGIA /
FOLKLORE /
LETTERPRESS /
SILKSCREEN /

03

Retro/Naïve   Ch. 12

04

Favored by many bands, bars, and breweries, this subset of logo design adds a touch of folklore and naïve exotica to overprinting, letterpress and silk-screen aesthetics, op-art patterns, wood cuts, and classic typography. Stir in a mid-twentieth century color palette and you get a contemporary take on modernism that flirts with youthful nostalgia, post-war optimism, and pioneering frontier aesthetics.

01
illDesigns

02
Alphabet
Arm Design

03
Mikey Burton

04, 05
Red Box Inc.

These retro references are currently enjoying a strong resurgence thanks to a yearning for nostalgia and to a rose-tinted, romantic view of hand-crafted quality and the good old days. People love a product with a good story and expressive heritage—even when it is based on a well-executed fake.

In these logos, aesthetics and technology go hand in hand. While the limited line-width or color options of traditional printing techniques demand new approaches to the design, the cheeky pleasures of deliberate mistakes, of smudges, splashes, and splurges, add a personal touch to the finished logo. Restricted to just one or two colors, the process

itself comes to the fore. By embracing these print-related limitations, the resulting identities convey a sense of straightforward candor, hands-on involvement, and down-to-earth integrity.

This style is in high demand. Many musicians, music venues, bars, restaurants, and family-run distilleries yearn for this sense of authenticity and unfiltered "honesty." They want something that is unique and sincere—none of that new-fangled digital stuff!

Proudly flaunting its inherent imperfections, its missing ink and misalignments, this rough and ready letterpress style is indelibly linked to early frontier fonts, vaudeville bonhomie, and spirited pioneers, to hand-printed notices pinned to the wall of a saloon or sheriff's office, announcing town gatherings, community dances, or today's specials.

Even designers who recreate this do-it-yourself aesthetic by digital means often bow to the intrinsic limitations of letterpress and silk-screen printing, to color limitations, faults, and fuzzy edges where the paper

05

335

06
ilovedust

07
Inksurge

08
Superlow

doesn't quite catch the ink. With their promise of faithful application and authenticity, the resulting logos cherish these imperfections as specks of humanity in an all-too-perfect world; an approach particularly suited to country retreats, high-end restaurants, bespoke beauty products, and one-off promotions such as Alphabet Arm Design's [02] wine tasting events.

On a similar note, the associated patina-tinged pastel shades, often combined with white typography, add a sense of lightness and approachability to the brand. Pristine, pure, and innocent, they hint at the promise of a sheltered life,

06

of a long-lost Americana as wholesome as apple pie. Infused with plenty of retro chic, these visuals say "we care" and—like Redbox's [04, 05] logo for the Shortbread Bakery, a boutique food brand treading the thin line between high-end exclusivity and cozy familiarity— convey a sense of homemade goodness.

Well-aware of these ingrained associations, some logo designers have started to take a more subversive look at this kitsch-infused essence of 1950s suburbia. In their design for Adidas Originals, Sellout-Industries [p.342] confront us with a cutesy innocence more at home in a housewife-populated knitwear emporium. With this deliberate exploration and exaggeration of gender clichés, they force us to take a closer look at our own preconceptions and at the brand itself.

07

08

Retro/Naïve   Ch. 12

01 Mikey Burton

02 G. Lacerda & R. Cunha Lima

03 Mikey Burton

04 Blake E. Marquis

05 Like Minded Studio

06 illDesigns

07 Hexanine

Ch.12　Retro/Naïve

01　Strohl

02　Jesse Kirsch

03　Giorgio Paolinelli

04　Jesse Kirsch

Retro/Naïve   Ch. 12

02 Weather Control

01 Subcommunication

03 Studio On Fire

04 Irving & Co   05 Jesse Kirsch   06 Strohl

 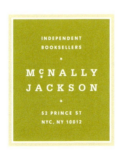 

07 Hatch Design   08 Strohl

Ch.12   Retro/Naïve

01   Alen 'Type08' Pavlovic

02   Ptarmak, Inc.

03   Ptarmak, Inc.

04   Ptarmak, Inc.

05   Ptarmak, Inc.

06   Ptarmak, Inc.

07   Ptarmak, Inc.

08   Ptarmak, Inc. & FÖDA Studio

09   Trademark™

Retro/Naïve Ch. 12

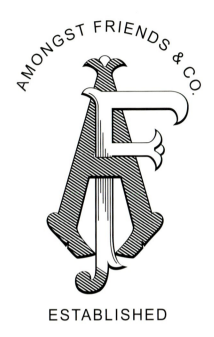

01 The KDU

02 Mash

03 Ptarmak, Inc.

04 Andy Mangold

05 Blake E. Marquis

06 DIE SEINER

07 Ptarmak, Inc.

08 Axel Raidt

Ch.12   Retro/Naïve

01   44flavours

02   sellout-industries™

03   Goldjunge Grafik & Design

04   Goldjunge Grafik & Design

05   Goldjunge Grafik & Design

06   Mikey Burton

07   Alphabet Arm Design

08   Luke Williams

01 HUSH

02 The Lousy Livincompany

03 Mitchell Paone

04 Michael Lashford

05 Red Box Inc.

06 A-Side Studio

07 John Beckers

Ch.12   Retro/Naïve

u c o n
———
A C R O B A T I C S

01 Falko Ohlmer

02 Mitchell Paone

03 Mitchell Paone

04 Mitchell Paone

PAROCHIA
LOCALLY GLOBAL

05 A-Side Studio

MELON
MOON

06 T. Hirter & A. Stebler

Retro/Naïve   Ch. 12

01 Trademark™

02 max-o-matic

03 Mitchell Paone

04 Toben

05 Weather Control

06 Studio On Fire

07 max-o-matic

345

Ch.12   Retro/Naïve

01   ROMstudio

02   Philipp Pilz

03   Allan Deas

04   Studio EMMI

05   Weather Control

06   Strohl

07   Weather Control

01 Mammal

02 Lapin Studio

03 Moxie Sozo

04 Moxie Sozo

Ch.12   Retro/Naïve

01   The Pressure

02   Floor Wesseling

03   Amy Jo

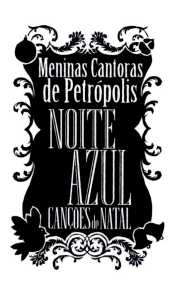

04   Boldº

05   U. Strasser & M. Baud

06   Trademark™

348

01 44flavours

02 sellout-industries™

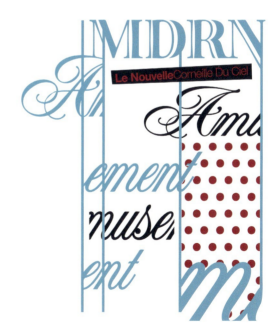

03 Kelly D. Williams

Ch.12   Retro/Naïve

01   Achilles Greminger

02   Achilles Greminger

03   Achilles Greminger

04   Achilles Greminger

05   Achilles Greminger

06   Achilles Greminger

07   Achilles Greminger

08   Achilles Greminger

09   Amy Jo

COOK COUTURE

01 Achilles Greminger   02 Bodara

03 Achilles Greminger   04 sellout-industries™   05 Studio On Fire

06 Matt W. Moore   07 anna-OM-line

Ch.12 Retro/Naïve

01 Barnbrook

01 A-Side Studio

02 Celeste Prevost   03 Mikey Burton   04 44flavours

05 Büro Destruct   06 Ptarmak, Inc.   07 INDASTRIACOOLHIDEA

Ch.13 Tactile

01

INSTALLATION /
MATERIALITY /
MISMATCHED /

13/
TAC
TILE

02

HAND-CRAFTED /
DIY /
TANGIBLE /

03

04

In an age where almost any information—be it newspaper articles, video clips, photographs, or music files—is only a few free clicks away, the unique immediacy of tangible objects, of sensory experiences and intense performances, is enjoying a resurgence of popularity.

Logo designers are also delighting in their newfound freedom and are increasingly swapping pen or screen for a more hands-on design experience. In their exploration of do-it-yourself culture, they toy with the rules of scope and perception to translate symbols into tangible space, and then back again to a logo-sized icon.

01
GWG inc.

02
BETA STUDIO

03
Kyle Bean

So, what comes first: 3D model or 2D image? In the case of logos and visual identities, the answer is a resounding "both!" While the pretty necklace that We love moules frites 04 designed for "Ladies & Girls" lays out the existing signature look in a pattern of real chains, Pandayoghurt 06, 07 picks a very different route by spinning a yarn for knitwear specialist Mayko. Starting from a real ball of wool, the designer later re-abstracts the image into a more versatile and scalable graphic icon.

Others leave the confines of the page and the safe office environment, taking their logos out into the world to celebrate the unique immediacy of a physical object. Ready to scale mountains or—in the case of Kyle Bean's 03 self-promotional web address—the nearest set of steps, they shake off the traditional ties of design and creation. If you don't come to us, we will simply take our identity to you!

Bean's letters are also a great example of cardboard in action. Cheap, sturdy, cheerful, and not a million miles away from the original creative blank slate, paper and board remain the most basic and popular building blocks, especially for outsized type. Some logo enthusiasts add a further dimension by cutting, folding, molding, perforating, embossing, slashing, and burning their logotypes. Or, like Toko's p.360 logo for Rainy Day Industries, they conjure up that personal touch with smudges and raindrops.

In their search for cheap and expendable materials, these pioneers of new and tactile realms try almost anything that comes to hand or from the nearest do-it-yourself store. The resulting logos brim with the joys of experimentation as they explore the intrinsic properties of their chosen material—from the

04
We love moules frites

05
Meatpack

05

355

above-mentioned cardboard to needles, thread, ribbons, pencils, nails, wires, silly putty, buttons, playing cards, found objects, clay, Styrofoam, fridge magnets, ice, water, stone, ink blobs, sequins, and even letters that grow into shape. If it's moveable or shapeable, it's fair game for appropriation!

Even food makes it into the mix to imbue the resulting identity with added sensory, even sensual qualities and emotions. Sean Freeman's **p.371** drizzled invitation for Cream, an event showcasing 20 top creative teams from around the world, is ephemeral and delicate by definition, which makes it all the more impressive.

Pitted against their own natural properties, such temporary designs and sculptures might not survive the pivotal moment, but captured on film (and sometimes retranslated into a more user-friendly and scalable digital version), they reveal the process and its short-lived intensity—the moment of something bursting into flames, of popping bubbles and ashy flakes literally going up in smoke—thereby mirroring the logo's intended use.

06, 07
Pandayoghurt

06

The majority of the following visual identities were created for a single event or purpose, for a festival, announcement, or limited edition, for something as short-lived, yet as special and intense, as the process of creation itself. As such, they briefly liberate the logo from the page or screen and literally take it outside the box.

01   ZEK

02   Gianni Rossi   03   Gianni Rossi

Ch.13   Tactile

01 Kyle Bean

02 Filmgraphik

358

Tactile   Ch. 13

01 HANDVERK
Veien Til København

The road to change?
Norwegian design studio Handverk have made it their mission to reveal the special, strange, and beautiful aspects hidden within every project.

Their identity for *Veien Til København (The Road To Copenhagen)*, a television show on climate change, took the concept and topic into the real world. They used recycled materials or actual humans and scattered them liberally around the city to spell out the theme of each episode, creating a visual hook before each show aired.

Unlike a slick channel or program IDs, this pre-show intro is no faceless logo. Starring those involved in and affected by the issues in the shows, it picks up on the transient, dynamic, and fragile nature of human and climate interactions. It shows people working together to get something done, then dispersing again into the city.

02 HANDVERK
Paradox Film

Paradox is an independent producer of commercials and films. Norwegian studio Handverk have created a range of filmed logos for the company, which are screened before every Paradox film. To find inspiration for these clips, Handverk delve deep into the production in question. More often than not, their brief urban interventions take place in a setting or scene taken from the film itself.

These short snippets provide a real link to what will follow and allow the public to participate in the mise-en-scène. They make Paradox part of the city's fabric and highlight the behind-the-scenes process of assembly and disassembly.

Ch.13   Tactile

01 Fons Hickmann m23   02 Toko

03 Linnea Andersson

JI LEE

New York/
USA

Pages
75, 230, 363—365

Born in Korea, raised in Brazil, and now a resident of NYC, Ji Lee likes to explore the delicate balance between graphic works and urban interventions, between professional assignments and personal projects.
So when he is not decorating his ceiling with miniature replicas of his own home, or building 3D chessboards with all the pieces perched high on opposing hills, Lee works as a freelance artist and designer and also as a creative director at Google Creative Lab.

Generally speaking, what is the essence of a great logo?

A logo is the simplest and most memorable visual means to communicate the fundamental nature of an entity. Simplicity and timelessness are the qualities shared by some of the best identities of all time—IBM, Apple, Volkswagen, and FedEx.

With this in mind, any words of advice for budding logo designers?

The key is to work with the right clients who are smart and open-minded. Try to really understand them and their particular needs. And don't be afraid to communicate the obvious!

In addition, I advise my students to avoid the temptation of designing their own logos. It is the ultimate over-design and a sign of self-indulgent amateurism. My own worst rookie mistake was to design my own logo.

Naturally, we would love to know a bit more about your work for the New Museum. How did this commission come about[p.361–363]**?**

01

Before the opening of the New Museum in downtown New York, the management approached several agencies to pitch for an ad campaign to announce the opening. At the time, I was working at one of the agencies, Droga5, and we submitted a proposal.

Could you take us through the creative process—from the initial idea to the final campaign choreography and its various permutations across the city?

The New Museum's striking new home was designed by Japanese star architects SANAA. They opted for a very simple, yet fascinating solution: a series of rectangular boxes stacked on top of each other. Inspired by the structure, we decided to focus the entire campaign on the building's unique outline.

After all, the campaign was going to be about the opening of the new building, and the single most striking aspect for the public would be this curious-looking outer facade.

So we sketched out the silhouette and made it our main design and core module. The shape became a window to reveal new and unexpected things, and a concept that could be applied literally everywhere: to posters, print ads, a billboard, and even a custom-shaped bicycle.

—

Did you encounter any particular pitfalls, challenges, or (un)pleasant surprises?

As the museum's marketing and media budget was rather small, we had to be very inventive and take the do-it-yourself approach. We had to improvise and make things ourselves, like all the Bloomingdale's window installations. We spent hours cutting the pieces, painting them, etc. Luckily, the client was very open-minded and—for the most part—let us do what we wanted. It was a lot of fun!

—

How did the New Yorkers react to this change in the fabric of their city?

For this project we played with the notion of mystery. Take the "defaced" billboard: to achieve the effect we poured magenta ink down a Calvin Klein billboard on one of the most prominent streets in downtown New York.

For days after it first appeared, people had no idea what was going on. The dripping increased as the days progressed and so did the mystery surrounding it. Some people thought it was vandalism and there was plenty of speculation in blogs and magazines.

In the end, you get the best advertising when others speak for you. And this is what happened with the New Museum campaign, because it was mysterious, engaging, and always changing.

—

Your team's Google design seems to follow a similar ethos by reducing an iconic logo to its basic shape and components. Did the briefing allow you to go wild or were there any particular restrictions?

There really was no brief. Google had a booth at Macworld and we had to come up with simple ideas for giveaways. Most companies resort to mouse pads, USB sticks, and logo stickers, but people don't tend to like such obvious branding.

02

So I abstracted the Google logo to the level where it does not look like a logo anymore, but more like a cool code. At the same time, the Google logo is powerful and recognizable enough to broadcast the brand. Now we had something fun people were happy to stick on their laptops and cell phones, or to wear on a T-shirt.

—

You seem to enjoy taking your work out onto the street. What drives you to these urban interventions? Are they always commissioned and sanctioned, like the New Museum campaign?

My first real experience with street art was the "Bubble Project." I placed more than 50,000 speech-bubble-shaped stickers on top of street-side advertising panels, inviting passers-by to fill them in. To me, streets are a great platform for expression and communication.

Street art is free, democratic, fresh, and scalable. And lessons learned from my personal street interventions also apply to my professional projects. They complement each other.

—

And how do you get the balance right between commercial work and your own projects? Is there any overlap or interference?

I always work on both. Personal projects give me the freedom to pursue what I feel really passionate about. There is no one to censor me or to stop me from doing something I believe in. I can explore things at my own pace and have fun doing it.

This fresh perspective, spirit, and positive energy then spill over into my professional projects. These commercial commissions, in turn, give me financial stability and the opportunity to collaborate, learn, and communicate with others on how to make the best use of mass media. Again, this helps me with my personal projects. It is a symbiotic relationship with constant, positive interactions.

03

Ch.13 Tactile

01 Derek A. Friday & Shawn English

02 No-Domain

03 Dennis Herzog   04 Toben   05 Christian Borstlap

01 Edhv

Ch.13 Tactile

02 KalleGraphics

03 Nicklas Hultman

01 Weather Control

04 Hype Type Studio

05 L. Barcellona & M. Klefisch

06 Red Design

07 Typejockeys

01 Faith

02 MH Grafik

03 Projekttriangle Design Studio

Ch.13 Tactile

01 dancemade

03 Nico Ammann

02 44flavours

04 Fabian Bertschinger

01 There is

ADDRESS INDEX

– A

#

1508 Denmark
info@1508.dk
1508.dk

Pages 220, 254, 289

0c/0m/0y/0k Germany
Daniel Adolph
daniel@0c0m0y0k.de
0c0m0y0k.de

Page 195

10 Associates
United Kingdom
hello@10associates.co.uk
10associates.co.uk

Page 262

21bis Netherlands
Frank Dresmé
frank@21bis.nl
21bis.nl

Page 208

310k Netherlands
info@310k.nl
310k.nl

Pages 118, 298, 333

3deluxe Germany
info@3deluxe.de
3deluxe.de

Pages 73, 121, 203, 211, 218

44flavours Germany
hello@44flavours.de
44flavours.de

Pages 131, 140, 150, 154, 155, 156, 157, 158, 161, 175, 179, 342, 349, 353, 368

903 Creative USA
Aaron Gibson
903creative.com

Pages 49, 215

A

A-Side Studio United Kingdom
contact@a-sidestudio.co.uk
a-sidestudio.co.uk

Pages 10, 23, 50, 113, 175, 217, 218, 262, 323, 343, 344, 353

Accident Grotesk! Germany
Timothy Santore & Patrick van den Heuvel
welovedesign@accidentgrotesk.com
accidentgrotesk.com

Pages 107, 292, 321

Achilles Greminger Switzerland
info@ashi.ch
ashi.ch

Pages 350, 351

Acme Industries Romania
acme@industries.ro
acmeindustries.ro

Pages 8, 14, 45, 62, 71, 101, 108, 163, 170, 208, 220, 262, 301

adam gf United Kingdom
info@adamgf.com
adamgf.com

Pages 50, 75

Advancedesign Czech Republic
Petr Bosák & Robert Jansa
info@advancedesign.org
advancedesign.org

Pages 243, 271

aim Designstudio Germany
info@aimdesignstudio.de
aimdesignstudio.de

Page 117

Akatre France
Valentin Abad, Julien Dhivert & Sébastien Riveron
akatre@akatre.com
akatre.com

Pages 66, 68, 72, 82, 83, 84, 85, 196

Akinori Oishi Japan
ceo@aki-air.com
aki-air.com

Page 139

Aldo Lugo Mexico
info@aldolugo.com
aldolugo.com

Pages 57, 87, 102, 111, 211, 322, 333

Alen 'Type08' Pavlovic Croatia
type08@gmail.com
type08.com

Pages 33, 44, 315, 340

Alessandro Mingione Italy
info@alessandromingione.com
alessandromingione.com

Pages 44, 49

Alex Trochut Spain
hello@alextrochut.com
alextrochut.com

Page 210

Alexander Penkin Germany
mail@alexanderpenkin.com
alexanderpenkin.com

Page 149

Alexander Spliid Denmark
contact@logointhegogo.com
alexanderspliid.com

Page 23

Ali Khorshidpour Iran
alikhorshidpour@yahoo.com

Pages 13, 56, 319

Allan Deas United Kingdom
info@allandeas.com
allandeas.com

Pages 163, 313, 346

Alphabet Arm Design USA
info@alphabetarm.com
alphabetarm.com

Pages 44, 98, 334, 342

ALVA Portugal
info@alva-alva.com
alva-alva.com

Pages 117, 185, 258, 259, 297

Amy Jo USA
hey@missamyjo.com
missamyjo.com

Pages 348, 350

Analog.Systm Iceland
Oscar Bjarnason
analog.sys.is

Pages 11, 98, 101, 213, 293

A N D USA
usa@and.ch
and.ch

Page 253

And Studio Australia
hello@andmelbourne.com
andmelbourne.com

Pages 99, 111

André Beato Portugal
mediaoneunltd@gmail.com
andrebeato.com

Pages 55, 99, 113, 208

Andrea Gustafson USA
lady.faya@gmail.com
artoffaya.com

Pages 10, 99, 103, 121, 150, 320, 325

Andreas Töpfer & Buchgut Germany
andreas.toepfer@kookbooks.de
andreastoepfer.blogspot.com

Page 20

Andreina Bello Canada
andreina.bello@yahoo.com
abello.ca

Pages 128, 129

Andy Mangold USA
andymangold@gmail.com
andymangold.com

Pages 37, 204, 225, 341

Anna Haas Switzerland
anna.haas@gmx.ch
annahaas.ch

Pages 122, 134

anna-OM-line Spain
Anna Maria Lopez Lopez
hello@anna-OM-line.com
anna-OM-line.com

Page 351

Annika Kaltenthaler Germany
ak@annikakaltenthaler.de
annikakaltenthaler.de

Pages 71, 206

Anónimo Studio Venezuela
anonimo@anonimostudio.com
anonimostudio.com

Pages 218, 258

Anthony Lane USA
hello@012485.com
012485.com

Pages 194, 292

Anti/Anti USA
sayhi@antiantinyc.com
antiantinyc.com

Page 152

Áron Jancsó Hungary
aronjancso@gmail.com
behance.net/milen

Pages 55, 103, 197, 207, 306, 319, 323, 324

Art Machine Germany
Julian Hrankov
info@julianhrankov.com
julianhrankov.com

Pages 153, 220

371

Address Index A–B

asmallpercent USA
Tim Ferguson Sauder
info@asmallpercent.com
asmallpercent.com

Pages 16, 32, 33, 43, 92

ASYL Japan
contact@asyl.co.jp
asyl.co.jp

Pages 81, 167, 240

atelier aquarium France
Jérémie Nuel & Simon Renaud
contact@atelieraquarium.com
atelieraquarium.com

Pages 12, 200, 224, 247

Atelier télescopique France
contact@ateliertelescopique.com
ateliertelescopique.com

Pages 77, 119, 214

ATTAK Netherlands
attak@attakweb.com
attakweb.com

Pages 64, 137, 152, 311, 318, 324

Autobahn Netherlands
info@autobahn.nl
autobahn.nl

Pages 54, 56, 69, 113, 181, 212, 222, 224, 301, 311

Avalanche France
hello@avalanche-designgraphique.com
avalanche-designgraphique.com

Pages 29, 270

Avantbras Italy
Stefano Bracci
info@avantbras.com
avantbras.com

Page 71

Axel Peemöller Germany
axel@axelpeemoeller.com
axelpeemoeller.com

Pages 86, 87, 100, 148, 152, 180

Axel Raidt Germany
axel@raidt.com
raidt.com

Pages 28, 341

B

backyard10 Germany
info@backyard10.com
backyard10.com

Pages 15, 127, 128, 293

Baldinger•Vu-Huu France
info@baldingervuhuu.com
baldingervuhuu.com

Page 67

BANK™ Germany
tellme@bankassociates.de
bankassociates.de

Page 49

Barnbrook United Kingdom
us@barnbrook.net
barnbrook.net

Pages 243, 352

Bas van Vuurde Netherlands
info@basvanvuurde.nl
basvanvuurde.nl

Pages 70, 203, 224

Base Belgium
infos@basedesign.com
basedesign.com

Pages 75, 77, 152, 173, 175, 206, 249, 317, 321

Ben Whitla USA
benwhitla@gmail.com
benwhitla.com

Page 330

Benjamin Metz Germany
benny_metz@hotmail.com
letsmetz.com

Pages 37, 77

Benny Gold USA
ben@bennygold.com
bennygold.com

Pages 102, 163, 310, 324

Benoît Bodhuin France
unpetitmot@benbenworld.com
benbenworld.com

Pages 31, 54, 81, 294

Benoit Lemoine Belgium
contact@benoitlemoine.eu
benoitlemoine.eu

Page 216

Bestial Design® Studio Argentina
hello@bestialdesign.com
bestialdesign.com

Pages 32, 50

BETA STUDIO Venezuela
info@beta-studio.com
beta-studio.com

Pages 94, 354

Bionic Systems Germany
info@bionic-systems.com
bionic-systems.com

Pages 39, 112, 131

Black-Marmalade USA
dechazier@black-marmalade.com
black-marmalade.com

Pages 88, 97, 258, 311

Blake E. Marquis USA
blake@camecrashing.com
blakeemarquis.com

Pages 112, 141, 158, 186, 212, 321, 337, 341

Bleed Norway
bleed@bleed.no
bleed.no

Pages 41, 194, 253, 323

Bo Lundberg Sweden
bo@bolundberg.com
bolundberg.com

Pages 10, 114, 215

**Bodara
Büro für Gebrauchsgrafik**
Switzerland
bodara@bodara.ch
bodara.ch

Pages 89, 301, 351

Bold° Brazil
contato@bolddesign.com.br
bolddesign.com.br

Pages 38, 150, 153, 250, 348

Braca Burazeri Serbia-Montenegro
dtzr@bracaburazeri.com
bracaburazeri.com

Page 163

Bram Nijssen Netherlands
info@bramnijssen.com
bramnijssen.com

Page 74

**Bram Nijssen &
Marnix de Klerk** Netherlands
info@bramnijssen.com
bramnijssen.com

Page 91

Brand New History™ Germany
info@brandnewhistory.net
brandnewhistory.net

Page 35

Breckon Gráfica Spain
info@breckon.es
breckon.es

Page 32

Brusatto Belgium
Geoffrey Brusatto
info@brusatto.be
brusatto.be

Pages 17, 54, 68, 262, 293

Büro Destruct Switzerland
Lopetz Gianfreda
bd@burodestruct.net
burodestruct.net

Pages 34, 57, 118, 215, 253, 293, 353

Büro Ink Germany
Markus Schäfer
hello@bueroink.com
bueroink.com

Page 198

Buro Reng Netherlands
welcome@buroreng.nl
buroreng.nl

Pages 147, 198, 214

**büro uebele visuelle
kommunikation** Germany
info@uebele.com
uebele.com

Pages 24, 151, 190, 198

Büro4 Switzerland
mail@buero4.ch
buero4.ch

Pages 38, 181, 256

Burro Design Singapore
perry@burrodesign.com
burrodesign.com

Page 310

C

C100 Purple Haze Germany
hello@c100purplehaze.com
c100purplehaze.com

Pages 102, 120, 149, 254, 305

cabina Argentina
info@espaciocabina.com.ar
espaciocabina.com.ar

Pages 110, 184, 219, 299, 302

Calango Netherlands
info@calango.nl
calango.nl

Pages 99, 192, 214, 215, 216, 220, 297

Canefantasma Studio Italy
m@canefantasma.com
canefantasma.com

Page 174

Cardamom USA
Julianna Goodman
julianna@cardamom.ws
cardamom.ws

Page 114

Carlos Ribeiro Portugal
carlosribeiro@sevenfiles.com
sevenfiles.com

Page 151

Carsten Raffel Germany
carsten@unitedstatesoftheart.com
unitedstatesoftheart.com

Page 118

Cassie Leedham United Kingdom
cassie@goodshowstudio.com
goodshowstudio.com

Page 30

Celeste Prevost USA
celeste@designisfine.com
designisfine.com

Pages 19, 114, 133, 147, 214, 353

cerotreees Venezuela
info@cerotreees.com
cerotreees.com

Pages 14, 102, 262, 303, 325, 330

chemicalbox Switzerland
Mario Buholzer
bureau@chemicalbox.com
chemicalbox.com

Page 102

Chragokyberneticks Switzerland
Chragi Frei,
chragi@chragokyberneticks.ch
chragokyberneticks.ch

Pages 86, 105, 130, 149, 158, 175, 179, 182

Chris Bolton Finland
chris@chrisbolton.org
chrisbolton.org

Pages 110, 165, 212

Chris Henley United Kingdom
chris@24exp.co.uk
24exp.co.uk

Pages 158, 204, 220

Chris Rubino USA
studio@chrisrubino.com
chrisrubino.com

Pages 13, 54, 95, 114, 311

Christian Borstlap Netherlands
hello@christianborstlap.com
christianborstlap.com

Pages 141, 364

Christian Cervantes USA
christiancervantes@gmail.com
christiancervantes.com

Pages 100, 111

Christian Rothenhagen Germany
moin@christianrothenhagen.com
christianrothenhagen.com

Pages 129, 301

CLAU.AS.KEE Spain
Claudia Mussett
hello@clauaskee.com
clauaskee.com

Pages 107, 194, 210, 223

Claus Gasque Denmark
gasque@gmail.com
cityfellaz.com

Pages 130, 159

Clusta United Kingdom
hello@clusta.com
clusta.com

Pages 19, 101

Coboi & Fageta Switzerland
Coboi / Katharina Reidy
Fageta / Philippe Egger & Adeline Mollard
katharina@coboi.ch
info@fageta.ch
coboi.ch
fageta.ch

Page 180

Coley Porter Bell United Kingdom
adam.ellis@cpb.co.uk
cpb.co.uk

Pages 44, 92, 123, 181, 240, 286

Côme de Bouchony France
hello@comedebouchony.com
comedebouchony.com

Pages 230, 231

COMMUNE Japan
info@commune-inc.jp
commune-inc.jp

Page 167

Company United Kingdom
studio@company-london.com
company-london.com

Pages 31, 35, 37, 63, 100, 263, 264, 291

Coolpuk Netherlands
puk@coolpuk.com
coolpuk.com

Page 133

Copenheroes Denmark
info@copenheroes.com
copenheroes.com

Pages 35, 96

Core60 Romania
hello@core60.com
core60.com

Pages 15, 34, 37, 92

COUP Netherlands
Erica Terpstra & Peter van den Hoogen
hello@coup.nl
coup.nl

Pages 15, 75, 99, 145, 201

Coutworks Japan
info@coutworks.com
coutworks.com

Pages 43, 160

Creative Inc Ireland
mel@creativeinc.ie
creativeinc.ie

Pages 19, 53, 98

cypher13 USA
info@cypher13.com
cypher13.com

Pages 19, 25, 289

D

dancemade Sweden
Jens Nilsson
jens@dancemade.com
dancemade.com

Pages 72, 368

Daniel Blik Hungary
blik@blikdsgn.com
blikdsgn.com

Pages 121, 321

Daniel Carlsten Sweden
daniel@danielcarlsten.com
danielcarlsten.com

Page 63

Daniel Medeiros Brazil
designboh@gmail.com
damned.com.br

Pages 140, 202

De Jongens Ronner Netherlands
info@dejongensronner.nl
dejongensronner.nl

Pages 72, 180

Deanne Cheuk USA
neomuworld@aol.com
deannecheuk.com

Pages 42, 189, 309

Demetrio Mancini Italy
me@demetriomancini.it
demetriomancini.it

Pages 101, 113, 195

Dennis Herzog Germany
dennis@derherzog.com
derherzog.com

Pages 302, 364

Denny Backhaus Germany
denny@zuckerundpfeffer.com
zuckerundpfeffer.com

Pages 14, 76, 133, 144

Derek A. Friday USA
Finndustry
derek@finndustry.com
finndustry.com

Pages 53, 312, 364

Designers United Greece
info@designersunited.gr
designersunited.gr

Pages 86, 101, 182, 250, 331

373

Designit Denmark
hasse.betak@designit.com
designit.com

Pages 133, 225

designJune France
Julien Crouigneau
june@designjune.com
designjune.com

Pages 19, 136

Device Spain
hello@devicers.org
devicers.org

Pages 28, 215

Di-Da Komunikakzioa Spain
inf@di-da.com
di-da.com

Pages 36, 77

Digitaluv Denmark
NC Stormgaard
nc@digitaluv.com
digitaluv.com

Page 97

Dimomedia Lab Italy
Massimo Sirelli
info@dimomedia.com
dimomedia.com

Page 36

Dog and Pony Netherlands
info@dogandpony.nl
dogandpony.nl

Page 310

Dogma Mexico
dogma@dogmaestudio.com
behance.net/dogma

Pages 190, 223, 224, 225, 258

Dongwoo Kim USA
contact@networkosaka.com
networkosaka.com

Page 51

Donuts Belgium
info@donuts.be
donuts.be

Pages 233, 250, 258

Dorota Wojcik France
conceptgraph2107@gmail.com
dorota.wojcik.free.fr

Pages 71, 220

Dtam – TM United Kingdom
Paul Heys
info@dtam.co.uk
dtam.co.uk

Pages 56, 71, 129, 217, 242, 292

DTM_INC Netherlands
dtm_inc@hotmail.com
behance.net/dtm_inc

Pages 13, 119, 150, 185, 219, 298, 310, 333

Dudu Torres Brazil
hello@dudutorres.com
dudutorres.com

Pages 132, 210

E

e-Types Denmark
info@e-types.com
e-types.com

Pages 41, 42, 51, 70, 74, 76

EBSL USA
Erik Kiesewetter
erik@erikbelowsealevel.com
erikbelowsealevel.com

Pages 56, 244

Eddie Brown USA
eddie@cyberpublishers.net
cyberpublishers.net

Pages 33, 44

Edgar Bąk Poland
poczta@edgarbak.info
edgarbak.info

Pages 11, 14, 38, 42, 68, 252

Edhv Netherlands
info@edhv.nl
edhv.nl

Pages 37, 73, 106, 197, 204, 272, 273, 274, 275, 365

Eduardo Vidales Mexico
evidalesc@yahoo.com
eduardovidales.tk

Pages 39, 56, 128

ehquestionmark United Kingdom
enquirehere@ehquestionmark.com
ehquestionmark.com

Pages 28, 39

Eivind Nilsen Norway
eiiviind@gmail.com
bensinstasjon.blogspot.com

Page 145

Ekaterina Tiouleikina Denmark
hello@itchyorange.com
itchyorange.com

Pages 33, 213, 217

EL MIRO Netherlands
sander@elmiro.nl
elmiro.nl

Pages 11, 32, 49, 107, 162, 194

elesefe Brazil
Friedrich Santana Lamego
hello@elesefe.com
elesefe.com

Page 163

ellenberg-martinez Argentina
Laura Ellenberg & Agustina Martínez
estudio@ellenbergmartinez.com.ar
ellenbergmartinez.com.ar

Pages 151, 312, 313

elRAiSE USA
Andy Risquez
raise@andresrisquez.com
**andresrisquez.com,
elraise.com**

Pages 73, 295

Emil Hartvig Studio Denmark
mail@eha.dk
eha.dk

Page 89

Emmanuel Rey Switzerland
contact@emmanuelrey.ch
emmanuelrey.ch

Pages 70, 71, 305

EMPK Venezuela
Diego Bellorin
hola@empk.net
empk.net

Pages 34, 35, 89, 96, 98, 217

eps51 Germany
mail@eps51.de
eps51.com

Pages 74, 113, 256, 304

Escobas Mexico
escobas@escobas.com.mx
escobas.com.mx

Page 257

espluga + associates Spain
info@espluga.net
espluga.net

Page 115

Esther Rieser Switzerland
estr@gmx.net
estr.ch

Pages 66, 88

Estudio Soma Argentina
info@estudiosoma.com.ar
estudiosoma.com.ar

Pages 153, 294

Extraverage Hungary
Karoly Kiralyfalvi
drez@extraverage.net
extraverage.net

Pages 37, 118, 170, 244, 258

EyesCream Germany
Matthias Wagner
matthias@matthiaswagner.org
**matthiaswagner.org
eyes-cream.org**

Pages 158, 160, 211, 213

F

Fabian Bertschinger
Switzerland
info@fabianbertschinger.com
fabianbertschinger.com

Pages 66, 164, 368

Fabio Lattanzi Antinori
United Kingdom
info@studiofla.com
studiofla.com

Page 259

Fabio Milito Italy
info@fabiomilito.com
fabiomilito.com

Page 220

Fabio Santoro Brazil
fabiosantoro@gmail.com
fabiosantoro.blogspot.com

Pages 28, 263

Face. Mexico
hello@designbyface.com
designbyface.com

Pages 41, 74, 101, 103, 111, 120, 148, 260, 322

Faith Canada
info@faith.ca
faith.ca

Pages 86, 93, 208, 286, 303, 310, 320, 367

Falko Ohlmer Germany
hello@falko-ohlmer.com
falko-ohlmer.com

Pages 90, 136, 175, 241, 300, 344

Federico Landini Italy
info@studioidom.com
studioidom.com

Pages 22, 311

FEED Canada
feed@studiofeed.ca
studiofeed.ca

Pages 19, 23, 56, 72, 96, 115, 120, 201, 216, 265

Felix Lobelius Australia
hello@felixlobelius.com
felixlobelius.com

Pages 44, 167, 198, 220

Felix Sockwell USA
Felix@felixsockwell.com
felixsockwell.com

Pages 45, 54, 213, 216, 223, 233, 234

Fieldtrip Netherlands
Joost Verhaak
studio@fieldtrip.nl
fieldtrip.nl

Pages 39, 184

Filippo Nugara Switzerland
hello@filipponugara.com
filipponugara.com

Page 72

Filmgraphik Germany
studio@filmgraphik.com
filmgraphik.com

Pages 114, 201, 310, 358

FLAMMIER Norway
alexander@flammier.com
flammier.com

Pages 148, 196

Floor 5 Germany
Marek Polewski & Jens Pieper
marek@floor5.de
floor5.de

Pages 57, 69, 129, 170, 290

Floor Wesseling Netherlands
floor@ixopusada.com
floorwesseling.nl

Pages 27, 104, 196, 202, 234, 324, 348

Floris Voorveld Netherlands
info@florisdesign.com
florisdesign.com

Pages 45, 250

Foan82 Portugal
mail@foan82.com
foan82.com

Pages 201, 214, 215, 219

Fons Hickmann m23 Germany
m23@fonshickmann.com
fonshickmann.com

Pages 14, 57, 129, 130, 149, 192, 198, 250, 252, 254, 293, 300, 360

Fontan2 Bulgaria
office@fontan2.com
fontan2.com

Pages 92, 96, 206, 214, 251, 260

Form+Format Germany
Daniel Neye
we@formandformat.com
formandformat.com

Pages 53, 70, 75

formdusche Germany
kontakt@formdusche.de
formdusche.de

Pages 107, 109

FoURPAcK ontwerpers
Netherlands
Tessa Hofman & Richard Pijs
post@fourpack.nl
fourpack.nl

Pages 172, 175, 202, 216

Frank Rocholl Germany
rocholl@miragemag.com
rocholl.cc

Page 70

Franz Falsch Germany
franzfalsch@googlemail.com
franzfalsch.com

Pages 121, 152, 304

Fresh Estudio Mexico
info@hola-fresh.com
hola-fresh.com

Pages 11, 118, 152, 322

FriendsWithYou USA
info@friendswithyou.com
fwystudios.com

Pages 37, 50, 53, 55, 128, 185, 253

FromKeetra USA
Keetra Dean Dixon
keetra@fromkeetra.com
fromkeetra.com

Pages 110, 229, 252

G

Gabe Ruane USA
gabe.ruane@gmail.com
gaberuane.com

Pages 25, 54, 120, 293

Gavillet & Rust Switzerland
mail@gavillet-rust.com
gavillet-rust.com

Pages 78, 79, 80, 193

gebrauchsgrafikundso Germany
post@gebrauchsgrafikundso.de
gebrauchsgrafikundso.de

Pages 56, 115, 190, 323

General Projects USA
ben@generalprojects.com
generalprojects.com

Pages 20, 30, 55, 75, 151, 248, 256

Gianni Rossi Italy
contact@giannirossi.net
giannirossi.net

Page 357

Giorgio Paolinelli Italy
giorgio@blumagenta.com
blumagenta.com

Pages 33, 338

Goldjunge Grafik & Design
Germany
kontakt@gold-junge.com
gold-junge.com

Pages 153, 342

Grandpeople Norway
post@grandpeople.org
grandpeople.org

Pages 22, 87, 99, 184, 248, 256

Graphical House United Kingdom
studio@graphicalhouse.com
graphicalhouse.co.uk

Pages 34, 35, 40, 51, 93, 94

Guapo Argentina
info@guapo.tv
guapo.tv

Pages 119, 189, 221, 252, 330

Guillaume Peitrequin
Switzerland
guillaume.peitrequin@gmail.com

Pages 69, 81

Gunnar Bauer Japan
gb@gunnarbauer.com
gunnarbauer.com

Page 74

Gustavo de Lacerda Brazil
gustavo@substantivo.net
substantivo.net

Pages 145, 201, 245, 261, 263, 337

GVA Studio Switzerland
info@gvastudio.com
gvastudio.com

Pages 52, 73, 218, 297

GWG inc. Japan
info@gwg.ne.jp
gwg.ne.jp

Pages 202, 354

Gytz Denmark
hg@gytz.com
gytz.com

Page 99

H

Haltenbanken Norway
post@haltenbanken.com
haltenbanken.com

Pages 163, 207, 263

Halvor Bodin Norway
halvor@bodin.no
halvorbodin.com

Page 96

HandGun USA
David Zack Custer
zack@hand-gun.org
iamhandgun.com
thisisalone.com

Page 118

Handverk Norway
contact@madebyhandverk.no
madebyhandverk.no

Pages 88, 359

H–J

Hansje van Halem Netherlands
hansje@hansje.net
hansje.net

Pages 165, 300

Happypets products Switzerland
info@happypets.ch
happypets.ch

Pages 135, 136

HarrimanSteel United Kingdom
mail@harrimansteel.co.uk
harrimansteel.co.uk

Pages 130, 238, 242

Hatch Design USA
info@hatchsf.com
hatchsf.com

Page 339

Hattomonkey Russia
mail@hattomonkey.ru
hattomonkey.ru

Pages 101, 103, 192, 236, 291

Haus CPH Denmark
felix@haus-cph.dk
haus-cph.dk

Pages 108, 198

Hayes Image Australia
Josh Hayes
mail@hayesimage.com.au
hayesimage.com.au

Pages 49, 133

HelloComputer South Africa
makefriends@hellocomputer.net
hellocomputer.net

Pages 40, 257

HelloMe Germany
Till Wiedeck
hello@tillwiedeck.com
tillwiedeck.com

Pages 52, 68, 91, 95, 197, 218, 248, 297, 302

Heloisa Dassie Genciauskas
Brazil
contact@heloisadassie.com
heloisadassie.com

Page 221

helvetic brands Switzerland
David Pache
info@helveticbrands.ch
helveticbrands.ch

Page 298

Heric Longe United Kingdom
hello@longedesign.com
longedesign.com

Pages 94, 137, 263, 294

Herr Metag Germany
Malte Metag
info@herrmetag.de
herrmetag.de

Page 74

Hexanine USA
connect@hexanine.com
hexanine.com

Pages 28, 140, 148, 201, 337

Hey Ho France
contact@heyho.fr
heyho.fr

Pages 22, 264

Heydays Norway
hey@heydays.info
heydays.info

Pages 62, 69, 148, 299

HEYHEYHEY Netherlands
Erik Sjouerman & Elske van der Putten
erik@heyheyheycreative.com
heyheyheycreative.com

Page 99

hintzegruppen Denmark
jesper@hintzegruppen.dk
hintzegruppen.dk

Pages 36, 38, 54, 141

Hold United Kingdom
hello@wearehold.com
wearehold.com

Page 288

HoohaaDesign United Kingdom
info@hoohaadesign.co.uk
hoohaadesign.co.uk

Pages 35, 94, 213

Hörður Lárusson Iceland
hordur@larusson.com
larusson.com

Pages 75, 100

HORT Germany
contact@hort.org.uk
hort.org.uk

Pages 295, 296

Hugh Frost United Kingdom
sportsdaymegaphone@gmail.com
hughfrost.com

Page 19

Hugo Mulder Netherlands
dhm@euronet.nl
dhmdesign.nl

Page 49

Hula+Hula Mexico
aloha@hulahula.com.mx
hulahula.com.mx

Pages 116, 259, 313

Human Empire Germany
post@humanempire.com
humanempire.com

Pages 141, 174, 179

Huschang Pourian China
huschang@pourian.com
pourian.com

Pages 50, 74, 116, 179

HUSH USA
shout@heyhush.com
heyhush.com

Pages 160, 182, 185, 343

Hype Type Studio United Kingdom
Paul Hutchison
info@hypetype.co.uk
hypetype.co.uk

Pages 22, 308, 324, 366

I

Ian Lynam Design Japan
ian@ianlynam.com
ianlynam.com

Page 39

Identity Estonia
info@Identity.ee
identity.ee

Pages 73, 294, 298

illDesigns Switzerland
Till Könneker
info@illdesigns.ch
illdesigns.ch

Pages 107, 334, 337

ilovedust United Kingdom
info@ilovedust.com
ilovedust.com

Pages 56, 112, 218, 336

Image Now Ireland
post@imagenow.ie
imagenow.ie

Page 36

INDASTRIACOOLHIDEA Italy
Luca Forlani
info@indastriacoolhidea.com
indastriacoolhidea.com

Pages 32, 353

Indyvisuals Greece
info@indyvisuals.net
indyvisuals.net

Pages 100, 162, 192

Inksurge Philippines
broadcast@inksurge.com
inksurge.com

Pages 325, 336

Insónia Portugal
mail@insonia.pt
insonia.pt

Page 224

Inventaire Switzerland
office@inventaire.ch
inventaire.ch

Pages 23, 43, 49, 151

Irving & Co United Kingdom
julian@irvingandco.com
irvingandco.com

Pages 71, 339

J

Jaime Narváez Spain
info@jaimenarvaez.com
jaimenarvaez.com

Pages 28, 52

Jan en Randoald Belgium
info@janenrandoald.be
janenrandoald.be

Pages 65, 81, 217, 291

Janine Rewell Finland
janine@janinerewell.com
janinerewell.com

Page 23

Jared Mirabile USA
Jared Mirabile
jared@sweyda.com
Sweyda.com

Pages 310, 322, 324, 325, 330, 332

Jarek Kowalczyk Poland
info@jarekkowalczyk.info
jarekkowalczyk.info

Pages 13, 19

Jarrik Muller Netherlands
jarrik@jarrik.com
jarrik.com

Page 31

Jesse Kirsch USA
design@jessekirsch.com
jessekirsch.com

Pages 50, 338, 339

Jessica Walsh USA
jessicavwalsh@gmail.com
jessicawalsh.com

Page 97

Jet Black Tribal Ink South Africa
info@jbti.co.za
jetblacktribalink.co.za

Pages 121, 186, 332

Jewboy Corp™ Israel
i@jewboy.co.il
jewboy.co.il

Pages 120, 207, 303

Ji Lee USA
writetojilee@gmail.com
pleaseenjoy.com

Pages 75, 361, 362, 363

JMSV Argentina
coralcoraza@gmail.com
jmsv.com.ar

Page 142

John Beckers Netherlands
info@john-beckers.nl
john-beckers.nl

Pages 86, 104, 213, 222, 224, 253, 304, 343

John L. Nguyen USA
john@jlnguyen.com
jlnguyen.com

Pages 13, 115

John Langdon USA
jlangdon12@comcast.net
johnlangdon.net

Pages 46, 47, 48

John Vingoe United Kingdom
john@wearerapscallion.co.uk
wearerapscallion.co.uk

Page 163

Jonathan Calugi Italy
hello@happyloverstown.eu
happyloverstown.eu

Pages 14, 128, 132, 147, 149, 171, 179, 184

Jonathan Gurvit Argentina
jonathan.gurvit@gmail.com
behance.net/JonathanGurvit

Page 94

Joseba Attard Spain
info@joseba.co.uk
joseba.co.uk

Page 206

Joseph Garner USA
ben@jgarnerdesign.com
jgarnerdesign.com

Pages 44, 49

Joshua Distler USA
hello@joshuadistler.com
joshuadistler.com

Pages 25, 28, 107, 173, 312

Josiah Jost Canada
contact@siahdesign.com
siahdesign.com

Page 41

Julia Heitmann Germany
giulia_silverstar@web.de
olympiaunddesign.de

Page 21

Julian Viera Venezuela
julian.viera.l@gmail.com
flickr.com/photos/causeweboom
causeweboom.com

Pages 105, 160, 209, 212, 221

Julien Vallée Canada
j@jvallee.com
jvallee.com

Page 223

Jum & Cargo Germany
jum@unitedstatesofheart.com
unitedstatesofheart.com

Page 105

Juntos otra vez Venezuela
Martin Allais
info@juntosotravez.com
juntosotravez.com

Pages 124, 125, 126, 127, 159, 210

Jürgen Frost Germany
hello@juergenfrost.com
juergenfrost.com

Pages 52, 141, 192, 224, 257

Just Smile And Wave Denmark
Anna Magnussen & Doris Poligrates
mail@jsaw.dk
jsaw.dk

Pages 100, 136, 153, 185, 223, 305

JUTOJO Germany
info@jutojo.de
jutojo.de

Pages 69, 146, 147

K

KalleGraphics Norway
email@kallegraphics.com
kallegraphics.com

Pages 88, 94, 116, 321, 366

Kate Moross United Kingdom
kate@katemoross.com
katemoross.com

Pages 105, 137, 140

Kelly D. Williams USA
info@kellydwilliams.com
kellydwilliams.com

Pages 57, 349

Ken United Kingdom
Simon Sparkes
hello@studioken.co.uk
studioken.co.uk

Pages 10, 98, 108, 260

Ken Tanabe USA
ken@kentanabe.com
kentanabe.com

Pages 53, 75

KesselsKramer Netherlands
ch@kesselskramer.nl
kesselskramer.com

Pages 54, 74

Kismanstudio Netherlands
Max Kisman
studio@kismanstudio.nl
kismanstudio.nl

Pages 124, 141, 180, 257

KismanVerhaak Netherlands
Max Kisman & Joost Verhaak
studio@kismanverhaak.nl
kismanverhaak.nl

Page 77

KMS TEAM Germany
info@kms-team.com
kms-team.com

Pages 58, 59, 60, 61

KOA France
Olivier Cramm
koa@koadzn.com
koadzn.com

Pages 127, 293, 333

Koehorst in 't Veld Netherlands
post@koehorstintveld.nl
koehorstintveld.nl

Pages 81, 175, 190, 304

Kokoro & Moi Finland
info@kokoromoi.com
kokoromoi.com

Pages 51, 66, 81, 108, 111, 113, 176, 177, 178, 293

Kummer & Herrman Netherlands
studio@kummer-herrman.nl
kummer-herrman.nl

Page 55

Kursiv Denmark
Peter Graabaek
kursiv@kursiv.dk
kursiv.dk

Page 287

Kyle Bean United Kingdom
kyle@kylebean.co.uk
kylebean.co.uk

Pages 354, 358

L

La Cáscara Amarga Spain
Jorge Chamorro
jorge@lacascaraamarga.com
lacascaraamarga.com

Pages 20, 88, 110, 173, 249, 292

Address Index · L–M

Lab2 Germany
info@lab-2.net
lab-2.net

Pages 105, 158, 202, 321

Laleh Torabi Germany
laleh@spookymountains.com
spookymountains.com

Page 159

LaMarca Venezuela
info@lamarca.com.ve
lamarca.com.ve

Pages 219, 323

Landor Associates France
jason.little@landor.com
landor.com

Pages 25, 32, 76, 124, 227, 233, 239, 246

Landor Tokyo France
jason.little@landor.com
landor.com

Page 75

Lapin Studio Spain
Jorge Navarro Herradón
jorge@lapinstudio.com
lapinstudio.com

Pages 130, 347

Leplancton Chile
leplancton@leplancton.cl
leplancton.cl

Pages 221, 299, 313

Lifter Baron USA
Rob Angermuller
info@lifterbaron.com
lifterbaron.com

Pages 14, 15, 75, 106, 214

Like Minded Studio Australia
Luca Ionescu
luca@likemindedstudio.com
likemindedstudio.com

Pages 112, 162, 216, 307, 316, 324, 332, 337

LIMA-KILO-WHISKEY
Switzerland
Thomas Lehner, Jacob Kadrmas
& Oliver Wehn
hello@lima-kilo-whiskey.com
lima-kilo-whiskey.com

Page 112

Linnea Andersson Sweden
bylinnea@gmail.com
bylinnea.com

Page 360

LLdesign Italy
ll@lldesign.it
lldesign.it

Pages 66, 68, 297

LogoOrange
Romania
logoorange.com

Pages 192, 220

Loic Sattler France
contact@lysergid.com
lysergid.com

Pages 102, 189, 309

Lorenzo Geiger Switzerland
hello@lorenzogeiger.ch
lorenzogeiger.ch

Pages 70, 71, 76, 252

Luca Barcellona Italy
luca.indelebile@gmail.com
lucabarcellona.com

Pages 248, 313, 333, 366

Luca Marchettoni Italy
luca@blumagenta.com
blumagenta.com

Pages 208, 247

Luke Williams USA
luke@lukelukeluke.com
lukelukeluke.com

Pages 99, 159, 247, 248, 342

Lundgren + Lindqvist Sweden
hello@lundgrenlindqvist.se
lundgrenlindqvist.se

Pages 27, 32, 95, 221, 263

M

Madhouse USA
info@madmadmad.com
madmadmad.com

Pages 159, 224, 299, 320

Mads Burcharth Denmark
info@mabu.dk
mabu.dk

Pages 17, 94, 102, 112, 115, 140, 261, 297

Mads Freund Brunse
Switzerland
hello@madsfreundbrunse.com
madsfreundbrunse.com

Pages 192, 301

Mads Jakob Poulsen Denmark
hello@madsjakobpoulsen.dk
madsjakobpoulsen.dk

Pages 72, 74, 193

Magdalena Czarnecki Italy
magdalena@tjaneski.com
tjaneski.com

Page 197

Mammal United Kingdom
info@mammaldesign.com
mammaldesign.com

Pages 256, 257, 309, 347

Maniackers Design Japan
Masayuki Sato
sato@mksd.jp
mksd.jp

Pages 22, 166

Manifiesto Futura Mexico
hola@manifiestofutura.com
manifiestofutura.com

Pages 76, 88, 95, 96, 150, 260, 290, 303

Marc van der Meer Netherlands
marc@marcvandermeer.nl
marcvandermeer.nl

Pages 90, 217

Marcelo Chelles Brazil
marcelochelles@yahoo.com
marcelochelles.com.br

Page 193

Markus Moström Sweden
studio@mostromdesign.se
mostromdesign.se

Pages 31, 76, 193, 201, 321

Martin Holm Norway
mail@martinholm.com
martinholm.com

Page 36

Martin Nicolausson Sweden
info@martinnicolausson.com
martinnicolausson.com

Pages 68, 209

MASA Venezuela
hello@masa.com.ve
masa.com.ve

Page 131

Mash Australia
hola@mashdesign.com.au
mashdesign.com.au

Pages 14, 92, 97, 131, 137, 162, 206, 219, 249, 292, 308, 341

Mash & Peta Kruger Australia
hola@mashdesign.com.au
mashdesign.com.au

Page 113

Masheen Sweden
Robert Wallis
rob@masheen.org
masheen.org

Pages 9, 118, 138, 288

Matt Carr United Kingdom
matt@hickindustries.com
hickindustries.com

Page 206

Matt Le Gallez United Kingdom
mattlegallez@me.com
mattlegallez.com

Pages 117, 118

Matt W. Moore USA
matt@mwmgraphics.com
mwmgraphics.com

Pages 22, 35, 69, 117, 120, 174, 196, 218, 226, 228, 250, 301, 351

Matteo Mastronardi France
matteo@worksisnotajob.com
worksisnotajob.com

Pages 36, 93, 129, 262

Matthew Manos USA
imattmanos@gmail.com
portfolio.mattmanos.com/

Page 322

Matthias Wagner Germany
matthias@matthiaswagner.org
matthiaswagner.org
eyes-cream.org

Page 138

max-o-matic Spain
Máximo Tuja
info@maxomatic.net
maxomatic.net

Pages 52, 148, 210, 345

Maximilian Baud & Uwe Strasser Germany
und@waskannstduso.com
waskannstduso.com

Page 32

Meatpack Belgium
info@meatpack.org
meatpack.org

Pages 150, 294, 355

Mehdi Saeedi Iran
mehdisaeedistudio@gmail.com
mehdisaeedi.com

Pages 318, 319

me studio Netherlands
look@mestudio.info
mestudio.info

Page 107

MetaDesign Germany
mail@metadesign.de
metadesign.de

Page 250

MH Grafik Switzerland
info@mhg.ch
mhg.ch

Pages 165, 186, 211, 367

Michael Lashford USA
howdy@michaellashford.com
michaellashford.com

Page 343

Mikey Burton USA
mikey@mikeyburton.com
mikeyburton.com

Pages 128, 130, 334, 337, 342, 353

milchhof : atelier Germany
post@milchhof.net
milchhof.net

Pages 133, 199, 220, 235, 240, 256, 259

Mind Design United Kingdom
info@minddesign.co.uk
minddesign.co.uk

Pages 108, 183, 266, 267, 268, 269

miniminiaturemouse USA
Fumi Mini Nakamura
contact@miniminiaturemouse.com
miniminiaturemouse.com

Pages 127, 131, 182, 309

minigram Germany
studio@minigram.de
minigram.de

Page 199

Mitchell Paone USA
mitch@dreamersinkaesthetics.net
dreamersinkaesthetics.net

Pages 40, 71, 112, 126, 206, 320, 343, 344, 345

modo Venezuela
Alexander Wright
alex@modovisual.com
modovisual.com

Pages 11, 15, 98, 99, 103, 118, 132, 219, 221, 224, 298

Monoblock Argentina
quiero@monoblock.tv
monoblock.tv

Pages 42, 92, 100, 181, 252

Moshik Nadav Israel
moshik@moshik.net
moshik.net

Pages 121, 305, 309

Moxie Sozo USA
info@moxiesozo.com
moxiesozo.com

Pages 33, 34, 35, 38, 103, 129, 313, 347

Mr. Brown – creative boutique Poland
boutique@mrbrown.pl
mrbrown.pl

Page 151

Mr. Kone Mexico
kone@kamikace.com
mrkone.com.mx

Page 57

Mr. Magenta Venezuela
edicsonn@hotmail.com

Page 261

Mutabor Germany
Mutabor Design GmbH
info@mutabor.de
mutabor.de

Pages 30, 41, 234

N

NALINDESIGN™ Germany
Andre Weier
andre@nalindesign.com
nalindesign.com

Pages 49, 310

Negro™ Argentina
Ariel Di Lisio
info@negronouveau.com
negronouveau.com

Pages 116, 119, 211, 215, 219, 257, 259

Nicklas Hultman Sweden
postmaster@nicklas-h.se
nicklas-h.se

Pages 246, 366

Nico Ammann Switzerland
info@nicoammann.com
nicoammann.com

Pages 10, 368

NNSS Argentina
contacto@nnss.com.ar
nnss.com.ar

Pages 223, 313

No-Domain Spain
ese@no-domain.com
no-domain.com

Pages 29, 145, 200, 258, 260, 261, 263, 322, 367

nocturn.ro Romania
office@nocturn.ro
nocturn.ro

Pages 36, 204, 252, 288

NODE Berlin Oslo Germany
mail@nodeberlin.com
nodeberlin.com

Pages 69, 90, 153, 182

Nohemí Dicurú Venezuela
contact@nohemidicuru.com
nohemidicuru.com
fashiongraphic.com

Page 90, 248

Non-Format USA
info@non-format.com
non-format.com

Pages 91, 94, 97, 201, 260

Norwegian Ink Norway
post@norwegianink.com
norwegianink.com

Pages 11, 113, 221

NR2154 Denmark
Troels Faber & Jacob Wildschiødtz
info@nr2154.com
nr2154.com

Pages 256, 276, 277, 278, 279, 280, 281

O

ODD United Kingdom
info@thankodd.com
oddlondon.com

Pages 104, 286

Ole Utikal Germany
post@oleutikal.de
oleutikal.de

Page 138

OMOCHI Japan
omochigraphics@mac.com
homepage.mac.com/omochigraphics

Pages 89, 259

OMOMMA™ Japan
Ohara Daijiro
ohara@omomma.in
omomma.in

Pages 137, 147, 166, 254, 318

one8one7 Australia
info@one8one7.com
one8one7.com

Pages 53, 93, 95, 249, 256

onlab Switzerland
Nicolas Bourquin & Thibaud Tissot
in@onlab.ch
onlab.ch

Pages 26, 286

OPX United Kingdom
post@opx.co.uk
opx.co.uk

Pages 86, 180

Otto Dietrich Germany
otto@ottodietrich.de
ottodietrich.de

Pages 64, 96

Address Index — O–S

Out Of Order Netherlands
info@outoforder.nl
outoforder.nl

Pages 32, 71, 95, 202

P

Pandayoghurt United Kingdom
info@pandayoghurt.co.uk
pandayoghurt.co.uk

Page 356

Patrik Ferrarelli Switzerland
hallo@patrikferrarelli.ch
patrikferrarelli.ch

Pages 31, 54, 76

Perndl + Co Austria
office@perndl.at
perndl.at

Page 105

Peter Gregson Serbia-Montenegro
mail@petergregson.com
petergregson.com/blog

Pages 43, 115, 148

Peter Schmidt Group Germany
info@peter-schmidt-group.de
peter-schmidt-group.de

Pages 44, 205, 293

Peter Sunna USA
petersunna@gmail.com
petersunna.com

Pages 104, 189, 262

Philipp Pilz Germany
fry@fry2k.de
fry2k.de

Pages 194, 203, 311, 313, 346

phospho Austria
Roland Hörmann
type@phospho.at
phospho.at

Pages 56, 95, 309

Pierre Jeanneret Switzerland
pierrejeanneret@dgeneral.com
pierrejeanneret.com

Pages 40, 194, 215

pleaseletmedesign Belgium
studio@plmd.me
plmd.me

Page 91

Pop Ovidiu Sebastian Romania
design@brandcore.ro

Pages 53, 116

Positron Co Ltd Japan
wada@the-positron.jp
the-positron.jp

Pages 12, 20, 56, 110, 261, 263

Power Graphixx Japan
support@power-graphixx.com
power-graphixx.com

Pages 10, 124, 253

Project 1000 Romania
oana@project1000.org
project1000.org

Pages 16, 45, 163, 195, 199, 242, 313

Projekttriangle Design Studio
Germany
mail@projekttriangle.com
projekttriangle.com

Pages 51, 96, 367

Ptarmak, Inc. USA
info@ptarmak.com
ptarmak.com

Pages 45, 340, 341, 353

Q

Q2 Design Austria
info@qzwei.com
qzwei.com

Pages 92, 194

R

Raf Vancampenhoudt Belgium
raf.vancampenhoudt@telenet.be
rafvancampenhoudt.be

Pages 56, 72, 197, 305, 330

Rasmus Snabb Denmark
rasmus@rasmussnabb.com
by.rasmussnabb.com

Pages 20, 172, 241, 312

Reaktor Lab Mexico
Jorge Aguilar
contacto@reaktorlab.com
reaktorlab.com

Pages 28, 209, 313

Red Box Inc. Canada
amy@creativeredbox.com
creativeredbox.com

Pages 251, 335, 343

Red Design United Kingdom
info@red-design.co.uk
red-design.co.uk

Pages 16, 43, 50, 110, 111, 117, 366

Regina Japan
republicofregina@hotmail.com
republicofregina.com

Pages 50, 152, 213, 220

Revivify Graphic Design Australia
Rich Scott
rich_s@tpg.com.au
revivifygraphicdesign.com

Pages 23, 34, 40, 44, 45, 132, 150

REX South Africa
za@rexcreative.com
rexcreative.com

Pages 34, 50, 140, 203, 236, 288, 293

Rick Klotz USA
contact@freshjive.net
sam@graphitela.com
freshjive.com
graphitela.com

Page 191

Rinzen Australia
they@rinzen.com
rinzen.com

Page 240

Rob van Hoesel Netherlands
post@robvanhoesel.nl
robvanhoesel.nl

Pages 27, 68, 72, 77

Robi Jöeleht Estonia
robi@robjoe.com
robjoe.com

Pages 50, 254

Rocholl Selected Designs
Germany
Frank Rocholl
rocholl.cc

Pages 110, 302

Rokac Croatia
Roko Kerovec
info@rokac.com
rokac.com

Pages 44, 49

ROMstudio Mexico
rom@romstudio.com.mx
romstudio.com.mx

Pages 116, 152, 346

Roy Smith United Kingdom
info@roysmithdesign.com
roysmithdesign.com

Pages 15, 25, 45, 102

ruiz + company Spain
estudio@ruizcompany.com
ruizcompany.com

Page 114

Ryan Crouchman Canada
ryan@ryancrouchman.com
ryancrouchman.com

Pages 25, 200

Ryan Massiah Canada
hello@ryan-massiah.com
ryan-massiah.com

Page 145

S

Sabina Keric Germany
hello@sabinakeric.de
sabinakeric.de

Pages 10, 11, 125, 131

Sagmeister Inc. USA
info@sagmeister.com
sagmeister.com

Pages 282, 283, 284, 285

Savas Ozay Turkey
mail@savasozay.com
savasozay.com

Pages 39, 93, 100, 101

Sawdust United Kingdom
studio@madebysawdust.co.uk
madebysawdust.co.uk

Pages 12, 94, 97, 100, 206, 207, 262, 263

Scandinavian DesignLab
Denmark
contact@scandinaviandesignlab.com
scandinaviandesignlab.com

Pages 18, 39, 72, 102, 193, 232, 262

DIE SEINER Switzerland
lain@sein.se
sein.se

Page 341

sellout-industries™ Germany
post@sellout-industries.org
sellout-industries.org

Pages 139, 163, 254, 342, 349, 351

Serif Mexico
contacto@serif.com.mx
serif.com.mx

Pages 206, 211, 247

Siggeir Hafsteinsson Iceland
digital@sys.is
digital.sys.is

Pages 86, 94, 116, 210, 250

Sister Arrow United Kingdom
sportsdaymegaphone@gmail.com
sisterarrow.com

Page 144

Sister Arrow & Hugh Frost
United Kingdom
sportsdaymegaphone@gmail.com
sisterarrow.com

Pages 38, 110

Skin Designstudio Norway
post@skin.no
skin.no

Pages 43, 217

SKKY Inc. Japan
ito_hen@skky.info
skky.info

Pages 168, 169

Slang Germany
Nathanaël Hamon
nat@slanginternational.org
slanginternational.org

Page 302

Søren Severin Denmark
hello@sorenseverin.dk
sorenseverin.dk

Pages 262, 294

Staynice Netherlands
staynice@staynice.nl
staynice.nl

Pages 34, 35, 304

Stefan Hornof Austria
info@artprophets.at
artprophets.at

Page 262

Stefan Romanu Romania
meetme@stefanromanu.com
stefanromanu.com

Pages 35, 51, 301, 304, 313

strange//attraktor: Canada
studio@strangeattraktor.com
strangeattraktor.com

Pages 36, 212, 288

Strohl USA
Eric Janssen Strohl &
Christine Celic Strohl
eric@strohlsf.com
strohlsf.com

Pages 28, 150, 338, 339, 346

Struggle inc. USA
info@struggleinc.com
struggleinc.com

Pages 22, 110, 132, 160, 174, 175

Strukt Austria
studio@strukt.com
strukt.com

Pages 33, 118, 138, 259

Studio Baum United Kingdom
hello@studiobaum.com
studiobaum.com

Page 317

Studio EMMI United Kingdom
Emmi Salonen
hello@emmi.co.uk
emmi.co.uk

Pages 68, 346

Studio On Fire USA
info@studioonfire.com
studioonfire.com

Pages 339, 345, 351

Studio Output United Kingdom
info@studio-output.com
studio-output.com

Pages 99, 113, 320

Studio Regular Germany
Carsten Giese
info@studio-regular.de
studio-regular.de

Pages 108, 115

StudioSpass Netherlands
Jaron Korvinus & Daan Mens
mail@studiospass.com
studiospass.com

Page 105

Stylism Netherlands
info@stylism.nl
stylism.nl

Page 302

Subcommunication Canada
Sébastien Théraulaz &
Valérie Desrochers
info@subcommunication.com
subcommunication.com

Page 339

SUNDAY VISION Japan
info@sunday-vision.com
sunday-vision.com

Pages 42, 206

Super Top Secret USA
hello@wearetopsecret.com
wearetopsecret.com

Page 36

superbüro Switzerland
Barbara Ehrbar
info@superbuero.com
superbuero.com

Page 43

superfried United Kingdom
info@superfried.com
superfried.com

Pages 102, 211, 239, 247

Superlow Norway
Halvor Bodin
halvor@bodin.no
halvorbodin.com

Pages 9, 336

Surface Germany
Surface Gesellschaft für Gestaltung GmbH
surface.de

Pages 108, 109

SWSP Design Germany
info@SWSP.de
swsp.de

Pages 29, 31, 41

T

Tabas France
cedric@tabas.fr
tabas.fr

Pages 105, 180

Taeko Isu Japan
info@nnnny.jp
nnnny.jp

Pages 12, 50, 57, 164, 166, 257

Tatiana Arocha Colombia
tatiana@servicio-ejecutivo.com
tatianaarocha.com

Pages 210, 244, 308, 316

Team Manila Philippines
info@teammanila.com
teammanila.com

Pages 70, 153, 189, 290

Technicolor Grayscale USA
info@technicolorgrayscale.com
technicolorgrayscale.com

Pages 104, 148

techvector USA
Reggie Gilbert
techvector@gmail.com
techvector.com

Page 40

The Action Designer Norway
the@actiondesigner.com
actiondesigner.com

Pages 23, 35, 81, 196, 289, 321

The Lousy Livincompany
Germany
Stefan Marx
stefan@livincompany.de
livincompany.com

Pages 122, 136, 179, 343

The KDU USA
general@thekdu.com
thekdu.com

Pages 38, 42, 90, 97, 102, 120, 210, 223, 252, 253, 259, 288, 289, 295, 301, 303, 316, 317, 318, 323, 325, 326, 327, 328, 329, 341

The Luxury of Protest
United Kingdom
Peter Crnokrak
info@theluxuryofprotest.com
theluxuryofprotest.com

Pages 23, 151, 251

The Pressure USA
Adam R. Garcia
adam.pressure@gmail.com
thepressure.org

Pages 55, 112, 119, 348

Address Index T–W

THE SKULL DEZAIN Japan
info@skull-dez.com
skull-dez.com

Pages 13, 122, 144, 145, 187, 203, 222, 306, 309, 310, 324, 332

Théo Gennitsakis France
theogennitsakis@gmail.com
theogennitsakis.com

Pages 69, 70, 302

There is United Kingdom
Sean Freeman
sean@thereis.co.uk
thereis.co.uk/

Page 369

**Thomas Hirter &
Andrea Stebler** Switzerland
thomas@olof.ch
thomashirter.ch

Pages 293, 344

Tilt Design Studio Germany
info@tiltdesignstudio.com
tiltdesignstudio.com

Page 171

Tim Bjørn Denmark
info@madebytim.com
madebytim.com

Pages 49, 120, 308

TNOP™ USA
Tnop Wangsillapakun
info@tnop.com
tnop.com

Pages 92, 224

Toben Australia
hello@toben.com.au
toben.com.au

Pages 52, 345, 364

Tobias Röttger Germany
tobias@hort.org.uk
tobiasroettger.de

Pages 52, 86

Toko Australia
info@toko.nu
toko.nu

Pages 22, 44, 51, 74, 105, 205, 232, 288, 298, 317, 360

Tomasz Politański Poland
info@tomaszpolitanski.com
tomaszpolitanski.com

Pages 20, 42

tomato United Kingdom
info@tomato.co.uk
tomato.co.uk

Pages 112, 215

Trademark™ USA
Tim Lahan
timlahan@gmail.com
trademark-trademark.com

Pages 31, 239, 340, 345, 348

Transfer Studio United Kingdom
Falko Grentrup & Valeria Hedman
we@transferstudio.co.uk
transferstudio.co.uk

Pages 53, 98

Tstout USA
Tyler Stout
tyler@tstout.com
tstout.com

Pages 127, 158

Tsuyoshi Hirooka Japan
hrk@hiro-ka.jpn.org
hiro-ka.jpn.org

Pages 254, 303, 305

TU SAIS QUI™ France
ok@tusaisqui.fr
tusaisqui.fr

Pages 31, 66, 81, 136, 138

TWhite design USA
Troy White
troy@twhitedesign.com
twhitedesign.com

Pages 116, 138, 209, 297, 319, 332

TwoPoints.Net Spain
info@twopoints.net
twopoints.net

Pages 112, 255

Typejockeys Austria
hello@typejockeys.com
typejockeys.com

Pages 52, 151, 366

typism Germany
format@typism.de
typism.de

Pages 117, 209

typotherapy + design inc. Canada
studio@typotherapy.com
typotherapy.com

Pages 99, 187

U

**Uwe Strasser &
Maximilian Baud** Germany
und@waskannstduso.com
waskannstduso.com

Page 348

ujidesign Japan
info@ujidesign.com
ujidesign.com

Pages 149, 167

unfolded Switzerland
we@unfolded.ch
unfolded.ch

Pages 93, 257

UNIT United Kingdom
James Sanderson & Si Billam
si@weareunit.com
weareunit.com

Pages 55, 119, 216, 260

Urbanskiworkshop Germany
Denis März
contact@urbanskiworkshop.com
urbanskiworkshop.com

Pages 71, 73, 190, 246, 253

urbn; interaction Germany
Franka Futterlieb & Jörn Alraun
reception@urbn.de
urbn.de

Pages 50, 175

UREDD Norway
uredd@uredd.no
uredd.no

Pages 172, 259

V

V15 Germany
hello@v15.com
v15.com
notfrombrooklyn.com

Pages 38, 208

Vänskap Finland
info@vanskap.fi
vanskap.fi

Page 29

Via Grafik Germany
info@vgrfk.com
vgrfk.com

Pages 117, 138, 148, 203, 214, 248

Vier5 France
contact@vier5.de
vier5.de

Page 144

Vilaz Portugal
info@vilaz.tv
vilaz.tv

Pages 119, 206

Viola Schmieskors Germany
Mail@violaschmieskors.com
violaschmieskors.com

Page 88

visualism Germany
hello@visualism.de
visualism.de

Pages 107, 163

Vivien Le Jeune Durhin France
vivien.ljd@gmail.com
vivienlejeunedurhin.com

Page 136

vonSüden Germany
studio@vonsueden.de
vonsueden.de

Pages 56, 77, 88, 96, 98, 149

W

W://THEM Germany
Floyd E. Schulze
info@wthm.net
wthm.net

Pages 71, 252

We love moules frites Belgium
welovemoulesfrites@gmail.com
welovemoulesfrites.com

Pages 307, 355

Weather Control USA
hello@weatherctrl.com
weatherctrl.com

Pages 143, 150, 158, 339, 345, 346, 366

weissraum.de(sign)° Germany
Bernd Brink & Lucas Buchholz
info@weissraum.de
weissraum.de

Page 121

Wissam Shawkat
United Arab Emirates
wissam@wissamshawkat.com
wissamshawkat.com

Pages 164, 306, 314, 315, 318

Wiyumi Germany
go@wiyumi.com
wiyumi.com

Pages 81, 128, 199

Wolff Olins USA
hello@wolffolins.com
wolffolins.com

Pages 72, 158, 237, 299

Working Format Canada
abi@workingformat.com
workingformat.com

Page 325

X

X3 Studios Romania
office@x3studios.com
x3studios.com

Pages 37, 117, 253, 317

Xavier Barrade France
xavier@xavierbarrade.com
xavierbarrade.com

Pages 290, 332

xy arts Australia
Quan
design@xyarts.com.au
xyarts.com.au

Pages 8, 10, 14, 15, 108, 248, 319

xyz.ch Switzerland
Alexander Meyer
office@xyz.ch
xyz.ch

Pages 13, 15

Y

yippieyeah cooperative
United Kingdom
yy@yippieyeah.co.uk
yippieyeah.co.uk

Page 256

YOK Australia
yok@theyok.com
theyok.com

Pages 125, 130

Young Jerks USA
Daniel Cassaro
dan.cassaro@gmail.com
youngjerks.com

Pages 14, 162, 163, 215, 219

Yucca Studio Singapore
hello@yuccastudio.com
yuccastudio.com

Pages 69, 225, 332

Yuu Imokawa Japan
contact@delotta.com
delotta.com

Page 127

Z

ZEK Slovenia
the.zek.crew@gmail.com
zek.si

Pages 139, 142, 188, 225, 244, 254, 305, 357

Zeroipocrisia Italy
webmaster@zeroipocrisia.com
zeroipocrisia.com

Page 236

Zigmunds Lapsa Latvia
zigmunds_lapsa@yahoo.com
82kg.net

Pages 93, 106, 234

Zion Graphics Sweden
ricky@ziongraphics.com
ziongraphics.com

Pages 190, 310, 320

WORK INDEX

008.01 xy arts
- Quan
- ◊ Art/unclassifiable

008.02 Acme Industries
- Paramon Ditu
- ◊ Political
- $ Fight the power association

009.03 Superlow
- Halvor Bodin
- ◊ Art/unclassifiable
- $ Bjørn Fredrik Gjerstad
- © Nygård Tatoo

009.04 Masheen
- Robert Wallis
- ◊ Culture
- $ Södra Teatern

010.01 Nico Ammann
- ◊ Culture
- $ Full House

010.02 Bo Lundberg & Jan Cafourek
- ◊ Fashion
- $ Cirque Deluxe
- © Anders Arnborger, Indre Singh

010.03 Power Graphixx
- ◊ Fashion
- $ Kanful

010.04 xy arts
- Quan
- ◊ Corporate
- $ bullion bourse

010.05 Sabina Keric
- ◊ Art/unclassifiable

010.06 Power Graphixx
- Sports
- $ Starfuckers

010.07 A-Side Studio
- Sports
- $ Loose-Fit

010.08 Andrea Gustafson
- Music
- $ Sam Roberts Band

010.09 Ken
- Simon Sparkes
- ◊ Art/unclassifiable

011.01 modo
- Alexander Wright
- ◊ Culture
- $ Gopher Illustrated

011.02 EL MIRO
- ◊ Corporate
- $ Das Lab
- © EL MIRO, Das Lab

011.03 Fresh Estudio
- ◊ Culture
- $ Flow

011.04 Norwegian Ink
- ◊ Music
- $ Madhatter Sandnes

011.05 Sabina Keric
- ◊ Art/unclassifiable

011.06 Analog.Systm
- Oscar Bjarnason
- ◊ Art/unclassifiable

011.07 Edgar Bąk
- ◊ Political
- $ Amnesty International

012.01 Sawdust
- Sneaky Raccoon
- ◊ Fashion
- $ Monsoon Accessorize Trust

012.02 atelier aquarium
- Jérémie Nuel & Simon Renaud
- ◊ Fashion
- $ appartement 16

012.03 Positron Co Ltd
- Hiroaki Doi & Kenichi Isogawa
- ◊ Culture

012.04 Taeko Isu
- ◊ Design
- $ NNNNY
- © GABIN ITO

013.01 John L. Nguyen
- ◊ Corporate
- $ Pen & Quill

013.02 Ali Khorshidpour
- ◊ Culture
- $ Iranian Tribes Museum

013.03 DTM_INC
- ◊ Corporate
- $ Big Tree

013.04 John L. Nguyen
- ◊ Corporate
- $ Pen & Quill

013.05 xyz.ch
- Alexander Meyer
- ◊ Design
- $ MilieuGrotesque
- © www.milieugrotesque.com

013.06 Jarek Kowalczyk
- ◊ Culture

013.07 Chris Rubino
- ◊ Art/unclassifiable

013.08 Ali Khorshidpour
- ◊ Culture
- $ National Library of Iran

013.09 THE SKULL DEZAIN
- ◊ Motion/Games/Media

014.01 Jonathan Calugi
- ◊ Corporate
- $ Vol de Nuit—Robert Pettena

014.02 Mash

014.03
- ◊ Design
- $ Alpha Box & Dice

014.04 Denny Backhaus
- ◊ Music
- $ hfn music

014.05 Acme Industries
- Paramon Ditu
- ◊ Fashion
- $ Praf, clothing company

014.06 Edgar Bąk
- ◊ Art/unclassifiable
- $ Photo month in Krakow

014.07 Lifter Baron
- ◊ Design
- © Rob Angermuller

014.08 Fons Hickmann m23
- Fons Hickmann & Gesine Grotrian-Steinweg (art directors); Sabina Keric (designer)
- ◊ Political
- $ Amnesty International

014.09 cerotreees
- Carlos Engel
- ◊ Motion/Games/Media
- $ Gamebombing

014.10 Acme Industries
- Octavian Budai
- ◊ Art/unclassifiable
- $ Est Etica

014.11 xy arts
- Quan
- ◊ Corporate
- $ majores

014.12 Young Jerks
- Daniel Cassaro
- ◊ Design
- $ maomao publications

015.01 Roy Smith
- ◊ Corporate
- $ Better Yet

015.02 COUP
- Peter van den Hoogen
- ◊ Corporate
- $ Kinderopvang Compagnie

015.03 Core60
- Eduard Muresan
- ◊ Corporate
- $ Geocip Palade

015.04 Lifter Baron
- ◊ Design
- © Rob Angermuller

015.05 modo
- Alexander Wright
- ◊ Culture
- $ massv

015.06 xyz.ch
- Alexander Meyer
- ◊ Design
- $ MilieuGrotesque
- © www.milieugrotesque.com

015.07 xy arts
- Quan
- ◊ Corporate
- $ Casafico

015.08 backyard10
- ◊ Music
- $ musikmachen.de

016.01 Project 1000
- Stefan Szakal
- ◊ Culture
- $ SCOP

016.02 Red Design
- ◊ Art / unclassifiable
- $ Bottletop

016.03 asmallpercent
- Tim Ferguson Sauder
- ◊ Culture
- $ Cape Ann Farmer's Market

017.04 Brusatto
- ◊ Culture
- $ Modemuseum Hasselt
- © Geoffrey Brusatto

017.05 Mads Burcharth
- ◊ Corporate
- $ CodeFish Carbon

018.06 Scandinavian DesignLab
018.07
- ◊ Corporate
- $ SuperBest

019.01 designJune
- Julien Crouigneau
- ◊ Art / unclassifiable
- $ Very Select Graphic Director's Club
- © Julien Crouigneau

019.02 Clusta
- Joe Mitchelmore
- ◊ Fashion
- $ Mr. Tod's

019.03 Hugh Frost
- ◊ Corporate
- $ TUFF

019.04 Jarek Kowalczyk
- ◊ Corporate
- $ Laney&Felter

019.05 FEED
- ◊ Corporate
- $ Amuse Integrative

019.06 cypher13
- ◊ Culture
- $ 15th Street Coffee Haus

019.07 Celeste Prevost
- ◊ Culture
- $ FreshSimple Café

019.08 Creative Inc
- Kathryn Wilson
- ◊ Art / unclassifiable
- $ Gills
- © Mel O'Rourke (art director)

020.01 Tomasz Politański
- ◊ Art / unclassifiable
- $ Museum of Art in Lodz
- © Museum of Art in Lodz

020.02 General Projects
- ◊ Corporate
- $ Iridesco LLC

020.03 Positron Co Ltd
- Hiroaki Doi, Kenichi Isogawa
- ◊ Corporate

020.04 Rasmus Snabb
- ◊ Design
- $ Aero Design Furniture

020.05 Andreas Töpfer & Buchgut
- ◊ Culture
- $ Aurora Verlag

020.06 La Cáscara Amarga
- Jorge Chamorro
- ◊ Corporate
- $ miss moneypenny

021.01 Julia Heitmann
- ◊ Sports
- $ IOC

022.01 Federico Landini
- ◊ Music
- $ Karl Marx was a broker
- © www.karlmarxwasabroker.com

022.02 Grandpeople
- ◊ Design
- $ Tveit & Tornoe, Knudsen & Hindenes, Circus Design, Geir Sætveit

022.03 Hype Type Studio
- Paul Hutchison
- ◊ Fashion
- $ 786

022.04 Struggle inc.
- ◊ Culture
- $ Mandible Projects

022.05 Toko
- ◊ Corporate
- $ Host Agency Sydney

022.06 Matt W. Moore
- ◊ Corporate
- $ CNC Builders
- © MWM Graphics

022.07 Maniackers Design
- Masayuki Sato
- ◊ Corporate
- $ CRAFTWORKS
- © CRAFTWORKS

022.08 Hey Ho
- ◊ Corporate
- $ XVIII Bordeaux

023.01 Alexander Spliid
- ◊ Corporate
- $ BEE

023.02 A-Side Studio
- ◊ Corporate
- $ Atlantic House

023.03 The Action Designer
- ◊ Fashion
- $ MiniMe

023.04 Inventaire
- ◊ Corporate
- $ Bureau Comptable Arnaud Privet

023.05 Janine Rewell
- ◊ Corporate
- $ Smiles for Miles / RISD

023.06 The Luxury of Protest
- Peter Crnokrak
- ◊ Design
- $ Daval

023.07 FEED
- ◊ Culture
- $ Barbe & Doucet

023.08 Revivify Graphic Design
- Rich Scott
- ◊ Motion / Games / Media

024.01 büro uebele visuelle kommunikation
- Katrin Dittmann, Daniel Fels, Andreas Uebele; Tristan Schmitz & Angela Klasar (project managers)
- ◊ Political
- $ Deutscher Bundestag

025.01 Joshua Distler
- ◊ Corporate
- $ MetaDesign / DAI

025.02 Ryan Crouchman
- ◊ Design
- $ Fahey and Associates
- © Bleublancrouge (agency); Marie-Hélène Trottier (creative director)

025.03 cypher13
- ◊ Culture
- $ Biennial of the Americas

025.04 Roy Smith
- ◊ Corporate
- $ Archant
- © Further

025.05 Gabe Ruane
- ◊ Corporate
- $ Sidewalk Connection

025.06 Landor Associates
- Rietje Gieskes & Craig Dobie
- ◊ Culture
- $ 9/11 Memorial

026.01 onlab
- Nicolas Bourquin & Thibaud Tissot
- ◊ Political
- $ City of Tramelan, Switzerland

027.01 Rob van Hoesel
- ◊ Music
- $ Mezz (concert venue)

027.02 Lundgren+Lindqvist
- ◊ Design

027.03 Floor Wesseling
- ◊ Art / unclassifiable
- $ Kultivator

028.01 Jaime Narváez
- ◊ Art / unclassifiable
- $ El Fotográfico
- © www.elfotografico.com

028.02 ehquestionmark
- ◊ Culture
- $ South Manchester Museum Of Keyboard Technology

028.03 Device
- ◊ Corporate

028.04 Fabio Santoro
- ◊ Corporate
- $ Biociência

028.05 Axel Raidt
- ◊ Corporate
- $ Abraham Energieprojekt GmbH

028.06 Reaktor Lab
- Jorge Aguilar
- ◊ Fashion
- $ Paulina y Cristina Castro

028.07 Strohl
- Eric Strohl
- ◊ Political
- $ Wiser Earth

028.08 Joshua Distler
- ◊ Corporate
- $ MetaDesign / DAI

028.09 Hexanine
- Tim Lapetino (designer); Jim Dygas (creative director)
- ◊ Corporate
- $ Ocean Dawn

029.01 Avalanche
- ◊ Culture
- $ Galerie des Projets / École supérieure des Arts décoratifs, Strasbourg

029.02 SWSP Design
- Georg Schatz
- ◊ Sports
- $ Yoga N Yoey

029.03 Vänskap
- ◊ Music
- $ MVSEVM

029.04 No-Domain
- ◊ Corporate
- $ Nomeno

030.01 Mutabor
- ◊ Corporate
- $ Beeftea Group
- © Mutabor Design GmbH

030.02 Mutabor
- ◊ Culture
- $ Seebühne Bremen
- © Mutabor Design GmbH

030.03 Mutabor
- ◊ Corporate
- $ Marxen Wein
- © Mutabor Design GmbH

030.04 Mutabor
- ◊ Corporate
- $ Sitag
- © Mutabor Design GmbH

030.05 Mutabor
- ◊ Fashion
- $ Gabor Footwear GmbH
- © Mutabor Design GmbH

030.06 Mutabor
- ◊ Sports
- $ Audi AG / Jacaranda Marketing
- © Mutabor Design GmbH

030.07 General Projects
- ◊ Music
- $ Panama

030.08 Mutabor
- ◊ Corporate
- $ Stadtwerke Kiel
- © Mutabor Design GmbH

030.09 Mutabor
- ◊ Sports
- $ DFL Deutsche Fußball Liga GmbH
- © Mutabor Design GmbH

030.10 Mutabor
- ◊ Sports
- $ Audi AG
- © Mutabor Design GmbH

030.11 Cassie Leedham
- ◊ Motion / Games / Media
- $ Good Show Studio

031.01 SWSP Design
- Georg Schatz
- ◊ Design
- $ German Mebel

031.02 SWSP Design
- Georg Schatz
- ◊ Corporate
- $ Orthopädie am Gasteig

031.03 Benoît Bodhuin
- ◊ Design
- © BENBENWORLD

031.04 TU SAIS QUI™
- Marc Armand
- ◊ Motion / Games / Media
- $ DGDP Productions

031.05 Markus Moström
- ◊ Corporate
- $ Citycon AB, Stockholm

031.06 Trademark™
- Tim Lahan
- ◊ Fashion
- $ The Organization Organization

031.07 Jarrik Muller
- ◊ Corporate
- $ Ooghduyne

031.08 Patrik Ferrarelli
- ◊ Corporate
- $ Alois Koller AG

031.09 Company
- ◊ Corporate
- $ PinPoint Events

032.01 Maximilian Baud & Uwe Strasser
- ◊ Art / unclassifiable
- $ Orignal Products GmbH

032.02 Landor Associates
- Pan Yamboonruang, Angela McCarthy & Jason Little
- ◊ Fashion
- $ Miller & Green

385

Work Index

032.03 asmallpercent
- Tim Ferguson Sauder
◊ Culture
$ Gloucester Community Arts Charter School
032.04 Bestial Design® Studio
◊ Art/unclassifiable
$ Computers Art Projects
032.05 asmallpercent
- Tim Ferguson Sauder
◊ Corporate
$ Jeffrey Keller Real Estate
032.06 INDASTRIACOOLHIDEA
- Luca Forlani
◊ Design
$ SERRANI ARREDAMENTI
032.07 Breckon Gráfica
◊ Culture
$ Ingrid Forbord Grafisk Design
032.08 EL MIRO
◊ Corporate
$ King Casting
© EL MIRO King Casting
032.09 Lundgren+Lindqvist
◊ Culture
$ Jennie Smith Photo
032.10 Out Of Order
◊ Motion/Games/Media
$ Bright Wide

033.01 Ekaterina Tiouleikina
◊ Corporate
$ Alg Börje
033.02 Alen 'Type08' Pavlovic
◊ Political
$ Africa Unite
033.03 Strukt
- Andreas Koller
◊ Design
$ Strukt Design Studio
033.04 asmallpercent
- Tim Ferguson Sauder
◊ Corporate
$ Northwest Cardiology Associates
033.05 Giorgio Paolinelli
◊ Corporate
$ Alejandra Garcia Travieso
033.06 asmallpercent
- Tim Ferguson Sauder
◊ Corporate
$ Chicago Family Asthma and Allergy
033.07 Eddie Brown
- Eddie Brown; typeface by Joe Prince
◊ Culture
$ Bio Glow
033.08 asmallpercent
- Tim Ferguson Sauder
◊ Corporate
$ Harvest
033.09 Moxie Sozo
◊ Corporate
$ Milton Taylor

034.01 Graphical House
◊ Design
$ Armando Ferrari
034.02 Moxie Sozo
◊ Sports
$ Traverse
034.03 Core60
- Eduard Muresan
◊ Corporate
$ The Phillips Collection
034.04 REX
◊ Culture
$ The Three Foxes
034.05 Revivify Graphic Design
- Rich Scott
◊ Design

034.06 Revivify Graphic Design
- Rich Scott
◊ Corporate
$ Australian Association for Cognitive and Behaviour Therapy
034.07 Revivify Graphic Design
- Rich Scott
◊ Motion/Games/Media
$ Copilot
034.08 Staynice
◊ Corporate
$ Plaisir du Vin
034.09 Core60
- Eduard Muresan
◊ Culture
$ Babel Education
034.10 Büro Destruct
- Lopetz
◊ Corporate
$ Perron8, Biel/Bienne
034.11 EMPK
- Diego Bellorin
◊ Corporate
$ GIOVANNIDRAFTFCB
© EMPK

035.01 Brand New History™
◊ Fashion
$ Murnau Textilien
035.02 Moxie Sozo
◊ Sports
$ Traverse
035.03 Stefan Romanu
◊ Sports
$ Alpin Carpatic Club
035.04 EMPK
- Diego Bellorin
◊ Design
$ Morfoxyz
035.05 Company
◊ Corporate
$ Global Canopy Programme—Forest Footprint Disclosure Project
035.06 Copenheroes
- Gringo Star
◊ Design
$ Furnld
035.07 Graphical House
◊ Motion/Games/Media
$ Filmcity Glasgow
035.08 The Action Designer
◊ Corporate
$ STRYVO—Stryn Vognfabrikk
035.09 Staynice
◊ Culture
$ AKV St.Joost
035.10 Matt W. Moore
◊ Design
$ HAI
© MWM Graphics
035.11 HoohaaDesign
◊ Art/unclassifiable
$ Unwind—De-stress Therapy Company

036.01 Image Now
- David Torpey
◊ Corporate
$ The Well
036.02 Matteo Mastronardi
◊ Corporate
$ Sam Music & Spherical Sound
036.03 Di-Da Komunikakzioa
- Asier Bilbao
◊ Corporate
$ Artez
© Di-Da Komunikakzioa

036.04 Dimomedia Lab
- Massimo Sirelli
◊ Culture
$ Torre di Babele School
036.05 Super Top Secret
◊ Corporate
$ Stackable
036.06 Di-Da Komunikakzioa
- Asier Bilbao
◊ Political
$ Chosen
© Asier Bilbao, Joseba Attard & Jane Ware
036.07 nocturn.ro
- Alex Tass
◊ Corporate
$ Trinidad & Tobago Energy Conference
© Alex Tass
036.08 nocturn.ro
- Alex Tass
◊ Corporate
$ The Caribbean Energy Conference
036.09 hintzegruppen
- Jesper Hintze
◊ Motion/Games/Media
$ PrintNinja
036.10 Martin Holm
◊ Culture
$ Litteraturuka Sarpsborg
036.11 strange//attraktor:
- Skødt D. McNalty
◊ Corporate
$ Karin Haumer

037.01 Benjamin Metz
◊ Corporate
$ Innovationszentrum Gestaltung von Lebensräumen, TU Berlin
037.02 Core60
- Eduard Muresan
◊ Corporate
$ Institut Dr. Nowak
037.03 X3 Studios
- Erik Erdokozi
◊ Corporate
$ Biosphaera
037.04 Edhv
◊ Corporate
$ SDK Vastgoed bv
© Eric de Haas & Remco van de Craats
037.05 Edhv
◊ Corporate
$ BKRS Crane Systems
© Remco van de Craats, Jeroen Braspenning & Jeroen Holthuis
037.06 Company
◊ Corporate
$ Olympic Air
© Dalton Maag
037.07 FriendsWithYou
◊ Design
037.08 Andy Mangold
◊ Design
$ Crowdstorms
037.09 Extraverage
- Karoly Kiralyfalvi
◊ Corporate
$ Class FM

038.01 Bold°
- Leonardo Eyer, Carlos Andre Eyer & Leandro Santos
◊ Corporate
$ Leão Júnior
© Bold° & Santa Clara Nitro

038.02 Sister Arrow & Hugh Frost
◊ Music
$ Lambs & Lions
038.03 The KDU
- Aerosyn-Lex
◊ Fashion
$ Ecko
038.04 Moxie Sozo
◊ Sports
$ Traverse
038.05 V15
◊ Corporate
$ White Hart
038.06 Büro4
◊ Corporate
$ Kanton Zürich, Switzerland
038.07 Edgar Bak
◊ Political
$ Amnesty International
038.08 hintzegruppen
- Jesper Hintze
◊ Corporate
$ Traetodo

039.01 Eduardo Vidales
◊ Corporate
$ Comision Iberoamericana de etica Judicial
039.02 Savas Ozay
◊ Design
$ Baykuş Medya
039.03 Ian Lynam Design
- Ian Lynam
◊ Culture
$ LePigeon
039.04 Fieldtrip
- Joost Verhaak
◊ Corporate
$ City of Utrecht, ProRail & Rijkswaterstaat
039.05 ehquestionmark
◊ Art/unclassifiable
$ POrigins of Pommery—Pommeranian Epoch
039.06 Bionic Systems
◊ Corporate
$ R.U.N. hospitality solutions, Germany
© Doris Fürst & Malte Haust
039.07 Scandinavian DesignLab
◊ Fashion
$ Munthe plus Simonsen
039.08 Bionic Systems
◊ Corporate
$ Kati Käss, Düsseldorf, Germany
© Doris Fürst & Malte Haust

040.01 techvector
- Reggie Gilbert
◊ Fashion
$ Foundry
© Reggie Gilbert/techvector.com
040.02 Pierre Jeanneret
◊ Corporate
$ Elite Galerie
040.03 Mitchell Paone
◊ Corporate
$ Tomorrow International
040.04 Graphical House
◊ Culture
$ University of Strathclyde
040.05 HelloComputer
◊ Sports
$ Basil Marcus
040.06 Revivify Graphic Design
- Rich Scott
◊ Corporate
$ PennyPuddle

Work Index

041.01 **e-Types**
◊ Culture
$ Egeskov Castle

041.02 **SWSP Design**
• Georg Schatz
◊ Corporate
$ SeafoodSylt

041.03 **Mutabor**
◊ Corporate
$ Torhaus Salzau
© Mutabor Design GmbH

041.04 **Josiah Jost**
◊ Motion / Games / Media
$ Josephine Publishing

041.05 **Face.**
• Rik
◊ Design
$ Salinas Lasheras

041.06 **Bleed**
◊ Culture
$ National Theatre Oslo

041.07 **Mutabor**
◊ Corporate
$ Beisser GmbH
© Mutabor Design GmbH

042.01 **Edgar Bąk**
◊ Corporate
$ Zielony Pomidor

042.02 **SUNDAY VISION**
• Shinsuke Koshio / SUNDAY VISION
◊ Fashion
$ AIM creates

042.03 **Tomasz Politański**
◊ Art / unclassifiable
$ Tastes of France
© Tastes of France

042.04 **e-Types**
◊ Political
$ Danish Arts Council

042.05 **Monoblock**
• Pablo Galuppo & Franziska Veh
◊ Corporate
$ Rooney's Boutique Hotel
© Pablo Galuppo

042.06 **Deanne Cheuk**
◊ Design
$ *TOKION* Magazine, Japan

042.07 **e-Types**
◊ Corporate
$ Nordea

042.08 **The KDU**
• Aerosyn-Lex
◊ Corporate
$ Qiviuk

043.01 **Red Design**
◊ Political
$ Elysee.fr

043.02 **superbüro**
• Barbara Ehrbar
◊ Corporate
$ Verein Bernischer Tierärztinnen und Tierärzte
© Anita Schneuwly

043.03 **Coutworks**
◊ Design

043.04 **Skin Designstudio**
◊ Music
$ Oslo String Quartet

043.05 **Inventaire**
◊ Corporate
$ Enjoy

043.06 **Inventaire**
◊ Culture
$ Rencontres Théâtrales

043.07 **Peter Gregson**
• Jovan Trkulja
◊ Corporate
$ ZAK Caffe & Restaurant

043.08 **asmallpercent & Return Design**
• Tim Ferguson Sauder
◊ Culture
$ Congregational Church of Topsfield

044.01 **Joseph Garner**
◊ Motion / Games / Media

044.02 **Eddie Brown**
◊ Culture
$ A&E Cyber Publishers
© Eddie Brown

044.03 **Revivify Graphic Design**
• Rich Scott
◊ Political

044.04 **Peter Schmidt Group**
◊ Design
$ Henkel Persil & BSH Bosch und Siemens Hausgeräte GmbH

044.05 **Alessandro Mingione**
◊ Corporate
$ Coffee Time

044.06 **Alphabet Arm Design**
• Chris Piascik
◊ Design
$ Placetailor

044.07 **Revivify Graphic Design**
• Rich Scott
◊ Art / unclassifiable

044.08 **Rokac**
• Roko Kerovec
◊ Corporate
$ mr. Vincent Busch

044.09 **Alen 'Type08' Pavlovic**
◊ Art / unclassifiable
$ Cakefilm

044.10 **Toko**
◊ Corporate
$ Bring Agency

044.11 **Coley Porter Bell**
• Adam Ellis
◊ Corporate
$ Gelert Pet Nutrition

044.12 **Felix Lobelius**
◊ Culture
$ Kaffe

045.01 **Felix Sockwell**
◊ Culture
$ The *New York Times*

045.02 **Revivify Graphic Design**
• Rich Scott
◊ Culture

045.03 **Floris Voorveld**
◊ Design
$ TiredChildren

045.04 **Revivify Graphic Design**
• Rich Scott
◊ Art / unclassifiable

045.05 **Roy Smith**
◊ Corporate
$ Advanta / The Point

045.06 **Ptarmak, Inc.**
◊ Culture
$ Eat Innovations
© JR Crosby & Zach Ferguson

045.07 **Acme Industries**
• Paramon Ditu
◊ Fashion
$ L'Armoire concept store

045.08 **Project 1000**
• Stefan Szakal
◊ Corporate
$ Ugly Duck Events

046.01 **John Langdon**
◊ Art / unclassifiable
$ Bobby Martin

047.02 **John Langdon**
◊ Corporate
$ Lotus Lille Alchemy

047.03 **John Langdon**
◊ Corporate
$ Janet Smith Warfield

048.04 **John Langdon**
◊ Corporate
$ The Guthrie Center

048.05 **John Langdon**
◊ Music
$ Lovekraft

048.06 **John Langdon**
◊ Corporate
$ Action Africa

048.07 **John Langdon**
• John Langdon
◊ Corporate
$ Shhhout Pte Ltd.

048.08 **John Langdon**
◊ Corporate
$ Department of Psychology, Drexel University

048.09 **John Langdon**
◊ Art / unclassifiable

049.01 **903 Creative**
• Aaron Gibson
◊ Design

049.02 **Hayes Image**
• Josh Hayes
◊ Art / unclassifiable

049.03 **Tim Bjørn**
◊ Design

049.04 **EL MIRO**
◊ Fashion
$ Nikita Clothing
© nikitaclothing.com

049.05 **EL MIRO**
◊ Design
$ Smit&Jansen
© smitenjansen.nl

049.06 **Alessandro Mingione**
◊ Design

049.07 **BANK™**
◊ Art / unclassifiable
$ Claudia Christoffel

049.08 **Joseph Garner**
◊ Design
$ Joseph Garner

049.09 **Hugo Mulder**
◊ Design
$ DHM Graphic Design
© DHM Graphic Design

049.10 **NALINDESIGN™**
• Andre Weier
◊ Fashion

049.11 **Inventaire**
◊ Corporate
$ Magic Woman

049.12 **Rokac**
◊ Design
$ Mr. Ivan Kerovec
© Roko Kerovec

050.01 **Regina**
◊ Motion / Games / Media
$ *TYO magazine*
© Bon Voyage / *TYO magazine*

050.02 **Red Design**
◊ Music
$ Tommy Sparks / Island Records

050.03 **Jesse Kirsch**
◊ Art / unclassifiable
$ Melt

050.04 **Bestial Design® Studio**
◊ Design
$ Madhouse

050.05 **REX**
◊ Fashion
$ KO KLEE KO

050.06 **Huschang Pourian**
◊ Fashion
$ Ragwear

050.07 **FriendsWithYou**
◊ Design

050.08 **A-Side Studio**
◊ Sports
$ Flatspot

050.09 **Taeko Isu**
◊ Culture
$ BOW
© BOW

050.10 **Robi Jõeleht**
◊ Fashion
$ HAW (Hello And Welcome)

050.11 **urbn; interaction**
• Franka Futterlieb, Jörn Alraun
◊ Culture
$ urbn; interaction

050.12 **adam gf**
◊ Motion / Games / Media
$ Polarpic

051.01 **e-Types**
◊ Design
$ Danish Design Center

051.02 **Dongwoo Kim**
◊ Fashion
$ Take Over

051.03 **e-Types**
◊ Culture
$ Substanz / Nordic Film

051.04 **Stefan Romanu**
◊ Design
$ Ctrl D
© Stefan Romanu (designer); Sorin Bechira (art director); Stefan Szakal (creative director)

051.05 **Projekttriangle Design Studio**
◊ Corporate
$ Frankfurt Hahn Airport

051.06 **Kokoro & Moi**
◊ Corporate
$ Moskito Group

051.07 **Toko**
◊ Corporate
$ Untitled Agency

051.08 **Graphical House**
◊ Corporate
$ Quarriers

052.01 **Toben**
◊ Design

052.02 **Jaime Narváez**
◊ Art / unclassifiable
$ La Más Bella

052.03 **Typejockeys**
◊ Music
$ Thomas A. Bec

052.04 **Tobias Röttger**
◊ Culture
$ Onkel & Onkel

052.05 **GVA Studio**
◊ Art / unclassifiable
$ Group8

052.06 **HelloMe**
• Till Wiedeck
◊ Music
$ Drei Groschen Studio

052.07 **max-o-matic**
• Máximo Tuja
◊ Art / unclassifiable
$ Sala de estar
© www.maxomatic.net

• Designer Name (if not identical with studio name) // ◊ Category // $ Client (if not identical with studio name) // © Credits (if not owned by studio or designer)

Work Index

052.08 Jürgen Frost
◊ Motion/Games/Media
$ Intro Magazin
053.01 one8one7
◊ Design
$ Powerhouse Museum
053.02 FriendsWithYou
053.03
◊ Design
053.04 Ken Tanabe
◊ Motion/Games/Media
$ Leo Ferguson
053.05 Form+Format
• Daniel Neye
◊ Corporate
$ The Little Gourmet Company
053.06 Pop Ovidiu Sebastian
◊ Corporate
$ nige
053.07 Derek A. Friday
• Derek A. Friday/Finndustry
◊ Corporate
$ Metropia
© Paul Pewterbaugh
053.08 one8one7
◊ Design
$ Food Wine and Design
053.09 Transfer Studio
• Falko Grentrup & Valeria Hedman
◊ Art/unclassifiable
$ Junco Films
053.10 Transfer Studio
• Falko Grentrup & Valeria Hedman
◊ Design
053.11 Creative Inc
• Ciara Cantwell
◊ Culture
$ The Lab

054.01 Benoît Bodhuin
◊ Culture
$ le vivat
© BENBENWORLD
054.02 Felix Sockwell
◊ Art/unclassifiable
054.03 KesselsKramer
• Fabienne Feltus
◊ Culture
$ Graphic Design Museum
054.04 Chris Rubino
◊ Corporate
$ dotcom
054.05 Autobahn
◊ Culture
$ Typisch Kim
054.06 Brusatto
◊ Culture
$ MijnErfgoed, Genk
© Geoffrey Brusatto
054.07 hintzegruppen
• Jesper Hintze
◊ Sports
$ All American Volleyball
054.08 Patrik Ferrarelli
◊ Sports
$ Basketball Alstom Baden
054.09 Gabe Ruane
◊ Culture
$ Hapa

055.01 Kummer & Herrman
◊ Culture
$ We are the world (Paradox & Three Shadows Photography Art Centre Beijing)
055.02 André Beato
◊ Corporate
$ Lisbon Lovers/Metropolis

055.03 UNIT
• Si Billam
◊ Fashion
$ Twist magazine
055.04 Áron Jancsó
◊ Music
$ Jingle Jungle
055.05 The Pressure
• Adam R Garcia
◊ Design
$ Personal
055.06 General Projects
◊ Design
$ Ben Pieratt
055.07 FriendsWithYou
◊ Design

056.01 Positron Co Ltd
• Hiroaki Doi
◊ Music
056.02 gebrauchsgrafikundso
◊ Fashion
$ meersachen.de
056.03 Dtam-TM
• Paul Heys
◊ Design
$ Dtam
056.04 vonSüden
◊ Music
$ 7 Golden Vampires
© Michael Luther
056.05 Ali Khorshidpour
◊ Political
$ The Center for Political and International Studies
056.06 Eduardo Vidales
◊ Art/unclassifiable
$ Universidad Autonoma de Guerrero
056.07 Raf Vancampenhoudt & Make Agency
◊ Fashion
$ Milkmade/Make Agency
056.08 FEED
◊ Art/unclassifiable
$ Melinda Pap/Atelier Punkt
056.09 Autobahn
◊ Music
$ Holland Baroque Society
056.10 EBSL
• Erik Kiesewetter
◊ Culture
$ Faub.org Creative Aid & Pleasure Club
056.11 phospho
• Roland Hörmann
◊ Design
056.12 ilovedust
◊ Fashion
$ Under Two Flags

057.01 Floor 5
• Marek Polewski & Jens Pieper
◊ Corporate
$ Caras Gourmet
057.02 Büro Destruct
• Lopetz
◊ Corporate
$ Hosoya Schaefer Architects AG Zurich & VW Autostadt Wolfsburg
057.03 Aldo Lugo
◊ Culture
$ Persigna Store
057.04 Fons Hickmann m23
• Fons Hickmann & Gesine Grotrian-Steinweg
◊ Music
$ Elektra Vision

057.05 Floor 5
• Marek Polewski & Jens Pieper
◊ Corporate
$ Luigi Zuckermann Deli
© Jan Stöwe (illustration)
057.06 Mr. Kone
◊ Culture
$ Kamikace Studio
057.07 Kelly D. Williams
• Kelly D. Williams on behalf of Distrikt Studio
◊ Corporate
$ Rolf Contemporary
© Distrikt Creative Group for respective client(s)
057.08 Taeko Isu
◊ Culture
$ MASANORI IKEDA
© ANDA ITOI

058.01 KMS TEAM
• Michael Keller (creative director); Chris Goennawein (designer)
◊ Culture
$ Dog Ear Films
058.02 KMS TEAM
• Knut Maierhofer (creative director); Patrick Märki (team manager design)
◊ Sports
$ Canyon Bicycles GmbH

059.03 KMS TEAM
• Knut Maierhofer (creative director), Chris Goennawein (designer)
◊ Culture
$ Bundesverband Deutscher Galerien und Editionen e.V.
059.04 KMS TEAM
• Knut Maierhofer (creative director); Julia Oesterle (team manager design); Carl Bartel (senior designer); Atli Hilmarsson (senior designer); Sandra Opiela (designer)
◊ Corporate
$ Warendorfer Küchen GmbH
059.05 KMS TEAM
• Knut Maierhofer (creative director); Helena Fruehauf (team manager design); Atli Hilmarsson (senior designer)
◊ Corporate
$ Deutsche Pfandbriefbank AG
059.06 KMS TEAM
• Knut Maierhofer (creative director); Patrick Märki (team manager design); Sarah Graf (designer)
◊ Design
$ ICSID (International Council of Societies of Industrial Design)
059.07 KMS TEAM
• Knut Maierhofer (creative director); Stefan Hecht (designer)
◊ Corporate
$ InterComponentWare Deutschland AG & Co. KG

060.08 KMS TEAM
• Knut Maierhofer (creative director); Susanne Elhardt (designer)
◊ Corporate
$ Klöpferholz GmbH & Co. KG
060.09 KMS TEAM
• Knut Maierhofer & Michael Keller (creative directors); Patrick Märki (team manager design); May Kato (designer)
◊ Corporate
$ feno GmbH

060.10 KMS TEAM
• Knut Maierhofer (creative director); Michael Keller (creative director); Patrick Märki (team manager design); Bettina Otto (senior designer); Daniel Perraudin (designer)
◊ Sports
$ Dr. Ing. h. c. F. Porsche AG
061.11 KMS TEAM
• Michael Keller (creative director); Stefan Bergmeier (designer interactive)
◊ Design
$ Armin Brosch Fotografie
061.12 KMS TEAM
• Knut Maierhofer (creative director); Carl Bartel (senior designer); Susanne Elhardt (designer)
◊ Corporate
$ Isaria Corporate Design AG
061.13 KMS TEAM
• Knut Maierhofer (creative director); Susanne Elhardt (designer)
◊ Corporate
$ Klöpferholz GmbH & Co. KG
061.14 KMS TEAM
• Michael Keller (creative director); Chris Goennawein (designer)
◊ Music
$ VOXYD GmbH

062.01 Acme Industries
• Paramon Ditu
◊ Culture
$ Zvak
062.02 Heydays
◊ Culture
$ Grip: kultur

063.03 Company
◊ Culture
$ Suzy Roston
063.04 Daniel Carlsten
• Daniel Carlsten for Acne Art Department
◊ Corporate
$ Oscar Properties

064.05 ATTAK
◊ Music
$ Plein79, 's-Hertogenbosch
© ATTAK • Powergestaltung
064.06 Otto Dietrich
◊ Corporate
$ Gallery Desaga, www.desaga.com

065.01 Jan en Randoald
◊ Culture
$ Kunstenfestivaldesarts Bruxelles

066.01 Fabian Bertschinger
◊ Corporate
$ Spitzbarth Zürich
066.02 Kokoro & Moi
◊ Design
$ Design Forum Finland
066.03 LLdesign
• Lorella Pierdicca
◊ Music
$ Scoolptures
066.04 Esther Rieser
◊ Fashion
$ Bolsopaseo

388

066.05 TU SAIS QUI™
- Marc Armand
◊ Corporate
$ Les Sommeliers Indépendants

066.06 Akatre
◊ Corporate
$ Mains d'Œuvres

067.01 Baldinger·Vu-Huu
◊ Culture
$ École Estienne Paris

068.01 Rob van Hoesel
◊ Culture
$ Graphic Design Festival Breda

068.02 Martin Nicolausson
◊ Motion/Games/Media
$ Erik Wåhlström

068.03 LLdesign
- Lorella Pierdicca
◊ Art/unclassifiable
$ Il paradiso dei calzini srl

068.04 Studio EMMI
- Emmi Salonen
◊ Culture
$ Contemporary Art Archipelago

068.05 Akatre
◊ Corporate
$ Cindy Van Acker

068.06 HelloMe
- Till Wiedeck
◊ Culture
$ Summa Summarum

068.07 Edgar Bąk
◊ Art/unclassifiable
$ Foundation of Visual Arts

068.08 Brusatto
- Geoffrey Brusatto
◊ Culture
$ De Queeste – Theater-makershuis, Hasselt

069.01 Autobahn
◊ Culture
$ Kletter

069.02 NODE Berlin Oslo
◊ Music
$ Mere Records

069.03 Matt W. Moore
◊ Fashion
$ Dress Code
© MWM Graphics

069.04 Heydays
◊ Fashion
$ Berg & Berg

069.05 Guillaume Peitrequin
◊ Culture
$ In Situ Galerie

069.06 JUTOJO
◊ Art/unclassifiable
$ Replik Republik

069.07 Théo Gennitsakis
◊ Fashion
$ axara

069.08 Floor 5
- Marek Polewski & Jens Pieper
◊ Fashion
$ Client Fashion

069.09 Yucca Studio
- Agnes Tan
◊ Design
$ Moods

070.01 Lorenzo Geiger
◊ Culture
$ Sinfonie Orchester Biel Bienne

070.02 Frank Rocholl
◊ Corporate
$ Lokale Medien Berlin

070.03 Team Manila
◊ Art/unclassifiable

070.04 e-Types
◊ Corporate
$ New Media Days

070.05 Emmanuel Rey
◊ Design
$ Le Bureau

070.06 Théo Gennitsakis & Nicolas Rouyer
◊ Design
$ la fabrique urbain

070.07 Bas van Vuurde
◊ Music
$ Muziekpaviljoen Zandvoort

070.08 Form+Format
- Daniel Neye
◊ Music
$ YZ International

070.09 e-Types
◊ Culture
$ DR Koncerthuset

071.01 Urbanskiworkshop
- Denis März
◊ Music
$ Quazedelic/ePISTROPHIC PEACH SOUND
© Quazedelic logo

071.02 Lorenzo Geiger
◊ Political
$ Arbeit und Bildung Thun Steffisburg

071.03 Acme Industries
- Andrei D. Robu
◊ Culture
$ Culturhalle

071.04 Emmanuel Rey
◊ Corporate
$ EPFL/SGM

071.05 Avantbras
- Stefano Bracci
◊ Design
$ dispenser Studio

071.06 Dtam–TM
- Paul Heys
◊ Culture
$ Sticks & Stones magazine
© Paul Heys, Dtam, Sticks & Stones magazine

071.07 Mitchell Paone
◊ Music
$ John Brewer Trio

071.08 Out Of Order
◊ Music
$ Only my music

071.09 Annika Kaltenthaler
◊ Corporate
$ Gesellschaft für angewandtes Markenwissen
© Logo Gam

071.10 W://THEM
- Floyd E. Schulze
◊ Music
$ Schacht Musikverlag GmbH & Co KG

071.11 Dorota Wojcik
◊ Culture
$ IKAR—art magazine of Torun City, Poland

071.12 Irving & Co
- Julian Roberts
◊ Design
$ Brompton Design District

072.01 Scandinavian DesignLab
◊ Fashion
$ Karen By Simonsen

072.02 FEED
◊ Fashion
$ Agence Satellite

072.03 Akatre
◊ Corporate
$ Collectif Jeune Cinema

072.04 Raf Vancampenhoudt
◊ Art/unclassifiable
$ Karolin Tampere (I Love Your Work)

072.05 Rob van Hoesel
◊ Art/unclassifiable
$ The Bonsai Project

072.06 Raf Vancampenhoudt
◊ Art/unclassifiable
$ Maarten Vanden Eynde

072.07 De Jongens Ronner
◊ Design
$ KEI expert centre urban regeneration

072.08 Filippo Nugara
◊ Political
$ CCSI/SOS Racisme

072.09 Wolff Olins
◊ Corporate
$ New York City

072.10 dancemade
- Jens Nilsson
◊ Motion/Games/Media
$ Domestic

072.11 Mads Jakob Poulsen
◊ Sports
$ Mikkel Kessler

073.01 Identity
- Maret Põldre, Ionel Lehari
◊ Culture
$ Estonian Centre of Architecture 3

073.02 3deluxe
◊ Sports
$ North Kiteboarding/Boards & More GmbH

073.03 Edhv
◊ Corporate
$ De Negende
© Sjoerd Koopmans, Lenneke Heeren & Remco van de Craats

073.04 Urbanskiworkshop
- Denis März
◊ Music
$ Look Records/San Francisco, CA
© Georgia & Dudley logo

073.05 elRAiSE
- Andy Risquez
◊ Sports
$ tita d'enjoy

073.06 GVA Studio
◊ Art/unclassifiable
$ Cultural affairs department, City of Geneva

074.01 Huschang Pourian
◊ Corporate
$ Voll Design and Communication (Ltd.)

074.02 KesselsKramer
- Krista Rozema
◊ Culture
$ Dutch Funeral Museum "Tot Zover" (So Far)

074.03 Toko
◊ Corporate
$ Terroir Architects

074.04 Gunnar Bauer
◊ Art/unclassifiable
$ kollektiv tokio

074.05 Mads Jakob Poulsen
◊ Culture
$ Smiley Days

074.06 Herr Metag
- Malte Metag
◊ Culture
$ Affekt Blog

074.07 Bram Nijssen
◊ Art/unclassifiable
$ Self-initiated (Volksrekorders, Rotterdam)

074.08 e-Types
◊ Culture
$ Nordisk Film

074.09 eps51
◊ Culture
$ Willau

074.10 Face.
- Rik
◊ Art/unclassifiable
$ Artvvork.

075.01 adam gf
◊ Music
$ Liberty Drums

075.02 Ken Tanabe
◊ Art/unclassifiable
$ Annie Kwon

075.03 Form+Format
- Daniel Neye
◊ Corporate
$ Trax Associates

075.04 General Projects
◊ Design

075.05 Landor Tokyo
◊ Corporate
$ Meiji Holdings Company Limited

075.06 COUP
- Peter van den Hoogen
◊ Design

075.07 Hörður Lárusson
◊ Art/unclassifiable
$ vin8

075.08 Lifter Baron
◊ Music
$ Iconotronic
© Rob Angermuller

075.09 Ji Lee
◊ Design
$ Infidel

075.10 Base
◊ Corporate
$ Jonathan Morr Group

076.01 Landor Associates
- Bina Kijmedee
◊ Corporate
$ Hertz

076.02 Manifiesto Futura
◊ Corporate
$ LOOL

076.03 Denny Backhaus
◊ Culture
$ Jüdisches Museum Berlin

076.04 Markus Moström
◊ Culture
$ Besttables, Portugal

076.05 e-Types
◊ Corporate
$ schmidt hammer lassen Architects

076.06 Lorenzo Geiger
◊ Art/unclassifiable
$ Wolfgang Zät

076.07 Patrik Ferrarelli
◊ Corporate
$ Bühlmann AG – Die Holzbaufachmänner

077.01 Atelier télescopique
◊ Motion/Games/Media
$ wéo, la télé Nord-Pas de Calais

077.02 vonSüden
◊ Culture
$ White Noise Club
© Thies Uthmöller, Michael Luther & Lutz Rüter

Work Index

077.03 KismanVerhaak
- Max Kisman & Joost Verhaak
◊ Corporate
$ S+RO magazine, Nirov publishers, The Hague, Netherlands
© Gerben Dollen, Typemafia (typographer)

077.04 Di-Da Komunikakzioa
- Joseba Attard
◊ Corporate
$ Topagunea
© Di-Da Komunikakzioa

077.05 Rob van Hoesel
◊ Art/unclassifiable
$ KOP

077.06 Benjamin Metz
◊ Culture
$ Media Innovation, Gentleys

077.07 Base
◊ Art/unclassifiable

078.01 Gavillet & Rust
078.02
◊ Culture
$ Frac Champagne-Ardenne

078.03 Gavillet & Rust
◊ Corporate
$ Microcrédit Solidaire Suisse

079.04 Gavillet & Rust
◊ Culture
$ Sibylle Axarlis & Kristin Stein

080.05 Gavillet & Rust
◊ Music
$ Roc Nation

081.01 Wiyumi
◊ Corporate
$ Potsdam Research Cluster for Georisk Analysis, Environmental Change and Sustainability

081.02 Benoît Bodhuin
◊ Corporate
$ PASBA
© BENBENWORLD

081.03 ASYL
◊ Culture
$ 3331 Arts Chiyoda

081.04 TU SAIS QUI™
- Marc Armand
◊ Culture
$ La Compagnie Désordres

081.05 Guillaume Peitrequin
◊ Culture
$ Agence Openculture

081.06 Kokoro & Moi
◊ Design
$ From

081.07 Jan en Randoald
◊ Culture
$ City of Antwerp

081.08 Koehorst in 't Veld
◊ Culture
$ Kunsthal KAdE

081.09 The Action Designer
◊ Culture

081.10 Koehorst in 't Veld
◊ Culture
$ Kunsthal KAdE

082.01 Akatre
◊ Art/unclassifiable
$ Mood Media

082.02 Akatre
◊ Art/unclassifiable
$ CNAP

082.03 Akatre
◊ Art/unclassifiable
$ Seulgi Lee, Les éditions de La Ferme du Buisson

083.04 Akatre
◊ Art/unclassifiable
$ TO RESUME

083.05 Akatre
◊ Corporate
$ Tu Nantes

083.06 Akatre
◊ Art/unclassifiable
$ Mood Media

084.07 Akatre
◊ Art/unclassifiable
$ Biennale of Design

085.08 Akatre
◊ Corporate
$ Louise 13

085.09 Akatre
◊ Corporate
$ Réseau Nord

085.10 Akatre
◊ Corporate
$ Fetart

085.11 Akatre
◊ Art/unclassifiable
$ Eleonore Didier (choreographer)

086.01 John Beckers
◊ Corporate
$ de spandoekfabriek

086.02 Chragokyberneticks
- Chragi Frei
◊ Music
$ Anyone Can Play Guitar Festival

086.03 Tobias Röttger
- Tobias Röttger & Timm Häneke
◊ Fashion
$ Haman Sutra

086.04 Faith
- Paul Sych
◊ Fashion
$ Bassett Media Group

086.05 Designers United
- designersunited.gr
◊ Corporate
$ Papasotiriou Bookstores
© Dimitris Koliadimas & Dimitris Papazoglou

086.06 Axel Peemöller
◊ Culture

086.07 OPX
- Jason Healey
◊ Corporate
$ British Council for Offices

086.08 Siggeir Hafsteinsson
◊ Fashion
$ 2ONCE

087.01 Grandpeople
◊ Culture
$ Bergen Kunsthall

087.02 Axel Peemöller
◊ Corporate
$ Market for Drama

087.03 Grandpeople
◊ Culture
$ Bergen Kunsthall

087.04 Aldo Lugo
◊ Fashion
$ Karime Salame

087.05 Axel Peemöller
◊ Corporate
$ Market for Drama

088.01 La Cáscara Amarga
- Jorge Chamorro
◊ Art/unclassifiable
$ Espacio Menos 1

088.02 Esther Rieser
◊ Art/unclassifiable

088.03 vonSüden
◊ Culture
$ ikono TV
© Thies Uthmöller, Michael Luther & Lutz Rüter

088.04 Handverk
◊ Music
$ Haaland & Eidsvåg Artist Management
© Kåre Martens

088.05 Manifiesto Futura
◊ Music
$ HELLOW

088.06 Viola Schmieskors
◊ Fashion
$ Sissi Goetze

088.07 KalleGraphics
◊ Corporate
$ NOBA Kitchen
© KalleGraphics™

088.08 Black-Marmalade
◊ Music
$ Keelay
© DeChazier Stokes-Johnson & Keelay

089.01 Emil Hartvig Studio
◊ Art/unclassifiable
$ Architecture without borders
© Emil Hartvig

089.02 EMPK
- Diego Bellorin
◊ Design
$ EMPK/Mobiles

089.03 OMOCHI
◊ Corporate
$ Ishimaru Takuma

089.04 Bodara
- Tobias Peier & Alain Scherer
◊ Art/unclassifiable
$ RKZ Zürich

090.01 Marc van der Meer
◊ Sports
$ Cheryl Maas

090.02 Marc van der Meer
◊ Art/unclassifiable
$ Drunk de la Drunk

090.03 The KDU
- Aerosyn-Lex
◊ Music
$ SOS magazine for Ryan Leslie

090.04 NODE Berlin Oslo
◊ Music
$ Ny Musikk (Norwegian section of the International Society for Contemporary Music)

090.05 Nohemí Dicurú
◊ Music
$ Monzter

090.06 Falko Ohlmer
◊ Fashion
$ Le Sucre Clothing

091.01 pleaseletmedesign
091.02
◊ Music
$ The Marquee

091.03 Bram Nijssen & Marnix de Klerk
◊ Political
$ Kraakpetitie.nl, Rotterdam

091.04 HelloMe
- Till Wiedeck
◊ Music
$ Schaltkreis

091.05 Non-Format
◊ Music
$ Lo Recordings

092.01 Monoblock
- Pablo Galuppo
◊ Music
$ Coni & the Clouds

092.02 Coley Porter Bell
- Paul Marsh
◊ Design
$ Coley Porter Bell
© Stephen Bell

092.03 Fontan2
◊ Design
$ F2TF
© Ivan Hristov

092.04 asmallpercent
- Tim Ferguson Sauder
◊ Art/unclassifiable
$ Christians in the Visual Arts

092.05 Core6o
- Eduard Muresan
◊ Corporate
$ Qiu Messe Hotel
© in colaboration with Stefan Lucut

092.06 Q2 Design
- Martin Agner
◊ Corporate
$ Alexander Oberndorfer Innenarchitektur

092.07 Mash
◊ Fashion
$ Michell 1870

092.08 Mash
◊ Fashion
$ Michell Yarn

092.09 TNOP™
- Tnop Wangsillapakun
◊ Fashion
$ Maria Pinto

093.01 one8one7
◊ Design
$ Native

093.02 Savas Ozay
◊ Fashion
$ Make
© Nihal Ozay

093.03 Faith
- Paul Sych
◊ Art/unclassifiable
$ Satoru Nihei

093.04 Matteo Mastronardi
◊ Corporate
$ M29

093.05 unfolded
◊ Culture
$ XPACE, Zürich

093.06 unfolded
◊ Culture
$ Departement Darstellende Künste und Film, Zürich

093.07 Zigmunds Lapsa
◊ Corporate
$ Orhid

093.08 Graphical House
◊ Design
$ ICA Architects
© Graphical House

094.01 Jonathan Gurvit
◊ Corporate
$ O la Lab (Ogilvy Argentina)

Work Index

094.02 Non-Format
◊ Culture
$ S magazine
© typo/photo image: Non-Format/ Jake Walters
094.03 Graphical House
◊ Fashion
$ Madame Gigis
© Graphical House
094.04 KalleGraphics
◊ Fashion
$ Carrot Clothing
© KalleGraphics™
094.05 Mads Burcharth
◊ Fashion
$ Andy Gore Photography
094.06 Siggeir Hafsteinsson
◊ Fashion
$ Cult of Chick
094.07 Heric Longe
◊ Sports
$ Carrot Clothing
094.08 BETA STUDIO
◊ Fashion
$ E! Entertainment TV
094.09 Sawdust
◊ Music
$ Angel-A
094.10 HoohaaDesign
◊ Fashion
$ Adore

095.01 HelloMe
• Till Wiedeck
◊ Design
$ New York Times Magazine
095.02 Lundgren+Lindqvist
◊ Music
$ Anton Kristiansson
095.03 Out Of Order
◊ Art/unclassifiable
$ Co2ro
095.04 one8one7
◊ Design
$ Pol Oxygen magazine
095.05 phospho
• Roland Hörmann
◊ Design
095.06 Chris Rubino
◊ Corporate
$ Adam Glickman/Idealists
095.07 Manifiesto Futura
◊ Fashion
$ ROCKOCO
095.08 Chris Rubino
◊ Corporate
$ Distrikt Hotel

096.01 vonSüden
◊ Culture
$ Summerize Festival
© Thies Uthmöller, Michael Luther, Lutz Rüter
096.02 EMPK
• Diego Bellorin
◊ Music
$ Black Hole
096.03 Copenheroes
• Gringo Star
◊ Music
$ Danish Jazz Federation
096.04 FEED
◊ Fashion
$ Les Étoffes
096.05 Fontan2
◊ Corporate
$ M Books
© Ivan Hristov
096.06 Manifiesto Futura
◊ Design

096.07 Otto Dietrich
◊ Music
$ E'de Cologne, www.e-de-cologne.de
096.08 Halvor Bodin
◊ Art/unclassifiable
$ Bjørn Fredrik Gjerstad
© Nygård Tatoo
096.09 Projekttriangle Design Studio
◊ Fashion
$ Cem Cako

097.01 Black-Marmalade
◊ Music
$ Iman Williams
© DeChazier Stokes-Johnson & Iman Williams
097.02 Mash
◊ Design
097.03 Non-Format
◊ Design
$ HypeForType
097.04 Jessica Walsh
◊ Music
$ Borealis Wind Quintet
097.05 Sawdust
◊ Art/unclassifiable
$ Sam Green Illustration
097.06 The KDU
• Aerosyn-Lex
◊ Sports
$ K2 SNOWBOARDING/SVSV
097.07 Digitaluv
• NC Stormgaard
◊ Political
$ Kost Consult

098.01 modo
• Alexander Wright
◊ Design
$ Alejandro Armas Vidal
098.02 vonSüden
◊ Art/unclassifiable
$ FEE
© Michael Luther
098.03 Analog.Systm
• Oscar Bjarnason
◊ Art/unclassifiable
098.04 Alphabet Arm Design
• Ryan Frease
◊ Culture
$ Laura Barisonzi
098.05 EMPK
• Diego Bellorin
◊ Fashion
$ Katerina Geislerova
098.06 Ken
• Simon Sparkes
◊ Fashion
$ Andre Bernard
098.07 Creative Inc
• Kathryn Wilson; Mel O'Rourke (art director)
◊ Art/unclassifiable
$ Saba
098.08 Transfer Studio
• Falko Grentrup & Valeria Hedman
◊ Music
$ Notes On Notes

099.01 André Beato
◊ Art/unclassifiable
$ Original Kollective
099.02 Calango
◊ Corporate
$ Rekers Makelaardij
099.03 modo
• Alexander Wright
◊ Motion/Games/Media
$ uff

099.04 Grandpeople
• Grandpeople
◊ Corporate
$ MK
099.05 typotherapy+design inc.
• Noel Nanton (creative director & designer)
◊ Fashion
$ Betty Hemmings Leathergoods
099.06 COUP
• Peter van den Hoogen
◊ Music
$ Felix Meritis
099.07 And Studio
◊ Design
099.08 Studio Output
• Stewart McMillan
◊ Corporate
$ Ink
099.09 HEYHEYHEY
• Erik Sjouerman & Elske van der Putten
◊ Culture
$ MU
099.10 Luke Williams
◊ Fashion
$ Nuria Frances
099.11 Gytz
◊ Corporate
$ TW Musik
099.12 Andrea Gustafson
◊ Fashion
$ Spoonfed

100.01 Savas Ozay
100.02 Hörður Lárusson
◊ Art/unclassifiable
$ Personal
100.03 Company
◊ Culture
$ Hellenic Ministry of Culture
100.04 Monoblock
• Pablo Galuppo
◊ Design
$ Monoblock
100.05 Sawdust
◊ Culture
$ Hoxton Hall
100.06 Indyvisuals
• til01/Indyvisuals
◊ Culture
$ Z gallery
100.07 Just Smile And Wave
• Anna Magnussen
◊ Culture
100.08 Christian Cervantes
◊ Music
$ Star Trak/Interscope
100.09 Axel Peemöller
100.10
◊ Corporate

101.01 Acme Industries
• Andrei D. Robu
◊ Design
$ Buckenmeyer & Co.
101.02 Acme Industries
• Paramon Ditu
◊ Music
$ Balanescu Quartet
101.03 Face.
• Rik
◊ Design
$ Salinas Lasheras
101.04 Savas Ozay
◊ Design
$ Neu

101.05 Hattomonkey
• Alexey Kurchin
◊ Corporate
$ AGZ
101.06 Designers United
• designersunited.gr
◊ Music
$ Mascarpone Blues Band
© Dimitris Koliadimas & Dimitris Papazoglou
101.07 Analog.Systm
• Oscar Bjarnason
◊ Art/unclassifiable
$ Ásta & Örn
101.08 Demetrio Mancini
◊ Sports
$ Jump4Joy Network
101.09 Clusta
• Joe Mitchelmore
◊ Culture
$ Vancouver Sons

102.01 Loic Sattler
◊ Corporate
$ Leonard de Leonard
102.02 The KDU
• Magomed Dovjenko
◊ Sports
$ K2 SNOWBOARDING
102.03 cerotreees
• Benkee Chang.
◊ Sports
$ NO FRIENDS
102.04 Benny Gold
◊ Fashion
102.05 C100 Purple Haze
◊ Fashion
$ 667
102.06 Roy Smith
◊ Corporate
$ Body Senses
102.07 Aldo Lugo
◊ Music
$ Booking Wolves
102.08 superfried
◊ Sports
102.09 chemicalbox
• Mario Buholzer
◊ Sports
$ mj
102.10 Mads Burcharth
◊ Corporate
$ Gordon Johnson & Associates
102.11 Scandinavian DesignLab
◊ Fashion
$ Dyrberg/Kern
102.12 Loic Sattler
◊ Corporate
$ Nicolas G./wood artist

103.01 Face.
• Rik
◊ Fashion
$ D+F
103.02 modo
• Alexander Wright
◊ Design
$ Alejandro Armas Vidal
103.03 Andrea Gustafson
◊ Fashion
$ Elizabeth Lebeis
103.04 Áron Jancsó
◊ Art/unclassifiable
103.05 Moxie Sozo
103.06
◊ Corporate
$ Milton Taylor
103.07 Hattomonkey
• Alexey Kurchin
◊ Corporate
$ DoorLock

• Designer Name (if not identical with studio name) // ◊ Category // $ Client (if not identical with studio name) // © Credits (if not owned by studio or designer)

Work Index

104.01 Peter Sunna
◊ Sports
$ Nike (Spirit Junkie)
104.02 ODD
• ODD London
◊ Design
104.03 Technicolor Grayscale
• Matt Benson
◊ Sports
$ NEU Productions
104.04 John Beckers
◊ Motion / Games / Media
$ MTV Networks Amsterdam / TMF
104.05 Peter Sunna
◊ Design
$ A&P
104.06 Floor Wesseling
◊ Art / unclassifiable
$ For the Love of Art

105.01 Chragokyberneticks
• Chragi Frei
◊ Art / unclassifiable
$ Media+Design Lab, ETH Lausanne
105.02 Perndl+Co
• Josef Perndl & Aleksandra Savic
◊ Corporate
$ Simtools
105.03 StudioSpass
• Jaron Korinus & Daan Mens
◊ Culture
$ Kijk op Zuid Foundation and AIR Foundation
105.04 Toko
◊ Corporate
$ Cranium Manly
105.05 Lab2
• Pixl Punx
◊ Corporate
$ Götz+Frass
105.06 Tabas
◊ Culture
$ Marseille in the box
105.07 Julian Viera
◊ Design
$ Hubba & Silica
105.08 Kate Moross
◊ Culture
$ *War!* magazine
105.09 Jum & Cargo
◊ Sports
$ United States Of The Art
© tron

106.01 Edhv
◊ Culture
$ Strp
© Sjoerd Koopmans & Remco van de Craats
106.02 Zigmunds Lapsa
◊ Culture
$ Kush!
106.03 Lifter Baron
106.04
◊ Music
$ Mike Swoop
© Rob Angermuller

107.01 formdusche
• Steffen Wierer, Svenja von Döhlen, Tim Finke & Timo Hummel & Matthias Rawald
◊ Culture
$ Kulturprojekte Berlin GmbH
107.02 Accident Grotesk!
• Timothy Santore
◊ Corporate
$ Convalid GmbH
107.03 formdusche
• Steffen Wierer, Svenja von Döhlen, Tim Finke & Timo Hummel
◊ Culture
$ Kulturprojekte Berlin GmbH
107.04 Joshua Distler
◊ Fashion
$ by:AMT
© with Mike Abbink
107.05 CLAU.AS.KEE
• Claudia Mussett
◊ Corporate
$ The Tall Target
107.06 visualism
◊ Music
$ Azzido da Bass
107.07 illDesigns
• Till Könneker
◊ Political
$ Juso Bern
107.08 EL MIRO
◊ Design
107.09 me studio
• Martin Pyper
◊ Music
$ perplex

108.01 Surface
• Oliver Kuntsche & Markus Weisbeck
◊ Corporate
108.02 Mind Design
◊ Corporate
$ John Lyall Architects
108.03 Acme Industries
• Andrei D. Robu
◊ Culture
$ Bookfest / Leo Burnett
108.04 Studio Regular
• Carsten Giese
◊ Fashion
$ The Medley Institute
108.05 Kokoro & Moi
◊ Corporate
$ Kämp Galleria
108.06 Ken
• Simon Sparkes
◊ Art / unclassifiable
$ Ken
108.07 Haus CPH
• Mikkel Bock
◊ Corporate
$ Junckers
108.08 xy arts
• Quan
◊ Corporate
$ melas

109.01 Surface
• Markus Weisbeck
◊ Corporate
109.02 formdusche
• Steffen Wierer, Svenja von Döhlen, Tim Finke & Timo Hummel
◊ Culture
$ Oper der Stadt Köln

110.01 Sister Arrow & Hugh Frost
◊ Music
$ Florence & The Machine / Island Records
110.02 Red Design
◊ Music
$ Elbow — Fiction Records
110.03 cabina
◊ Fashion
$ toufic Areda
© La Chemise
110.04 Chris Bolton
◊ Corporate
$ Anton & Anton
110.05 Positron Co Ltd
• Kenichi Isogawa
◊ Corporate
110.06 Rocholl Selected Designs
• Frank Rocholl
◊ Fashion
$ Nomad Parfume
110.07 La Cáscara Amarga
• Jorge Chamorro
◊ Music
$ Europa Galante
110.08 Struggle inc.
◊ Culture
$ Longman & Eagle
110.09 FromKeetra
110.10
• Keetra Dean Dixon
◊ Art / unclassifiable

111.01 Red Design
◊ Music
$ Noisettes — Vertigo Records
111.02 Christian Cervantes
• AR New York: Raul Martinez & David Israel (creative directors); Christian Cervantes & Nobi Kashiwagi (art directors)
◊ Corporate
$ Denihan Hospitality Group
111.03 Kokoro & Moi
◊ Corporate
$ Tommila Architects
111.04 Face.
• Rik
◊ Corporate
$ IHO Espacios | Knoll
111.05 And Studio
◊ Art / unclassifiable
111.06 Aldo Lugo
◊ Music
$ Seitrack

112.01 Blake E. Marquis
◊ Design
$ Giant Artists
112.02 The Pressure
• Adam R Garcia
◊ Music
$ U.City
112.03 LIMA-KILO-WHISKEY
◊ Corporate
$ LägereBräu AG, brewery for beer specialities, Switzerland
© Thomas Lehner, Jacob Kadrmas & Oliver Wehn
112.04 Blake E. Marquis
◊ Design
$ Mistress Creative
112.05 Bionic Systems
◊ Corporate
$ R.U.N. Hospitality, Düsseldorf, Germany
© Doris Fürst, Malte Haust
112.06 ilovedust
◊ Corporate
$ Vanilla Splits
112.07 tomato
◊ Motion / Games / Media
$ Intelligent Life / *The Economist*
112.08 Like Minded Studio
• Luca Ionescu
◊ Fashion
$ RVCA
112.09 Mads Burcharth
◊ Culture
$ la Galliano Bar
112.10 Mitchell Paone
◊ Corporate
$ Vinifest
112.11 TwoPoints.Net
◊ Fashion
$ bambi / bylaura

113.01 A-Side Studio
◊ Music
$ Sony
113.02 Norwegian Ink
◊ Fashion
$ Bad Butler
113.03 André Beato
◊ Culture
$ Lisbonlovers
113.04 eps51
◊ Fashion
$ Ibn·Nas
113.05 Demetrio Mancini
◊ Corporate
$ Pasta Montagna
113.06 Studio Output
• Dan Moore
◊ Art / unclassifiable
$ The Fancy Baker
113.07 Autobahn
◊ Corporate
$ Poike Stomps Photography
113.08 Kokoro & Moi
◊ Art / unclassifiable
$ Artnet
113.09 Mash & Peta Kruger
◊ Music
$ 4AD Records

114.01 Bo Lundberg
◊ Corporate
$ Klockargården
© Åsa Sundin
114.02 Celeste Prevost
◊ Design
$ K.I.D. Collective
114.03 Celeste Prevost
◊ Culture
114.04 ruiz+company
◊ Corporate
$ Carrasco Guijuelo
114.05 Celeste Prevost
◊ Design
$ K.I.D. Collective
114.06 Cardamom
• Julianna Goodman
◊ Fashion
114.07 Chris Rubino
◊ Corporate
$ AARP
114.08 Filmgraphik
◊ Music
$ Blitzen GmbH

115.01 Peter Gregson
• Jovan Trkulja
◊ Motion / Games / Media
$ The Government of the Republic of Serbia, Ministry for Sustainable Development
115.02 Mads Burcharth
◊ Fashion
$ Elias Gunnar Studio
115.03 Studio Regular
• Carsten Giese
◊ Fashion
$ Stylist Pamela Büttner
115.04 gebrauchsgrafikundso
◊ Culture
115.05 John L. Nguyen
◊ Design
$ Red Inc.

Work Index

115.06 espluga+associates
◊ Corporate
$ hesperia
115.07 FEED
◊ Culture
$ Agence littéraire
Patrick Leimgruber

116.01 ROMstudio
• Rodrigo Maceda del Río
◊ Music
$ Reactor 105.5/YYY
116.02 Hula+Hula
• Quique Ollervides
◊ Music
$ Sony Music
116.03 Siggeir Hafsteinsson
◊ Music
$ Krook
116.04 Negro™
• Ariel Di Lisio
◊ Corporate
$ Livearealabs
116.05 TWhite design
• Troy White
◊ Fashion
$ Billabong
116.06 Huschang Pourian
◊ Fashion
$ Ragwear
116.07 KalleGraphics
◊ Art/unclassifiable
$ Self initiated
© KalleGraphics™
116.08 Pop Ovidiu Sebastian
◊ Corporate
$ cnvm

117.01 Red Design
◊ Music
$ Frankmusik–Island Records
117.02 typism
◊ Art/unclassifiable
$ blouzaat
© Ahmad Sabbagh
117.03 X3 Studios
• Erik Erdokozi
◊ Music
$ Caras Adventure Tours
117.04 Matt Le Gallez
◊ Art/unclassifiable
$ Centre Fold Gallery
117.05 aim Designstudio
◊ Design
117.06 Matt W. Moore
◊ Fashion
$ Official
© MWM Graphics
117.07 ALVA
◊ Music
© Alva Multidisciplinary Design Studio
117.08 Via Grafik
• André Nossek
◊ Motion/Games/Media
$ imf usa

118.01 Fresh Estudio
◊ Music
$ Kaki Co.
118.02 Strukt
• Andreas Koller
◊ Design
$ Strukt Design Studio
118.03 310k
◊ Music
$ Paradiso
118.04 Matt Le Gallez
◊ Art/unclassifiable
$ Readerswives Collective
118.05 Carsten Raffel
◊ Art/unclassifiable
$ United States of the Art
© Carsten Raffel/Usota
118.06 HandGun
• David Zack Custer
◊ Sports
$ 529/The Code Project
© Mitch Morse/The Code Project (director)
118.07 modo
• Alexander Wright
◊ Music
$ simpl3
118.08 Masheen
• Robert Wallis
◊ Music
$ Playground Music Scandinavia
118.09 Extraverage
• Karoly Kiralyfalvi
◊ Art/unclassifiable
$ Agh Marton
118.10 Büro Destruct
• MB
◊ Art/unclassifiable

119.01 The Pressure
• Adam R Garcia
◊ Music
$ Yak Ballz
119.02 UNIT
• James Sanderson
◊ Music
$ Deadsound DJ
119.03 Vilaz
• Cátia Oliveira & Pedro Vilas-Boas
◊ Corporate
$ Microsoft (proposal)
119.04 Atelier télescopique
◊ Fashion
$ Wassingue™, Floor Clothes Design
119.05 DTM_INC
◊ Fashion
$ Frogbite.nl
119.06 Negro™
• Ariel Di Lisio
◊ Music
$ Rockmonamour
119.07 Guapo
◊ Motion/Games/Media
$ Shango.tv

120.01 Matt W. Moore
◊ Sports
$ Burton - Artist Series 13
© MWM Graphics
120.02 Jewboy Corp™
◊ Music
120.03 The KDU
• Aerosyn-Lex
◊ Political
$ Shepard Fairey, Obama YES WE CAN
120.04 Matt W. Moore
◊ Fashion
$ For All To Envy
© MWM Graphics
120.05 C100 Purple Haze
◊ Fashion
$ 667
120.06 Tim Bjørn
◊ Corporate
$ Spasiba
120.07 FEED
◊ Design
$ Réalisons Montréal, Ville Unesco de design
120.08 Face.
• Rik
◊ Design
$ BLOC
120.09 Gabe Ruane
◊ Culture
$ Hapa

121.01 Andrea Gustafson
◊ Music
$ Dustan Louque
121.02 Jet Black Tribal Ink
◊ Design
121.03 Moshik Nadav
◊ Design
$ Institue of Hebrew Typography Research
121.04 Andrea Gustafson
◊ Music
$ Guns N' Roses
121.05 weissraum.de(sign)°
• Bernd Brink & Lucas Buchholz
◊ Music
$ Dabrink, DJ Phly (Clubveranstaltungsreihe)
121.06 Daniel Blik
◊ Fashion
$ Akrobatx Clothing
121.07 Franz Falsch
◊ Design
121.08 3deluxe
◊ Sports
$ ION essentials/ Boards & More GmbH

122.01 THE SKULL DEZAIN
◊ Fashion
$ bishop inc.
122.02 Anna Haas
◊ Culture
$ Rignier
122.03 The Lousy Livincompany
• Stefan Marx
◊ Fashion

123.04 Coley Porter Bell
• Adam Ellis
◊ Corporate
$ It's that Organic Place

124.01 Kismanstudio
• Max Kisman
◊ Culture
$ Erasmus House/Dutch Consulate, Jakarta, Indonesia
124.02 Kismanstudio
• Max Kisman
◊ Motion/Games/Media
$ The One Minutes Foundation, Amsterdam, Netherlands
124.03 Power Graphixx
◊ Motion/Games/Media
$ ASCII MEDIA WORKS
124.04 Juntos otra vez
• Martin Allais
◊ Music
$ Disboot record label
124.05 Juntos otra vez
• Martin Allais
◊ Music
$ Allrice
124.06 Landor Associates
• Richard Westendorf & Adam Waugh
◊ Political
$ Global Handwashing Day

125.01 Juntos otra vez
• Martin Allais
◊ Art/unclassifiable
$ Juntos otra vez
125.02 YOK
◊ Art/unclassifiable
125.03 Sabina Keric
◊ Art/unclassifiable
125.04 Juntos otra vez
• Martin Allais
◊ Design
125.05 Juntos otra vez
125.06
• Martin Allais
◊ Music
$ Lunchmeat Sessions

126.01 Juntos otra vez
• Martin Allais
◊ Culture
$ Sid lee Collective
126.02 Mitchell Paone
◊ Corporate
$ Microsoft Messenger

127.01 miniminiaturemouse
• Fumi Mini Nakamura
◊ Art/unclassifiable
127.02 KOA
• Olivier Cramm
◊ Music
$ Fash
127.03 miniminiaturemouse
• Fumi Mini Nakamura
◊ Music
$ Amonie
127.04 Juntos otra vez
• Martin Allais
◊ Music
$ Chacho Brodas
127.05 Yuu Imokawa
◊ Fashion
$ Collaboration
127.06 Tstout
• Tyler Stout
◊ Sports
$ Forum Snowboards
127.07 backyard10
◊ Sports
$ Völkl

128.01 Andreina Bello
◊ Design
$ Bello Brothers
128.02 Eduardo Vidales
◊ Art/unclassifiable
$ Goverment of the State of Guerrero
128.03 FriendsWithYou
◊ Design
128.04 backyard10
◊ Sports
$ Völkl
128.05 Jonathan Calugi
◊ Music
$ China Surprise
128.06 Wiyumi
◊ Art/unclassifiable
$ UhuShan
128.07 Mikey Burton
◊ Fashion
$ Burton Jewelry Repair Shop

129.01 Dtam-TM
• Paul Heys
◊ Design

• Designer Name (if not identical with studio name) // ◊ Category // $ Client (if not identical with studio name) // © Credits (if not owned by studio or designer)

Work Index

129.02 Floor 5
- Marek Polewski, Jens Pieper & Eva Hückmann
◊ Music
$ Supersoul Recordings
129.03 Matteo Mastronardi
◊ Music
$ Sam Music
129.04 Andreina Bello
◊ Fashion
$ Hand 11
© Gaby Burger & Isa Traverso-Burger
129.05 Fons Hickmann m23
- Gesine Grotrian-Steinweg
◊ Art/unclassifiable
$ Clownnixen Theater
129.06 Christian Rothenhagen
◊ Fashion
$ CARHARTT
© Campaign
129.07 Moxie Sozo
◊ Art/unclassifiable
$ Rattlecan Films

130.01 HarrimanSteel
- Matt Blease (designer); Julian Harriman-Dickinson & Nick Steel (creative directors)
◊ Corporate
$ Terrier Research
130.02 Lapin Studio
- Jorge Navarro Herradón
◊ Culture
$ Fatal fatalitas
130.03 Chragokyberneticks
- Chragi Frei & Helm Pfohl
◊ Corporate
$ cedac
130.04 Mikey Burton
◊ Art/unclassifiable
$ Society of Gluttony
130.05 YOK
◊ Art/unclassifiable
130.06 Fons Hickmann m23
- Gesine-Grotrian Steinweg & Thomas Schrott (art directors)
◊ Culture
$ Bayerische Staatsoper
130.07 Claus Gasque
◊ Fashion
$ CityFellaz

131.01 MASA
◊ Corporate
$ BREED Ltd
131.02 44flavours
◊ Music
131.03 miniminiaturemouse
- Fumi Mini Nakamura
◊ Art/unclassifiable
$ Wheat Toast
131.04 Mash
◊ Design
$ Misfits Wine Co.
131.05 Bionic Systems
◊ Culture
$ Einzelkind
© Doris Fürst & Malte Haust
131.06 Sabina Keric
◊ Art/unclassifiable

132.01 Revivify Graphic Design
- Rich Scott
◊ Design
$ B&T Magazine / Design Bay
132.02 Struggle inc.
◊ Fashion
$ Stussy

132.03 modo
- Alexander Wright
◊ Music
$ Carl Matthes
132.04 Dudu Torres
◊ Fashion
$ Ruta
132.05 modo
- Alexander Wright
◊ Art/unclassifiable
$ sheyla
132.06 Jonathan Calugi
◊ Fashion
$ noodle park

133.01 Hayes Image
- Josh Hayes
◊ Art/unclassifiable
$ Jacobs & Sons
133.02 milchhof : atelier
- Andreas Töpfer für tinkerbelle
◊ Corporate
$ Unilever Europe Savoury supply chain
133.03 Celeste Prevost
◊ Design
$ HauteNature
133.04 Celeste Prevost
◊ Corporate
$ General Mills
© Agency: Zeus Jones
133.05 Denny Backhaus
◊ Art/unclassifiable
$ TPTP
133.06 Coolpuk
- TOKO73/Coolpuk
◊ Culture
$ Warmoesstraat entrepreneurs in collaboration with Kunstenaars & Co
133.07 Designit
133.08
◊ Culture
$ IFHP
133.09 Coolpuk
- TOKO73/Coolpuk
◊ Culture
$ Warmoesstraat entrepreneurs in collaboration with Kunstenaars & Co

134.01 Anna Haas
◊ Culture
$ RINGIER

135.01 Happypets products
◊ Music
$ Pully For Noise Festival

136.01 Falko Ohlmer
◊ Music
$ Beatsteaks, Formsalon
136.02 Happypets products
◊ Culture
$ Graphic Design Museum of Breda
136.03 designJune
136.04
- Julien Crouigneau
◊ Culture
$ Keith magazine
136.05 The Lousy Livincompany
- Stefan Marx
◊ Fashion
$ Cleptomanicx
© Cleptomanicx
136.06 TU SAIS QUI™
- Marc Armand & Florent d'Heilly
◊ Art/unclassifiable
$ Frappe magazine

136.07 Vivien Le Jeune Durhin
◊ Culture
$ Le Jardin Moderne
136.08 Just Smile And Wave
- Doris Poligrates
◊ Design

137.01 ATTAK
◊ Fashion
$ Blont Hairdressers
© ATTAK • Powergestaltung
137.02 Kate Moross
◊ Music
$ Glastonbury
© Agency TBWA
137.03 OMOMMA™
- Daijiro Ohara
◊ Music
$ Kakubarhythm
137.04 Mash
◊ Design
$ Alpha Box & Dice
137.05 Heric Longe
◊ Sports
$ Burton Snowboards

138.01 TWhite design
138.02
- Troy White
◊ Fashion
$ Nike 6.0
© Craig Metzger
138.03 Strukt
- Andreas Koller
◊ Design
$ Strukt Design Studio
138.04 Ole Utikal
◊ Culture
$ Radar Hamburg Film Festival
138.05 Masheen
◊ Motion/Games/Media
$ TheOne.tv
© 10:00 AM
138.06 Matthias Wagner
◊ Design
138.07 Via Grafik
- André Nossek
◊ Culture
$ 18 bit
138.08 TU SAIS QUI™
- Marc Armand
◊ Art/unclassifiable
$ PM LAUZ

139.01 sellout-industries™
◊ Fashion
$ adidas Originals
© adidas Originals
139.02 sellout-industries™
◊ Fashion
$ adidas Originals
139.03 ZEK
◊ Music
$ k4
139.04 Akinori Oishi
◊ Art/unclassifiable
139.05 sellout-industries™
◊ Fashion
$ adidas Originals

140.01 44flavours
◊ Music
$ out now
140.02 Kate Moross
◊ Music
$ Master Shortie
140.03 REX
◊ Culture
$ Bouffant Films

140.04 Mads Burcharth
◊ Art/unclassifiable
$ Self-initiated
140.05 Hexanine
- Jason Adam
◊ Art/unclassifiable
$ Nerdcore
140.06 Daniel Medeiros
◊ Music
$ Prince Leo / 420

141.01 Christian Borstlap
◊ Design
$ graniph.com
141.02 Human Empire
◊ Art/unclassifiable
141.03 Blake E. Marquis
◊ Design
$ You Work For Them
141.04 Jürgen Frost
◊ Art/unclassifiable
141.05 hintzegruppen
- Jesper Hintze
◊ Corporate
$ Take The Cake
141.06 Kismanstudio
- Max Kisman
◊ Sports
$ Boyle Park Tennis, Mill Valley, California, USA

142.01 JMSV
◊ Music
$ Somos Una Triste Banda de Rock
142.02 ZEK
◊ Music
$ k4

143.03 Weather Control
- Silvia Cordero Vega (calligrapher); Josh Oakley (art director)
◊ Political
$ School's Out Washington

144.01 Denny Backhaus
◊ Music
$ Kis
144.02 Vier5
◊ Art/unclassifiable
144.03 Denny Backhaus
◊ Music
$ Kis
144.04 Sister Arrow
◊ Music
$ Florence & The Machine / Island Records
144.05 THE SKULL DEZAIN
145.01
◊ Fashion
$ ROUTEBURN Co., ltd
145.02 Eivind Nilsen
◊ Design
$ La Familia
145.03 No-Domain
◊ Design
$ J&B
145.04 Ryan Massiah
◊ Fashion
$ Jason Small
145.05 COUP
- Peter van den Hoogen
◊ Culture
$ Lars Eijssen
145.06 Gustavo de Lacerda
◊ Art/unclassifiable
$ Teatro Oficina

Work Index

145.07 No-Domain
◊ Design
$ No Name Horses

146.01 JUTOJO
◊ Music
$ HOME clubnight
(Dirk Rumpff & Alex Barck)

147.01 OMOMMA™
• Ohara Daijiro
◊ Culture
$ mozine

147.02 JUTOJO
◊ Culture
$ Soquiet Filmproduktion

147.03 OMOMMA™
• Ohara Daijiro
◊ Music
$ Kakubarhythm

147.04 Buro Reng
◊ Design
$ Penduka

147.05 Jonathan Calugi
◊ Fashion
$ gold

147.06 JUTOJO
◊ Music
$ Sonar Kollektiv

147.07 Celeste Prevost
◊ Fashion
$ Ashi Dashi

148.01 Heydays
◊ Fashion
• The Streethearts

148.02 FLAMMIER
◊ Culture
$ Artisan—set construction and art direction

148.03 Axel Peemöller
◊ Fashion

148.04 Via Grafik
• André Nossek
◊ Design
$ Accept & proceed
© via Grafik

148.05 Peter Gregson
• Jovan Trkulja
◊ Corporate
$ LTC/Language and Translation Centre

148.06 Technicolor Grayscale
• Matt Benson
◊ Music
$ Hope Management UK

148.07 Face.
• Blast
◊ Music
$ Page.

148.08 Hexanine
• Jason Adam
◊ Art/unclassifiable
$ Nerdcore

148.09 max-o-matic

148.10
• Maximo Tuja
◊ Music
$ Miqui Puig/Razzmatazz

149.01 C100 Purple Haze

149.02
◊ Fashion
$ 667

149.03 Chragokyberneticks
• Chragi Frei
◊ Music
$ Anyone Can Play Guitar Festival

149.04 Alexander Penkin, Lilli Langenheim & Roman Schultze
◊ Design
$ LA-PESCH

149.05 vonSüden
◊ Culture
$ death by pop Club
© Thies Uthmöller, Michael Luther & Lutz Rüter

149.06 Jonathan Calugi
◊ Fashion
$ noodle park

149.07 ujidesign
◊ Music
$ Sawori Namekawa

149.08 Fons Hickmann m23
• Barbara Bättig & Fons Hickmann (designers); Fons Hickmann & Gesine Grotrian-Steinweg (art directors)
◊ Design
$ Graphic Europe

150.01 Andrea Gustafson
◊ Corporate
$ Dee Liciously Gluten Free

150.02 DTM_INC
◊ Fashion
$ Frogbite.nl

150.03 Revivify Graphic Design
• Rich Scott
◊ Design
$ Cheb Deez

150.04 Weather Control
• Silvia Cordero Vega (calligrapher); Josh Oakley (art director)
◊ Political
$ School's Out Washington

150.05 Meatpack

150.06
◊ Music
$ Libertine Supersport Nightclub
© Caracostas Nicolas & Labro Richard

150.07 Strohl
• Eric Strohl
◊ Culture
$ The Bold Italic

150.08 Manifiesto Futura
◊ Corporate
$ RENDER SOLUTIONS

150.09 Boldº
• Leonardo Eyer & Billy Bacon
◊ Culture
$ SKY

150.10 44flavours
◊ Corporate
$ Amadeus—Pflege mit Empathie

151.01 ellenberg-martinez
• Laura Ellenberg & Agustina Martínez
◊ Corporate
$ clorophile

151.02 Typejockeys
◊ Music
$ Moonshaker Sunnymaker

151.03 Carlos Ribeiro
◊ Design
$ Rodrigo Abreu

151.04 büro uebele visuelle kommunikation
• Beate Kapprell (project management); Andreas Uebele
◊ Corporate
$ Werner Sobek Ingenieure GmbH & Co. KG

151.05 General Projects
◊ Art/unclassifiable
$ Lee Reedy Fine Art

151.06 Typejockeys
◊ Corporate
$ Immobilien Rohr

151.07 Inventaire
◊ Corporate
$ Le Buro

151.08 Mr. Brown - creative boutique
• Artur Augustyniak
◊ Design

151.09 The Luxury of Protest
• Peter Crnokrak (designer); Stefan Boubil (creative director)
◊ Corporate
$ Me Time

152.01 ATTAK
◊ Design
$ Self
© ATTAK • Powergestaltung

152.02 Regina
◊ Art/unclassifiable

152.03 ROMstudio
• Rodrigo Maceda del Río
◊ Design
$ María José Baez

152.04 Axel Peemöller
◊ Corporate

152.05 Fresh Estudio
◊ Fashion
$ Safari Clothing Company

152.06 Axel Peemöller
◊ Corporate
$ Florian Schneider

152.08 Base
◊ Fashion
$ BELLEROSE

152.09 Anti/Anti
◊ Design
$ Anti/Anti
© Ros Knopov

153.01 Team Manila
◊ Music
$ Locked Down Entertainment

153.02 NODE Berlin Oslo
◊ Music
$ Ny Musikk (Norwegian section of the International Society for Contemporary Music)
© NODE Berlin Oslo, Calligraphy by Bård Ydén

153.03 Estudio Soma
◊ Music
$ Genoma del Eter Rock Band

153.04 Goldjunge Grafik & Design
◊ Music
$ The Life After

153.05 NODE Berlin Oslo
◊ Art/unclassifiable
$ The Contemporary Art Centre, Vilnius (CAC) / Nomeda & Gediminas Urbonas

153.06 Boldº
• Billy Bacon
◊ Music
$ Som Livre
© Boldº

153.07 Just Smile And Wave
• Anna Magnussen
◊ Culture

153.08 Art Machine
• Julian Hrankov
◊ Art/unclassifiable
$ Logo Concept

154.01 44flavours
◊ Music
$ Robot Koch

154.02 44flavours
◊ Culture
$ Run Vie—SuperCity

154.03 44flavours
◊ Culture
$ Run Vie

154.04 44flavours
◊ Culture
$ SuperCity

155.05 44flavours
◊ Corporate
$ 44flavours

155.06 44flavours
◊ Music
$ Robot Koch

155.07 44flavours
◊ Fashion
$ Carlo

156.08 44flavours

156.09
◊ Music
$ The Knights of Love

156.10 44flavours
• 44flavours
◊ Sports
$ fies & matschig

156.11 44flavours
◊ Music
$ Robot Koch

157.12 44flavours
◊ Music
$ Sneaky

157.13 44flavours
◊ Fashion
$ E.

157.14 44flavours
◊ Music
$ not for sale

158.01 Wolff Olins
◊ Corporate
$ Macmillan Cancer Support

158.02 Chris Henley
◊ Culture
$ Totally Theatre

158.03 Blake E. Marquis
◊ Design
$ Microsoft

158.04 Chragokyberneticks
• Chragi Frei
◊ Culture
$ Fool's Proof Theatre

158.05 Weather Control
• Josh Oakley
◊ Music
$ Hair Envelope

158.06 Lab2
◊ Fashion
$ Paperboi Wear

158.07 EyesCream
• Matthias Wagner
◊ Design

158.08 44flavours
◊ Music
$ Sneaky

158.09 Tstout
• Tyler Stout
◊ Music
$ Pelican

159.01 Juntos otra vez
• Martin Allais
◊ Music
$ Friends of Friends

• Designer Name (if not identical with studio name) // ◊ Category // $ Client (if not identical with studio name) // © Credits (if not owned by studio or designer)

Work Index

159.02 Claus Gasque
◊ Fashion
$ CityFellaz

159.03 Juntos otra vez
• Eva Puyuelo Muns
◊ Fashion
$ Ubiquity Records

159.04 Luke Williams
◊ Music
$ End the Century

159.05 Madhouse
• Tyler Fortney
◊ Music
$ The Climates

159.06 Laleh Torabi
◊ Art/unclassifiable
$ transmediale – festival for art and digital culture berlin

160.01 EyesCream
• Matthias Wagner
◊ Design

160.02 Coutworks
◊ Design

160.03 Julian Viera
◊ Music
$ PIPPO

160.04 HUSH
• Laura Alejo
◊ Culture
$ Booklyn

160.05 Struggle inc.
◊ Culture
$ Devening Projects

160.06 Struggle inc.
◊ Sports
$ Nike

161.01 44flavours
◊ Culture
$ proud

162.01 Like Minded Studio
• Luca Ionescu
◊ Culture
$ BMF, Tooheys Extra Dry

162.02 Mash
◊ Design
$ Redheads Studio

162.03 EL MIRO
◊ Motion/Games/Media
$ Smit&Jansen
© smitenjansen.nl, EL MIRO

162.04 Indyvisuals
• til01/Indyvisuals
◊ Art/unclassifiable
$ design walk 2009

162.05 Indyvisuals
• til01 & Indyvisuals
◊ Music
$ Cast A Blast

162.06 Young Jerks
• Daniel Cassaro
◊ Culture
$ Nik Ruckert

162.07 Young Jerks
• Daniel Cassaro
◊ Art/unclassifiable
$ God Bless the Midwest

162.08 Young Jerks
• Daniel Cassaro
◊ Corporate
$ Budweiser

163.01 John Vingoe
◊ Fashion
$ Kirsty Calnan—Hair and Make-Up

163.02 Project 1000
• Stefan Szakal
◊ Culture
$ Upper Crazy Society
© Project 1000

163.03 Acme Industries
• Octavian Budai
◊ Fashion
$ AAH

163.04 elesefe
• Friedrich Santana Lamego
◊ Music
$ Dj Mush (Portugal)

163.05 Braca Burazeri
• Necone & Braca Burazeri
◊ Fashion
$ Dechkotzar T-shirts

163.06 Young Jerks
• Daniel Cassaro
◊ Corporate
$ Bud Light Lime

163.07 Haltenbanken
◊ Culture
$ Jazz Akks

163.08 Benny Gold
◊ Fashion

163.09 sellout-industries™
◊ Corporate
$ laden 12

163.10 Allan Deas
◊ Fashion

163.11 visualism
◊ Fashion
$ Mantis Lifestore

164.01 Taeko Isu
◊ Culture
$ Erika Kasai
© Erika Kasai

164.02 Fabian Bertschinger
◊ Culture
$ 11 Club/Bar/Restaurant Amsterdam

164.03 Wissam Shawkat & Xandi
◊ Sports
$ Mahra Polo Team, Ursula Winzel
© Wissam Shawkat, Xandi, Mahra Polo Team

164.04 Wissam Shawkat
◊ Sports
$ Brash Branding
© Brash Branding

164.05 Wissam Shawkat
◊ Sports
$ Turquoise Branding, UK
© Turquoise Branding, UK

165.01 MH Grafik
◊ Sports
$ Safari Clothing

165.02 Hansje van Halem
◊ Design

165.03 Chris Bolton
◊ Music
$ N.E.W.S./Music Man

165.04 Hansje van Halem
◊ Design
$ Schrank8, Amsterdam (NL)

165.05 Hansje van Halem
◊ Design
$ Hotel Mariakapel, Hoorn (NL)

166.01 Taeko Isu
◊ Culture
$ NNNNY
© Gabin Ito, Kei Hagiwara

166.02 Taeko Isu
◊ Corporate
$ icca
© Katsuki Tanaka, Gabin Ito

166.03 Taeko Isu
◊ Motion/Games/Media
$ UPLINK
© Takuji Uehara

166.04 OMOMMA™
• Ohara Daijiro
◊ Music
$ commmons

166.05 Maniackers Design
• Masayuki Sato
◊ Culture
$ A DROWNING CROCODILE BOOK SERVICE
© A DROWNING CROCODILE BOOK SERVICE

166.06 Taeko Isu
◊ Motion/Games/Media
$ Columbia Music Entertainment
© Atsuko Takeyari

167.01 ASYL
◊ Culture
$ CET (Central East Tokyo)

167.02 Felix Lobelius
◊ Culture
$ Kinokuniya

167.03 ujidesign
◊ Culture
$ Mitsubishi Ichigokan Museum

167.04 ujidesign
◊ Culture
$ Suntory Museum of Art

167.05 COMMUNE

167.06
• Ryo Ueda
◊ Corporate
$ A-TO

167.07 COMMUNE
• Ryo Ueda
◊ Art/unclassifiable
$ Theatrical company Inadagumi

168.01 SKKY Inc.
◊ Art/unclassifiable
$ Shiori Nishino

168.02 SKKY Inc.
◊ Art/unclassifiable
$ AKO

168.03 SKKY Inc.
◊ Art/unclassifiable
$ mirocomachiko

168.04 SKKY Inc.
◊ Art/unclassifiable
$ Swimy Project

168.05 SKKY Inc.
◊ Art/unclassifiable
$ TACO

169.01 SKKY Inc.
• SKKY Inc.
◊ Art/unclassifiable
$ Yusuke Mashiba

169.02 SKKY Inc.
◊ Art/unclassifiable
$ TUNE GRAPHIC

169.03 SKKY Inc.
◊ Art/unclassifiable
$ Tomoyo Kawase

170.01 Extraverage
• Karoly Kiralyfalvi
◊ Culture
$ Hungarian National Gallery

170.02 Floor 5
• Marek Polewski & Jens Pieper
◊ Design
$ Artschoolvets.com

170.03 Acme Industries
• Paramon Ditu
◊ Music
$ KOKOLO

171.04 Jonathan Calugi
◊ Music
$ a smile for timbuctu

171.05 Tilt Design Studio
• Marc Antosch
◊ Culture

172.01 Rasmus Snabb
◊ Art/unclassifiable
$ Aalto University

172.02 Rasmus Snabb
◊ Art/unclassifiable
$ Aalto University
© Competition entry. Not finalized. Winning proposal for Aalto University logo.

172.03 UREDD
◊ Art/unclassifiable
$ Art Hotel Norway

172.04 FoURPAcK ontwerpers
• Tessa Hofman
◊ Corporate
$ Liesbeth Kalderling

173.01 La Cáscara Amarga
• Jorge Chamorro
◊ Corporate
$ FEDACE

173.02 Joshua Distler
◊ Culture
$ Saffron/Visit London
© with Mike Abbink

173.03 Base
◊ Art/unclassifiable
$ BLUE LABEL

174.01 Canefantasma Studio
◊ Art/unclassifiable
$ Dsu Siena

174.02 Human Empire
◊ Fashion
$ Uniqlo

174.03 Struggle inc.
◊ Fashion
$ The Quiet Life

174.04 Matt W. Moore
◊ Culture
$ Creative Kegger Event
© MWM Graphics

175.01 urbn; interaction
• Franka Futterlieb & Jörn Alraun
◊ Fashion
$ F&M

175.02 FoURPAcK ontwerpers
• Richard Pijs
◊ Culture
$ Cultuurhuis Patronaat, Heerlen

175.03 Base
◊ Culture
$ Greene Hill Food Co-op

175.04 Falko Ohlmer
◊ Culture
$ Limitees.com

175.05 44flavours
◊ Music
$ RQM

175.06 Chragokybernetiks
• Chragi Frei
◊ Corporate
$ Friedlgraeser

175.07 Struggle inc.
◊ Culture
$ *Monster Children* magazine

396

175.08 Koehorst in't Veld
◊ Culture
$ Market Academy
175.09 A-Side Studio
◊ Sports
$ Trans Surf
176.01 Kokoro & Moi
◊ Design
$ City of Lahti
177.02 Kokoro & Moi
◊ Design
$ Design Forum Finland
178.03 Kokoro & Moi
◊ Design
178.04 Kokoro & Moi
• Kokoro & Moi
◊ Design
$ Vallila Interior
178.05 Kokoro & Moi
◊ Fashion
$ Jim & Jill
178.06 Kokoro & Moi
◊ Corporate
$ Helsinki Regional Transport Authority
179.01 Chragokyberneticks
• Chragi Frei
◊ Design
179.02 Chragokyberneticks
• Chragi Frei
◊ Corporate
$ Convergeo Architects
179.03 44flavours
◊ Corporate
179.04 Jonathan Calugi
◊ Art/unclassifiable
$ Personal show
179.05 Human Empire
◊ Fashion
$ Human Empire Shop
179.06 Huschang Pourian
◊ Corporate
$ Voll Design and Communication (Ltd.)
179.07 The Lousy Livincompany
• Stefan Marx
◊ Corporate
$ Cleptomanicx
© Cleptomanicx
179.08 The Lousy Livincompany
• Stefan Marx
◊ Culture
179.09 The Lousy Livincompany
• Stefan Marx
◊ Corporate
$ Cleptomanicx
© Cleptomanicx
180.01 Kismanstudio
• Max Kisman
◊ Culture
$ International Film Festival Rotterdam
180.02 Kismanstudio
• Max Kisman
◊ Art/unclassifiable
$ Stedelijk Museum of Modern Art, Amsterdam, Netherlands
180.03 Kismanstudio
• Max Kisman
◊ Design
$ Staatsliederlijk choir, Amsterdam, Netherlands
180.04 Tabas
◊ Music
$ Label note

180.05 De Jongens Ronner
◊ Culture
$ Platform Gras
180.06 Coboi & Fageta
• Katharina Reidy, Philippe Egger & Adeline Mollard
◊ Music
$ Bad Bonn Kilbi
180.07 Axel Peemöller
◊ Art/unclassifiable
180.08 OPX
• Risa Sano
◊ Sports
$ Look mum no hands!
© Risa Sano, Graham Bignell, David Bennett & Simon Goodall
181.01 Coley Porter Bell
• Helen Hartley & Paul Marsh
◊ Culture
$ Museum of London
© Stephen Bell
181.02 Büro4
◊ Culture
$ Schweizer Radio DRS, Zürich, Switzerland
181.03 Monoblock
• Pablo Galuppo
◊ Political
$ Unicef
181.04 Autobahn
◊ Music
$ SJU
182.01 NODE Berlin Oslo
• Felix Weigand
◊ Music
$ Ny Musikk
182.02 Chragokyberneticks
• Chragi Frei
◊ Design
$ CHKY
182.03 Designers United
• designersunited.gr
◊ Corporate
$ Papasotiriou bookstores
© Dimitris Koliadimas, Dimitris Papazoglou
182.04 miniminiaturemouse
• Fumi Mini Nakamura
◊ Art/unclassifiable
$ Together We Make
182.05 HUSH
• Laura Alejo
◊ Design
182.06 miniminiaturemouse
• Fumi Mini Nakamura
◊ Music
$ Himitsu no Doukutsu (Secret Cave)
183.01 Mind Design
• Mind Design in collaboration with Simon Egli
◊ Fashion
$ Tess Management
183.02 Mind Design
◊ Art/unclassifiable
$ Gumbo TV
184.01 Jonathan Calugi
◊ Corporate
$ himalaya
© himalaya
184.02 cabina
◊ Corporate
$ Toufic Areda
© tô Sushi

184.03 Fieldtrip
• Joost Verhaak
◊ Culture
$ Project bureau Belvedere, Utrecht, Netherlands
184.04 Jonathan Calugi
◊ Design
$ paul paper
184.05 Grandpeople
◊ Music
$ Escalator Records
185.01 HUSH
• Laura Alejo
◊ Design
$ Hush
185.02 Just Smile And Wave
• Anna Magnussen
◊ Political
185.03 ALVA
◊ Corporate
$ The Hood
© Alva Multidisciplinary Design Studio
185.04 FriendsWithYou
• FriendsWithYou
◊ Design
185.05 DTM_INC
◊ Culture
$ ATCB
185.06 FriendsWithYou
185.07
185.08
◊ Design
186.01 Blake E. Marquis
◊ Art/unclassifiable
$ This LA
186.02 MH Grafik
◊ Sports
$ Safari Clothing
186.03 Jet Black Tribal Ink
◊ Design
$ Jet Black Tribal ink
187.04 THE SKULL DEZAIN
◊ Design
$ THE SKULL DEZAIN
187.05 typotherapy+design inc.
• Noel Nanton
◊ Corporate
$ PMA Landscape Architects
188.06 ZEK
◊ Music
189.01 Team Manila
◊ Design
189.02 Loic Sattler
◊ Art/unclassifiable
189.03 Guapo
◊ Motion/Games/Media
$ Dalmiro.tv
189.04 Deanne Cheuk
◊ Design
$ Tokion magazine, Japan
189.05 Peter Sunna
◊ Sports
$ Maverik
190.01 Koehorst in't Veld
◊ Culture
$ Netherlands Architecture institute
190.02 büro uebele visuelle kommunikation
• Jan Filek (project manager); Andreas Uebele
◊ Culture
$ Bundesministerium für Verkehr, Bau und Stadtentwicklung

190.03 Zion Graphics
• Ricky Tillblad
◊ Corporate
$ B-Reel
190.04 Dogma
◊ Music
$ Jorge HM
190.05 Urbanskiworkshop
• Denis März
◊ Culture
$ TAKE COPY magazine, London
© Magazine contributed by Aleks Catina & Nicolas Lobo Brennan
190.06 gebrauchsgrafikundso
◊ Culture
191.01 Rick Klotz
◊ Fashion
192.01 Mads Freund Brunse/Ecal
◊ Corporate
$ Green Oil-X
192.02 Hattomonkey
• Alexey Kurchin
◊ Corporate
$ Security cameras OCOCAM
192.03 Indyvisuals
• til01/Indyvisuals
◊ Culture
$ designworkshop
192.04 Fons Hickmann m23
• Barbara Bättig (designer); Fons Hickmann (art director & designer)
◊ Political
$ IFA Gallery
192.05 Jürgen Frost
◊ Culture
$ Projekt Bilderschlachten
192.06 LogoOrange
• Mihai Licanescu
◊ Design
$ Revolverne
192.07 Calango
◊ Fashion
$ BINC
193.01 Markus Moström
◊ Design
$ Thorbjörn Andersson
193.02 Scandinavian DesignLab
◊ Corporate
$ Alectia
193.03 Gavillet & Rust
◊ Culture
$ Ormond Contemporary Editions
193.04 Mads Jakob Poulsen
◊ Culture
$ Copenhagen Parts
© Goodmorning Technology
193.05 Marcelo Chelles
◊ Music
$ Headlesssheep
194.01 Pierre Jeanneret
◊ Motion/Games/Media
$ Zunit
© Pierre Jeanneret/Plurial
194.02 Bleed
◊ Art/unclassifiable
$ K+I+A. KREATIV INTERSJON I ARBEJDSLIVET
© Bleed
194.03 CLAU.AS.KEE
• Claudia Mussett
◊ Music
$ Mubarak bar
194.04 Q2 Design
◊ Sports
$ Allied Bikes

• Designer Name (if not identical with studio name) // ◊ Category // $ Client (if not identical with studio name) // © Credits (if not owned by studio or designer)

397

Work Index

194.05 **Anthony Lane**
◊ Art / unclassifiable
194.06 **Philipp Pilz**
◊ Music
$ Sebastian Kaufung & Leonhard Brandeis Gbr
194.07 **EL MIRO**
◊ Design
$ Voor de Stijl
© www.voordestijl.nl

195.01 **Project 1000**
• Stefan Szakal
◊ Corporate
$ Think Advertising
© Project 1000
195.02 **Demetrio Mancini**
◊ Corporate
$ Marco Serafini
195.03 **Demetrio Mancini**
◊ Design
$ Civico
195.04 **Oc/Om/Oy/Ok**
• Daniel Adolph
◊ Design
$ Royal Grafico

196.01 **Floor Wesseling**
◊ Music
$ Chaos & L-dopa
196.02 **FLAMMIER**
◊ Culture
$ After Sunrise Productions
196.03 **Matt W. Moore**
◊ Music
$ DJ Benzi
© MWM Graphics
196.04 **The Action Designer**
◊ Design
196.05 **Akatre**
◊ Culture
$ MO'FO'10, Mains d'Œuvres

197.01 **HelloMe**
• Till Wiedeck
◊ Music
$ Schaltkreis
197.02 **Magdalena Czarnecki**
◊ Culture
$ Venezia Biennale
© (Self-initiated, proposal only)
197.03 **Raf Vancampenhoudt & Joris Van Aken**
◊ Art / unclassifiable
$ Ans Nys
197.04 **Edhv**
◊ Corporate
$ Studio Jspr
© Remco van de Craats
197.05 **Áron Jancsó**
◊ Design
$ personal

198.01 **Fons Hickmann m23**
• Fons Hickmann & Thomas Schrott (art directors)
◊ Culture
$ roc-berlin
198.02 **Büro Ink**
• Markus Schäfer
◊ Art / unclassifiable
$ Moonblinx Gallery
© with SiteSeeing / Interaktive Medien
198.03 **Felix Lobelius**
◊ Culture
$ Perspective
198.04 **Haus CPH**
• Felix Børgesen
◊ Corporate
$ Akuart/Phart Directors
198.05 **Buro Reng**
◊ Design
$ VdpArchitecten
198.06 **büro uebele visuelle kommunikation**
• Alexandra Busse (project manager); Katrin Dittmann, Katrin Häfner, Daniel Perraudin, Maragrethe Saxler, Andreas Uebele
◊ Corporate
$ evangelische stiftung alsterdorf, hamburg

199.01 **Wiyumi**
◊ Corporate
$ Gekonntext, Ilka Russy
199.02 **minigram**
◊ Culture
$ Kunstfabrik am Flutgraben e.V.
199.03 **milchhof : atelier**
• Andreas Töpfer
◊ Culture
$ ham.lit / lange nacht junger literatur und musik
199.04 **Project 1000**
• Stefan Szakal
◊ Design
$ VSF

200.01 **atelier aquarium**
• Jérémie Nuel & Simon Renaud
◊ Culture
$ Trace et Empreintes Publishing
200.02 **Ryan Crouchman**
◊ Design
$ Plania: urban planning
© Agency: Bleublancrouge, Creative Direction: Marie-Hélène Trottier
200.03 **No-Domain**
◊ Corporate

201.01 **Coup**
• Peter van den Hoogen
◊ Culture
$ S.M.A.K. / Lars Eijssen
201.02 **Gustavo de Lacerda**
◊ Art / unclassifiable
$ Carpe Diem
201.03 **FEED**
◊ Fashion
$ Productions L'Éloi
201.04 **Hexanine**
• Jason Adam
◊ Motion / Games / Media
$ Bernie Su
201.05 **Markus Moström**
◊ Art / unclassifiable
$ Kulturhuset, Stockholm
201.06 **Foan82**
◊ Fashion
$ Gliese
201.07 **Filmgraphik**
◊ Motion / Games / Media
$ One Two Films
© Oliver Peters, Sven Zuege
201.08 **Non-Format**
◊ Music
$ Polydor
© Images by Non-Format / Jake Walters

202.01 **Floor Wesseling**
◊ Music
$ Afrikan Vibrations
202.02 **GWG inc.**
◊ Sports
$ AIR TO GROUND A-SEVEN
202.03 **Lab2**
• Pixl Punx
◊ Music
$ Sick Soul
202.04 **FoURPAcK ontwerpers**
• Richard Pijs
◊ Motion / Games / Media
$ B-There Festival, 's-Hertogenbosch
202.05 **Daniel Medeiros**
◊ Fashion
$ Hanfmanner
202.06 **Out Of Order**
◊ Design
$ Alynia

203.01 **3deluxe**
◊ Sports
$ ION essentials / Boards & More GmbH
203.02 **Bas van Vuurde**
◊ Culture
$ Scratch and sniff
203.03 **THE SKULL DEZAIN**
◊ Design
203.04 **Via Grafik**
• André Nossek
◊ Culture
$ kunstclub Stuttgart
203.05 **Philipp Pilz**
◊ Design
$ ideensturm
© Moritz Dünkel
203.06 **REX**
◊ Culture
$ Liquid Chefs

204.01 **Edhv**
◊ Corporate
$ Lebesque
© Kim Hemmes, Wendy Plomp, Remco van de Craats
204.02 **Chris Henley**
◊ Art / unclassifiable
$ Arts Gateway
204.03 **nocturn.ro**
• Alex Tass
◊ Art / unclassifiable
$ Delice
204.04 **Andy Mangold**
◊ Art / unclassifiable

205.05 **Toko**
◊ Corporate
$ ShopAround Agency
205.06 **Peter Schmidt Group**
◊ Political
$ Hamburg Marketing GmbH

206.01 **Mash**
◊ Design
$ Genesin Studio
206.02 **Mitchell Paone**
◊ Corporate
$ Douglas B. Paone MD, PA
206.03 **Annika Kaltenthaler**
◊ Fashion
$ Marcel Shirts
© M Shirt
206.04 **Matt Carr**
◊ Fashion
$ Hick Industries T Shirts
206.05 **Serif**
◊ Corporate
$ The Brand Agency
© Carolina Rodriguez
206.06 **Vilaz**
• Pedro Vilas-Boas, Cátia Oliveira
◊ Motion / Games / Media
206.07 **Base**
◊ Fashion
$ CAMPER
206.08 **Joseba Attard**
◊ Corporate
$ Eden Hope
206.09 **Fontan2**
◊ Design
$ F2TF
© Ivan Hristov
206.10 **SUNDAY VISION**
• Shinsuke Koshio / SUNDAY VISION
◊ Sports
$ F.C. Tokyo, Beams
206.11 **Fontan2**
◊ Corporate
$ Lessno
© Ivan Hristov
206.12 **Sawdust**
◊ Music
$ Middle Boop

207.01 **Áron Jancsó**
◊ Art / unclassifiable
207.02 **Jewboy Corp™**
◊ Corporate
$ Ben Riftin PR & Management
207.03 **Sawdust**
◊ Music
$ Be Events
207.04 **Áron Jancsó**
207.05
◊ Art / unclassifiable
207.06 **Haltenbanken**
◊ Culture
$ Avgarde
207.07 **Haltenbanken**
◊ Culture
$ Avgarde

208.01 **21bis**
• Frank Dresmé
◊ Sports
$ Taste Snowboard Magazine
208.02 **Luca Marchettoni**
◊ Art / unclassifiable
$ Blumagenta
208.03 **Faith**
• Paul Sych
◊ Corporate
$ Huge Paper Company
208.04 **André Beato**
◊ Fashion
$ BAPE
208.05 **V15**
◊ Fashion
$ Feral
208.06 **Acme Industries**
• Octavian Budai
◊ Culture
$ Radio Zu
© Design director Andrei D. Robu
208.07 **Faith**
• Paul Sych
◊ Music
$ Freedom Jazz

209.01 **TWhite design**
• Troy White
◊ Fashion
$ Elemeny
209.02 **typism**
◊ Design

398

Work Index

209.03 Reaktor Lab
◊ Art/unclassifiable
$ Solera Typeface
© Jorge Aguilar

209.04 Martin Nicolausson
◊ Art/unclassifiable

209.05 Julian Viera
◊ Music
$ Hard Candy
© Roedor & Group, Massiva.org

210.01 The KDU
• Magomed Dovjenko
◊ Sports
$ 361 Sports

210.02 Tatiana Arocha
◊ Fashion
$ Burton

210.03 CLAU.AS.KEE
• Claudia Mussett
◊ Music
$ Dj drop

210.04 Siggeir Hafsteinsson
◊ Fashion
$ 2ONCE

210.05 Juntos otra vez
• Martin Allais
◊ Culture
$ Iconographic Magazine

210.06 Alex Trochut
◊ Sports
$ Adidas
© www.alextrochut.com

210.07 Dudu Torres
◊ Art/unclassifiable

210.08 max-o-matic
• Maximo Tuja
◊ Art/unclassifiable
$ Picnic
© www.maxomatic.net

211.01 EyesCream
• Matthias Wagner
◊ Design

211.02 MH Grafik
◊ Sports
$ Safari Clothing

211.03 Negro™
• Ariel Di Lisio
◊ Art/unclassifiable
$ Chispum

211.04 superfried
◊ Design

211.05 Serif
◊ Culture
$ Sonidos Urbanos
© Carolina Rodriguez/Rodrigo Maceda

211.06 3deluxe
◊ Sports
$ North Kiteboarding/Boards & More GmbH

211.07 Aldo Lugo
◊ Culture
$ Mercadorama

212.01 Chris Bolton
◊ Culture
$ Kiasma Contemporary Art Museum

212.02 Blake E. Marquis
◊ Music
$ Le Rev

212.03 strange//attraktor:
• Sködt D. McNalty
◊ Corporate
$ Indoor Recess

212.04 Chris Bolton
212.05
212.06
◊ Culture
$ Kiasma Contemporary Art Museum

212.07 Autobahn
◊ Fashion
$ Clean and Unique

212.08 Julian Viera
◊ Corporate
$ a la parrilla *grill food

212.09 Julian Viera
◊ Art/unclassifiable
$ OT@

213.01 Felix Sockwell
◊ Culture
$ new york magazine

213.02 Regina
◊ Motion/Games/Media
$ alma creations

213.03 Analog.Systm
• Oscar Bjarnason
◊ Art/unclassifiable

213.04 EyesCream
• Matthias Wagner
◊ Design

213.05 John Beckers
◊ Culture
$ MTV Networks Amsterdam

213.06 HoohaaDesign
◊ Music
$ DJ Milly

213.07 Ekaterina Tiouleikina
◊ Fashion

213.08 HoohaaDesign
◊ Music

214.01 Buro Reng
◊ Corporate
$ Cygnis

214.02 Celeste Prevost
◊ Design
$ MIMA
© Agency: Zeus Jones

214.03 Foan82
◊ Design

214.04 Lifter Baron
◊ Sports
$ Sevnthsin
© Rob Angermuller

214.05 Calango
◊ Sports
$ Zumbi

214.07 Fontan2
◊ Design
$ F2TF
© Ivan Hristov

214.08 Via Grafik
• Leo Volland
◊ Motion/Games/Media
$ eclectica magazine

214.09 Atelier télescopique
◊ Fashion
$ Wassingue™, Floor Clothes Design

215.01 tomato
• Dylan Kendle
◊ Motion/Games/Media
$ dabhandmedia

215.02 Young Jerks
• Daniel Cassaro
◊ Corporate
$ Souther Comfort

215.03 Calango
◊ Design
$ Dylan & Van Laatum

215.04 Büro Destruct
• H1
◊ Culture
$ PROGR, Zentrum für Kulturproduktion, Bern, Switzerland

215.05 Pierre Jeanneret
◊ Music
$ Poor Records & heidi.com

215.06 Büro Destruct
• MB
◊ Art/unclassifiable
$ Olmo, Switzerland

215.07 Foan82
◊ Design
$ Flaya

215.08 Bo Lundberg & Jan Cafourek
◊ Fashion
$ Cirque Deluxe
© Clients: Anders Arnborger, Indre Singh

215.09 903 Creative
• Aaron Gibson
◊ Culture
$ City Church of Richmond

215.10 Negro™
• Ariel Di Lisio
◊ Corporate
$ Piaf

215.11 Foan82
◊ Design
$ Taxi Communication

215.12 Device
◊ Corporate
$ NGFX

216.01 FoURPAcK ontwerpers
• Richard Pijs
◊ Culture
$ Kunstbalie, Tilburg

216.02 Felix Sockwell
• Felix Sockwell (designer), Jonah Bloom (ED)
◊ Fashion

216.03 Like Minded Studio
• Luca Ionescu
◊ Fashion
$ RVCA

216.04 UNIT
• Si Billam
◊ Art/unclassifiable
$ Studio U/S

216.05 UNIT
• Si Billam
◊ Art/unclassifiable
$ Studio U/S
© Si Billam/Ged Walker

216.06 Benoit Lemoine
◊ Corporate
$ Good telecom

216.07 Calango
◊ Art/unclassifiable

216.08 FEED
◊ Motion/Games/Media
$ Department of Design and Computation Arts, Concordia University

217.01 Jan en Randoald
◊ Culture
$ theater Artemis

217.02 Marc van der Meer
◊ Art/unclassifiable
$ Taste Magazine

217.03 Jan en Randoald
◊ Culture
$ theater Artemis

217.04 Skin Designstudio
◊ Culture
$ Nord

217.05 A-Side Studio
◊ Corporate
$ The Vine Marketing

217.06 Ekaterina Tiouleikina
◊ Art/unclassifiable

217.07 EMPK
• Diego Bellorin
◊ Design
$ Hasta la victoria colectif
© EMPK/Monsieur t

217.08 Dtam-TM
• Paul Heys
◊ Design
$ Dtam

218.01 GVA Studio
◊ Design

218.02 A-Side Studio
◊ Sports
$ Trans Surf

218.03 Anónimo Studio
• Hector Do Nascimento
◊ Culture

218.04 ilovedust
◊ Design
$ Self-initiated

218.05 Matt W. Moore
◊ Culture
$ Symptoms Collective
© MWM Graphics

218.06 HelloMe
• Till Wiedeck
◊ Corporate
$ Lucky Viral Branded Content NY

218.07 3deluxe
◊ Corporate
$ Lalaland

219.01 Foan82
◊ Art/unclassifiable
$ Carrot Clothing

219.02 Negro™
• Ariel Di Lisio
◊ Art/unclassifiable
$ La Feliz

219.03 Young Jerks
• Daniel Cassaro
◊ Art/unclassifiable
$ Amanda Axelson

219.04 LaMarca
◊ Fashion
$ Pow Clothing

219.05 modo
• Alexander Wright
◊ Music
$ simpl3

219.06 Mash
◊ Design
$ Gourmet Glaze

219.07 cabina
◊ Fashion
$ Juana de Arco
© Rural Invierno 2010

219.08 DTM_INC
◊ Music
$ Buskruit

220.01 Calango
• Jeroen Krielaars
◊ Culture
$ CitID

220.02 Art Machine
• Julian Hrankov
◊ Art/unclassifiable
$ MetalBrands

220.03 Chris Henley
◊ Art/unclassifiable
$ Bend+Fold

• Designer Name (if not identical with studio name) // ◊ Category // $ Client (if not identical with studio name) // © Credits (if not owned by studio or designer)

Work Index

220.04 Regina
◊ Corporate
$ ballet studio rise
220.05 Dorota Wojcik
◊ Culture
$ IKAR, art magazine of Torun City (Poland)
220.06 milchhof : atelier
• Michael Rudolph & Carsten Stabenow
◊ Corporate
$ A24 LANDSCHAFT
220.07 Fabio Milito
◊ Music
$ TYNA party
220.08 Acme Industries
• Octavian Budai
◊ Design
$ Zurich
220.09 1508
• Tore Rosbo
◊ Corporate
$ Danish Pig Production
220.10 Felix Lobelius
◊ Corporate
$ Icehouse
© Designed at There
220.11 LogoOrange
• Mihai Licanescu
◊ Motion / Games / Media
$ Irompler

221.01 Guapo
◊ Corporate
$ Fierro Hotel Buenos Aires
221.02 Leplancton
◊ Design
221.03 Lundgren+Lindqvist
◊ Music
$ Ante Up
221.04 Julian Viera
◊ Fashion
$ S.O.F
221.05 modo
• Alexander Wright
◊ Design
$ Alejandro Armas Vidal
221.06 Heloisa Dassie Genciauskas
◊ Design
$ William Albert
221.07 Norwegian Ink
◊ Music
$ Anders Brochman Hansken

222.01 THE SKULL DEZAIN
◊ Fashion
$ ROUTEBURN Co., Ltd
222.02 Autobahn
◊ Music
$ SJU
222.03 John Beckers
◊ Art / unclassifiable

223.01 Felix Sockwell
• Felix Sockwell (designer); Stefan Sagmeister (creative director), Matthias Ernstberger (art director)
◊ Art / unclassifiable
$ AIDS NQC, NY
223.02 NNSS
• Laura Ocampo
◊ Sports
$ Argentine Quad Rugby Team
© NNSS
223.03 Julien Vallée
◊ Corporate
$ Swatch

223.04 The KDU
• Aerosyn-Lex
◊ Fashion
$ BREAD & BUTTER BERLIN
223.05 Dogma
◊ Music
$ Elide
223.06 Julien Vallée
◊ Corporate
$ Swatch
223.07 The KDU
• Aerosyn-Lex
◊ Fashion
$ Ecko
223.08 Just Smile And Wave
• Doris Poligrates
◊ Sports
223.09 CLAU.AS.KEE
• Claudia Mussett
◊ Music
$ Os surfistas electronic band

224.01 Madhouse
• Tyler Fortney, Mike Gump & Garret Bodette
◊ Culture
$ Manifest Equality
224.02 Bas van Vuurde
◊ Culture
$ De Zingende Zaag, Haarlem
224.03 atelier aquarium
• Jérémie Nuel & Simon Renaud
◊ Culture
$ MJC Laennec Mermoz
224.04 John Beckers
◊ Motion / Games / Media
$ MTV Networks Amsterdam / Jamba
224.05 TNOP™
• Tnop Wangsillapakun
◊ Design
$ The Kenichi Yoshida Design, Japan
224.06 modo
• Alexander Wright
◊ Corporate
$ caracas catering
224.07 Jürgen Frost
◊ Music
$ Melt! Festival
224.08 Autobahn
◊ Culture
$ Sowieso 030
224.09 Dogma
◊ Music
$ MAXIMA FM
224.10 Insónia
◊ Music
$ Levelclub
© Insónia – Dreams don't sleep

225.01 Dogma
◊ Fashion
$ Chocolat
225.02 Andy Mangold
◊ Art / unclassifiable
$ Art for Hope
225.03 ZEK
◊ Culture
$ Mglc
225.04 Yucca Studio
• Gerard Tan
◊ Corporate
$ ada
225.05 Designit
◊ Design
$ Danish Architecture Centre

226.01 Matt W. Moore
226.02
◊ Motion / Games / Media
$ Google
© MWM Graphics
227.03 Landor Associates
• Jason Little, Jefton Sungkar, Sam Pemberton & Ivana Martinovic
◊ Political
$ City of Melbourne

228.04 Google Creative Lab
◊ Corporate
$ Google
© Google Creative Lab
228.05 Matt W. Moore
◊ Motion / Games / Media
$ Google
© MWM Graphics

229.01 FromKeetra
• Keetra Dean Dixon
◊ Design
$ Time and Place Workshop

230.01 Côme de Bouchony

231.01
◊ Design
$ La Surprise

232.01 Toko
◊ Corporate
$ The Communications Council
232.02 Scandinavian DesignLab
◊ Culture
$ Nørrebro Theater

233.01 Donuts
◊ Culture
$ Les Biennales de Lyon
233.02 Landor Associates
• Jason Little, Mike Staniford, Joao Peres, Serhat Ferat
◊ Culture
$ Worldeka
© Landor Associates
233.03 Felix Sockwell & Thomas Fuchs
◊ Sports
$ h2h
© Felix Sockwell, Thomas Fuchs, Steven Heller

234.01 Mutabor
◊ Culture
$ Theater Bremen
© Mutabor Design GmbH
234.02 Zigmunds Lapsa
◊ Design
$ Hungry Lab
234.03 Floor Wesseling
◊ Culture
$ Ymere
234.04 Felix Sockwell, Thomas Fuchs & Steven Heller
◊ Political
$ gop100

235.01 milchhof : atelier
• Andreas Töpfer
◊ Culture
$ Residenz Verlag, Salzburg

236.01 REX
◊ Corporate
$ RMB Properties

236.02 REX
◊ Corporate
$ ALDAR
236.03 Zeroipocrisia
• Matteo Marchetti
◊ Corporate
$ Sam Schultze
236.04 Hattomonkey
• Alexey Kurchin
◊ Fashion
$ RooshMoosh

237.01 Wolff Olins
◊ Corporate
$ AOL

238.01 HarrimanSteel
• Julian Harriman-Dickinson & Nick Steel (creative directors); Julian Harriman-Dickinson (designer)
◊ Corporate
$ BBC Learning

239.01 Landor Associates
• Nicolas Aparicio, Paul Chock, JJ Ha & Henri Kusbiantoro
◊ Culture
$ First Graduate
239.02 Trademark™
• Tim Lahan
◊ Design
$ Commercial Pop
239.03 superfried
◊ Music
$ GloryHoleMusic

240.01 Rinzen
• Karl Maier
◊ Culture
$ Right Angle Studio
240.02 milchhof : atelier
• Michael Rudolph, Carsten Stabenow & Andreas Töpfer
◊ Corporate
$ Hochschulübergreifendes Zentrum Tanz
240.03 Coley Porter Bell
• Simon Adamson
◊ Sports
$ Equilbrium
© Adam Ellis
240.04 ASYL
◊ Culture
$ ENSEMBLES Committee

241.01 Falko Ohlmer
◊ Corporate
$ Acht Frankfurt, Radio Televisionne Svizzera
© Falko Ohlmer & Simon Mayer
241.02 Rasmus Snabb
◊ Design
$ Design Studio Muotohiomo

242.01 HarrimanSteel
• Julian Harriman-Dickinson & Nick Steel (creative directors); Julian Harriman-Dickinson & George Wu (Designers)
◊ Art / unclassifiable
$ Touchpoint
242.02 Project 1000
• Stefan Szakal
◊ Design
$ VSF

242.03 Dtam-TM
- Paul Heys & Jeffery Bowman
◊ Art / unclassifiable
$ Crim Collective, The Univeristy of Huddersfield, UK – School of Art
© Paul Heys, Dtam, Jeffery Bowman, Mr Bowlegs, The Univeristy of Huddersfield, UK – School of Art

243.01 Advancedesign
- Petr Bosák & Robert Jansa
◊ Corporate
$ Prinz Prager Gallery

243.02 Barnbrook
◊ Corporate
$ Daichi Wo Mamoru Kai

243.03 Barnbrook
◊ Corporate
$ Dignity

244.01 EBSL
- Erik Kiesewetter
◊ Art / unclassifiable
$ CANO / Creative Alliance of New Orleans

244.02 Tatiana Arocha
◊ Design

244.03 ZEK
◊ Music
$ k4

244.04 Extraverage
- Karoly Kiralyfalvi
◊ Music
$ Future Funk Squad

245.05 Paloma Valls & Gustavo de Lacerda
◊ Corporate
$ Kas Reformas

246.01 Nicklas Hultman
◊ Fashion
$ ICONS of ECO

246.02 Landor Associates
- Malin Holmstrom & Jason Little
◊ Culture
$ Design Institute of Australia

246.03 Urbanskiworkshop
- Denis März
◊ Music
$ ePISTROPHIC PEACH SOUND
© ePS logo design

247.01 Serif
◊ Culture
$ Esquina Norte
© Hector Montes de Oca

247.02 Luke Williams
◊ Culture
$ Production Club of Baltimore

247.03 superfried
◊ Design

247.04 Luca Marchettoni
◊ Fashion
$ Donadata

247.05 atelier aquarium
- Jérémie Nuel & Simon Renaud
◊ Culture
$ Bzz

248.01 HelloMe
- Till Wiedeck
◊ Design
$ Bureau 91c

248.02 Luca Barcellona
◊ Corporate
$ M.A.P.C.
© www.mapc.eu.com

248.03 Grandpeople
◊ Music
$ Ekko Festival

248.04 Luke Williams
◊ Fashion
$ Nuria Frances

248.05 xy arts
- Quan
◊ Design
$ vekt

248.06 General Projects
◊ Culture
$ Wikipenny Press

248.07 Via Grafik
- Leo Volland
◊ Motion / Games / Media
$ Eclectica magazine

248.08 Nohemí Dicurú
◊ Music
$ Monzter

249.01 one8one7
◊ Corporate
$ NineteenFiftyThree

249.02 Mash
◊ Fashion
$ Claire Inc.

249.03 La Cáscara Amarga
- Jorge Chamorro
◊ Corporate
$ navaho

249.04 Base
◊ Fashion
$ LOEWE

250.01 Donuts
◊ Design
$ tamawa

250.02 Boldº
- Leonardo Eyer
◊ Corporate
$ WeDo Marketing Promocional

250.03 Fons Hickmann m23
- Fons Hickmann & Simon Gallus (art directors); Barbara Bättig & Caro Hansen (designers)
◊ Art / unclassifiable
$ seesaw

250.04 Matt W. Moore
◊ Music
$ AUX

250.05 Siggeir Hafsteinsson
◊ Music
$ Naibu

250.06 MetaDesign
◊ Corporate
$ MunichRe

250.07 Floris Voorveld
◊ Corporate
$ Teamworks

250.08 Designers United
◊ Sports
$ Euroleague Basketball
© Dimitris Koliadimas & Dimitris Papazoglou

251.01 Fontan2
◊ Design
$ ZKA
© Ivan Hristov

251.02 Red Box Inc.
- Tatjana Green
◊ Culture
$ Nadege Patisserie
© Red Box Inc.

251.03 The Luxury of Protest
- Peter Crnokrak
◊ Music
$ MTV Networks

252.01 Edgar Bąk
◊ Sports
$ University of Warsaw

252.02 Fons Hickmann m23
- Fons Hickmann (art director); Till Wiedeck (designer)
◊ Culture
$ Ruhrpot

252.03 Lorenzo Geiger
◊ Political
$ Landplan

252.04 The KDU
- Aerosyn-Lex
◊ Music
$ SOS magazine for Ryan Leslie

252.05 FromKeetra
- Keetra Dean Dixon
◊ Art / unclassifiable

252.06 W://Them
- Floyd E. Schulze
◊ Sports
$ b&d Verlag

252.07 Fons Hickmann m23
- Fons Hickmann & Lena Panzlau (art directors)
◊ Corporate
$ navi

252.08 Monoblock
- Pablo Galuppo
◊ Political
$ Unicef

252.09 nocturn.ro
- Alex Tass
◊ Art / unclassifiable
$ DOL

252.10 Guapo
◊ Design
$ Lola

253.01 Urbanskiworkshop
- Denis März
◊ Music
$ Georgia Anne Muldrow / ePISTROPHIC PEACH SOUND

253.02 A N D
- Jean-Benoit Levy (designer); Noemi Rav (creative director)
◊ Motion / Games / Media
$ Big Book Media

253.03 Büro Destruct
- Lopetz
◊ Design
$ Nu-Shi, Japan

253.04 Bleed
◊ Art / unclassifiable

253.05 Power Graphixx
◊ Art / unclassifiable

253.06 The KDU
- Aerosyn-Lex
◊ Sports
$ 361 Sports

253.07 X3 Studios
- Erik Erdokozi
◊ Art / unclassifiable
$ Cros

253.08 FriendsWithYou
◊ Design

253.09 John Beckers
◊ Art / unclassifiable

254.01 1508
- Clea Simonsen & Tore Rosbo
◊ Corporate
$ Aarhus University

254.02 Robi Jõeleht
◊ Culture
$ Rotermann Quarter

254.03 Fons Hickmann m23
- Fons Hickmann, Gesine Grotrian-Steinweg (art directors); Thomas Kronbichler (designer)
◊ Corporate
$ Bayerisches Staatsballett

254.04 sellout-industries™
◊ Corporate

254.05 OMOMMA™
- Daijiro Ohara
◊ Music
$ Kakubarhythm

254.06 Tsuyoshi Hirooka
◊ Music
$ KAMMAI RECORDS

254.07 C100 Purple Haze
◊ Fashion
$ Vicelona

254.08 ZEK
◊ Music
$ k4

255.01 TwoPoints.Net
◊ Music
$ Banjo Music

256.01 Grandpeople
◊ Music
$ Safe As Milk Festival

256.02 yippieyeah cooperative
- Bauer / Borkowski
◊ Corporate
$ Stofanel Investment AG

256.03 General Projects
◊ Corporate
$ Iridesco LLC

256.04 eps51
◊ Culture
$ Contemparabia

256.05 NR2154
- Troels Faber & Jacob Wildschiødtz
◊ Political
$ Ministry of Foreign Affairs of Denmark

256.06 Büro4
◊ Culture
$ SRG SSR idée suisse, Eidg. Bundesamt für Kultur BAK, Swissfilms

256.07 milchhof : atelier
- Andreas Töpfer
◊ Culture
$ Ignaz Schick / The International Turntabel Festival

256.08 Mammal
◊ Motion / Games / Media
$ ITV

256.09 one8one7
◊ Corporate
$ Euroluce Lighting Australia

257.01 Escobas
◊ Music
$ Tokyo Pop Club

257.02 unfolded
◊ Art / unclassifiable
$ Theater der Künste, Zürich

257.03 Negro™
- Ariel Di Lisio
◊ Corporate
$ GOA

257.04 Kismanstudio
- Max Kisman
◊ Design
$ Rietveld Museum project, Utrecht, Netherlands

• Designer Name (if not identical with studio name) // ◊ Category // $ Client (if not identical with studio name) // © Credits (if not owned by studio or designer)

Work Index

257.05 Taeko Isu
◊ Culture
$ E.N.gallery
© YOSHINORI ARAI
257.06 Mammal
◊ Design
$ 67 + 69 Turnmill Street
257.07 HelloComputer
◊ Corporate
$ Ingenuity Property Investments
257.08 Jürgen Frost
◊ Music
$ Gornsewo / Rank

258.01 No-Domain
◊ Art / unclassifiable
$ Carlitos y Patricia
258.02 Dogma
◊ Music
$ YOYO breakers
258.03 Donuts
◊ Culture
$ Ambassade de France in Belgium
258.04 ALVA
◊ Corporate
$ Big Punch
© Alva Multidisciplinary
  Design Studio
258.05 Anónimo Studio
• Hector Do Nascimento
◊ Corporate
$ Nose Code Productions
258.06 Black-Marmalade
◊ Culture
• Jessica Stokes-Johnson
© DeChazier Stokes-Johnson &
  Jessica Stokes-Johnson
258.07 Extraverage
• Karoly Kiralyfalvi
◊ Culture
$ Ludwig Museum, Budapest

259.01 The KDU
• Aerosyn-Lex
◊ Corporate
$ United Visual Artists
259.02 UREDD
◊ Culture
$ Teaterhuset Avant Garden
259.03 Hula+Hula
• Quique Ollervides
◊ Culture
$ Festival de la Ciudad de México
259.04 milchhof : atelier
• Carsten Stabenow &
  Andreas Töpfer
◊ Culture
$ ausland
259.05 ALVA
◊ Art / unclassifiable
$ Red Bull
© Alva Multidisciplinary
  Design Studio
259.06 Fabio Lattanzi Antinori
◊ Culture
$ SUSO
259.07 Negro™
• Ariel Di Lisio
◊ Culture
$ 2021 Magazine
259.08 OMOCHI
◊ Music
$ beatica
259.09 Strukt
• Andreas Koller
◊ Design
$ Strukt Design Studio

260.01 No-Domain
◊ Corporate

260.02 Face.
• Blast
◊ Music
$ Nokia
260.03 Fontan2
◊ Design
$ Kliment
© Ivan Hristov
260.04 Non-Format
◊ Music
$ Lo Recordings
© Photos: Donald Christie
260.05 No-Domain
◊ Corporate
260.06 Ken
• Simon Sparkes
◊ Art / unclassifiable
$ Shift — Japan-based international
  online magazine
260.07 Manifiesto Futura
◊ Music
$ THE HYPE
260.08 UNIT
• Si Billam
◊ Design
$ UNIT
© Si Billam / UNIT /
  The Archetypal
260.09 Fontan2
◊ Culture
$ Gorichka
© Ivan Hristov

261.01 No-Domain
261.02
261.03
◊ Corporate
261.04 Mr. Magenta
◊ Design
$ Bricolaje
© Edicson Nieto
261.05 Positron Co Ltd
• Hiroaki Doi
◊ Music
261.06 Gustavo de Lacerda
◊ Corporate
$ Hormônios comunicação
  estratégica
261.07 Mads Burcharth
◊ Design
$ KARMA
© Mads Burcharth
261.08 No-Domain
261.09
◊ Corporate

262.01 Peter Sunna
◊ Fashion
$ Klayco
262.02 Matteo Mastronardi
◊ Sports
$ Aaro Vainio
262.03 cerotreees
• Benkee Chang
◊ Sports
$ NO FRIENDS
262.04 10 Associates
• Michael Freemantle & Jill Peel
◊ Design
$ Chapter Eight
262.05 Stefan Hornof
◊ Corporate
262.06 Acme Industries
• Paramon Ditu
◊ Corporate
$ Business Coaching Company
262.07 Sawdust
262.08
◊ Corporate
$ CloserStill

262.09 Brusatto
• Geoffrey Brusatto
◊ Culture
$ Z33, Hasselt
262.10 Søren Severin
◊ Design
$ Self-initiated
© Søren Severin
262.11 Scandinavian DesignLab
◊ Corporate
$ 1:1 Architects
262.12 A-Side Studio
◊ Motion / Games / Media
$ Awen Productions

263.01 Fabio Santoro
◊ Design
$ MBC — Mostra Brasil é Cosi
263.02 Sawdust
◊ Corporate
$ Green Cuisine Cook Shop
263.03 Positron Co Ltd
• Hiroaki Doi & Kenichi Isogawa
◊ Music
263.04 Company
◊ Motion / Games / Media
$ Neon
263.05 Lundgren + Lindqvist
◊ Culture
$ Filmbyte / Anthem&Friends
263.06 Haltenbanken
◊ Culture
$ Bergen Arkitektforening
263.07 Gustavo de Lacerda
◊ Design
$ verso
263.08 Heric Longe
◊ Fashion
$ Niho
263.09 Heric Longe
◊ Sports
$ Zoo York
263.10 No-Domain
◊ Music
$ Cristian Vogel /
  Snork Enterprises

264.01 Hey Ho
◊ Corporate
$ Max Bordeaux
© photo left: Hey Ho;
  photo right: Gregoire
  Grange, www.jumomedia.com
264.02 Company
◊ Corporate
$ Almo Office

265.01 FEED
◊ Motion / Games / Media
$ Mobile Media Lab

266.01 Mind Design
◊ Corporate
$ Znips
© Znips

267.02 Mind Design
◊ Corporate
$ Paramount

268.03 Mind Design
◊ Corporate
$ Circus
© Circus logos

269.04 Mind Design
◊ Corporate
$ Hive London
© Hive logo

270.01 Avalanche
◊ Culture
$ Toulouse Observatory (FR)

271.01 Advancedesign
• Petr Bosák & Robert Jansa
◊ Corporate
$ The Brno House of Arts

272.01 Edhv
273.02
◊ Design
$ Bits 'n Pieces
© Lenneke Heeren &
  Remco van de Craats

274.03 Edhv
◊ Design
$ Design Connection Brainport
© Remco van de Craats & Jeroen
  Braspenning

275.04 Edhv
◊ Culture
$ De Negende
© Lenneke Heeren &
  Remco van de Craats

276.01 NR2154
• UNIT-1391 / NR2154
◊ Culture
$ Royal Theatre / Turbinehallerne
© Troels Faber, Jacob Wildschiødtz,
  Satoru Inoue & Jonas Hz
276.02 NR2154
• UNIT-1391 / NR2154
◊ Culture
$ Royal Theatre / Turbinehallerne
© A UNIT collaboration
276.03 NR2154
• Troels Faber & Jacob Wildschiødtz
◊ Culture
$ LiveWired Music

277.04 NR2154
• Troels Faber & Jacob Wildschiødtz
◊ Culture
$ Hz
277.05 NR2154
277.06
• Troels Faber & Jacob Wildschiødtz
◊ Corporate
$ NR2154

278.07 NR2154
278.08
• Troels Faber & Jacob Wildschiødtz
◊ Political
$ Post Danmark

279.09 NR2154
280.10
281.11
• Troels Faber & Jacob Wildschiødtz
◊ Political
$ Ministry of Foreign Affairs of
  Denmark / United Nations
© Troels Faber, Jacob Wild-
  schiødtz & Ulrik Ejlers (ass.)

282.01 Sagmeister Inc.
282-285
◊ Music

286.01 Coley Porter Bell
• Adam Ellis & John Kubale
◊ Corporate
$ Inishturkbeg

402

Work Index

286.02 Faith
- Paul Sych
- ◊ Corporate
- $ Suzy Johnston Associates Artist Representation

286.03 ODD
- ◊ Design
- $ Brandcast.tv

286.04 onlab
- Nicolas Bourquin & Thibaud Tissot
- ◊ Corporate
- $ soundcloud

287.01 Kursiv
- Peter Graabaek
- ◊ Corporate
- $ Copenhagen Natureschools, City of Copenhagen
- © Photo: Torben Nielsen

288.01 nocturn.ro
- Alex Tass
- ◊ Motion/Games/Media
- $ VideoArt

288.02 strange//attraktor:
- Sködt D. McNalty
- ◊ Art/unclassifiable
- $ The Good Project—Kanye West

288.03 The KDU
- Aerosyn-Lex
- ◊ Corporate
- $ MTV2

288.04 REX
- ◊ Culture
- $ Myriad

288.05 Toko
- ◊ Corporate
- $ Southpaw Agency

288.06 Hold
- ◊ Music
- $ Concrete Plastic

288.07 Masheen
- ◊ Culture
- $ Södra Teatern

289.01 The KDU
- Aerosyn-Lex
- ◊ Fashion
- $ SVSV

289.02 The Action Designer
- ◊ Motion/Games/Media
- $ Studio 8

289.03 cypher13
- ◊ Corporate
- $ Sapphire Click

289.04 1508
- Tore Rosbo
- ◊ Corporate
- $ Headnet

290.01 Manifiesto Futura
- ◊ Design
- $ soyculturadeldiseno.org

290.02 Team Manila
- ◊ Art/unclassifiable

290.03 Floor 5
- Marek Polewski, Jens Pieper & Eva Hückmann
- ◊ Corporate
- $ Bar Tausend Berlin

290.04 Xavier Barrade & Mathieu Laroussinie
- ◊ Music
- $ School project (Philharmonie de Paris)

291.01 Jan en Randoald
- ◊ Culture
- $ City of Antwerp

291.02 Company
- ◊ Political
- $ European Interagency Security Forum

291.03 Hattomonkey
- Alexey Kurchin
- ◊ Music
- $ Music project Touchscream

292.01 Mash
- ◊ Design
- $ Glasshouse Projects

292.02 Accident Grotesk!

292.03
- Timothy Santore
- ◊ Corporate
- $ Bon Immobilien

292.04 Accident Grotesk!
- Timothy Santore
- ◊ Music
- $ D6

292.05 Accident Grotesk!
- Timothy Santore
- ◊ Corporate
- $ Convalid GmbH

292.06 Anthony Lane
- ◊ Art/unclassifiable

292.07 Dtam-TM
- Paul Heys
- ◊ Music
- $ The Six Hills
- © Paul Heys, Dtam, The Six Hills

292.08 La Cáscara Amarga
- Jorge Chamorro
- ◊ Culture
- $ santillana ediciones

293.01 Kokoro & Moi
- ◊ Music
- $ Renaissance Man

293.02 KOA
- Olivier Cramm
- ◊ Corporate

293.03 backyard10
- ◊ Sports
- $ Völkl

293.04 Büro Destruct
- Lopetz
- ◊ Music
- $ Bomb The Bass, K7!

293.05 Brusatto
- Geoffrey Brusatto
- ◊ Culture
- $ Musica, Neerpelt

293.06 Analog.Systm
- Oscar Bjarnason
- ◊ Culture

293.07 Gabe Ruane
- ◊ Corporate
- $ Flare

293.08 Andrea Stebler & Thomas Hirter
- ◊ Music
- $ Der Letzte Schrei Records

293.09 Fons Hickmann m23
- Fons Hickmann & Gesine Grotrian-Steinweg (art directors); Viola Smieskors & Susanne Stahl (designers)
- ◊ Culture
- $ Bayerische Staatsoper

293.10 Peter Schmidt Group
- ◊ Culture
- $ Nezu Museum Tokyo, Japan

293.11 REX
- ◊ Design
- $ M-Design

294.01 Søren Severin
- ◊ Corporate
- $ Hou+Partnere Arkitekter A/S

294.02 Identity
- Maret Põldre & Ionel Lehari
- ◊ Corporate
- $ Tretimber OÜ

294.03 Estudio Soma
- ◊ Corporate
- $ Red del Teatro Español de América

294.04 Benoît Bodhuin
- ◊ Culture
- $ Le Vivat
- © BENBENWORLD

294.05 Meatpack
- ◊ Music
- $ Libertine Supersport Nightclub
- © Caracostas Nicolas & Labro Richard

294.06 Heric Longe
- ◊ Sports
- $ Burton Snowboards

295.01 elRAiSE
- Andy Risquez
- ◊ Corporate
- $ BARU urbano

295.02 HORT
- ◊ Music
- $ Grafisch Papier Hier

295.03 The KDU

295.04
- Diego Quintana
- ◊ Sports
- $ 361 Sports

296.01 HORT
- ◊ Music
- $ Booka Shade

297.01 TWhite design
- Troy White
- ◊ Fashion
- $ Von Zipper

297.02 GVA Studio
- ◊ Culture
- $ Apotheek

297.03 LLdesign
- Lorella Pierdicca
- ◊ Corporate
- $ Tigellapoint

297.04 HelloMe
- Till Wiedeck
- ◊ Fashion
- $ OAMAO

297.05 Mads Burcharth
- ◊ Art/unclassifiable
- $ KARMA

297.06 ALVA
- ◊ Art/unclassifiable
- $ Parq magazine
- © Alva Multidisciplinary Design Studio

297.07 Calango
- ◊ Culture
- $ CitID

298.01 310k
- ◊ Music
- $ electronation

298.02 DTM_INC
- ◊ Corporate
- $ Knappe Koppen

298.03 helvetic brands
- David Pache
- ◊ Design
- $ simic

298.04 Identity
- Kristian Paljasma & Ionel Lehari
- ◊ Corporate
- $ Peetri Secondary School

298.05 modo
- Alexander Wright
- ◊ Culture
- $ imaginarios

298.06 Toko
- ◊ Culture
- $ Australian Institute of Architecture

299.01 Heydays
- ◊ Corporate
- $ ITI

299.02 cabina
- ◊ Corporate
- $ The Techint Group
- © T Jobs

299.03 Madhouse
- Mike Gump
- ◊ Art/unclassifiable
- $ the CAVE lab

299.04 Leplancton
- ◊ Art/unclassifiable
- $ Vicerrectoría de Extensión, Universidad de Chile

299.05 Wolff Olins
- ◊ Sports
- $ London 2012 Olympics

300.01 Fons Hickmann m23
- Fons Hickmann & Gesine Grotrian-Steinweg (art directors); Thomas Schrott (designer)
- ◊ Culture
- $ Bayerische Staatsoper

300.02 Fons Hickmann m23
- Fons Hickmann & Gesine Grotrian-Steinweg & Thomas Schrott
- ◊ Corporate
- $ roc-berlin

300.03 Hansje van Halem

300.04
- ◊ Design
- $ TNT Post, The Hague (NL)

300.05 Falko Ohlmer
- ◊ Corporate
- $ Acht Frankfurt
- © Acht Logo: Simon Mayer, (corporate designer, type designer); Firsteight Logo: Falko Ohlmer

301.01 Acme Industries
- Paramon Ditu
- ◊ Motion/Games/Media
- $ NEON

301.02 Christian Rothenhagen
- ◊ Music
- $ Several Degrees

301.03 Stefan Romanu
- ◊ Corporate
- $ Allnet Telecom

301.04 Matt W. Moore
- ◊ Fashion
- $ Glyph Cue
- © MWM Graphics

301.05 Bodara
- Tobias Peier & Alain Scherer
- ◊ Motion/Games/Media
- $ Republik Verlag

301.06 The KDU
- Aerosyn-Lex
- ◊ Sports
- $ 361 Sports

301.07 Autobahn
- ◊ Corporate
- $ AEF Academy

301.08 Mads Freund Brunse, Mathias Clottu & Andrey Zouari/ECAL
- ◊ Corporate
- $ ECAL

• Designer Name (if not identical with studio name) // ◊ Category // $ Client (if not identical with studio name) // © Credits (if not owned by studio or designer)

Work Index

302.01 Théo Gennitsakis
◊ Culture
$ Lifo magazine
302.02 Stylism
◊ Culture
$ Kunstroute Amsterdam
© Djordi Luymes
302.03 Théo Gennitsakis
◊ Culture
$ The New York Times
302.04 Slang
• Nathanaël Hamon
◊ Music
$ Death Sentence: Panda!
302.05 Dennis Herzog
◊ Music
$ Club Travolta
302.06 HelloMe
• Till Wiedeck
◊ Design
$ ZWEIDREI
302.07 Rocholl Selected Designs
• Frank Rocholl
◊ Music
$ Fudge Club
© Gunther Gebauhr
302.08 cabina
◊ Corporate
$ Axoft Argentina
© Tango

303.01 cerotreees
• Benkee Chang
◊ Sports
$ LMNOP
303.02 The KDU
• Aerosyn-Lex
◊ Design
$ Nontype
303.03 Jewboy Corp™
◊ Culture
$ Maria Kong Dance Group
303.04 Manifiesto Futura
◊ Music
$ ACCES
303.05 Faith
• Paul Sych
◊ Fashion
$ Bassett Media Group
303.06 Tsuyoshi Hirooka
◊ Art/unclassifiable

304.01 Koehorst in't Veld
◊ Culture
$ Kunsthal KAdE
304.02 eps51
◊ Culture
$ Willau
304.03 John Beckers
304.04
304.05
◊ Culture
304.06 Stefan Romanu
◊ Art/unclassifiable
304.07 Staynice
◊ Art/unclassifiable
$ Playgrounds
304.08 Franz Falsch
◊ Music
$ Blitzdelta

305.01 Tsuyoshi Hirooka
◊ Music
$ MTV Networks
© MTV Networks
305.02 Just Smile And Wave
• Doris Poligrates
◊ Sports

305.03 Moshik Nadav
◊ Political
$ OCAD
© Frederick Burbach
305.04 C100 Purple Haze
◊ Fashion
$ 667
305.05 Raf Vancampenhoudt
◊ Music
$ Esther Venrooy
305.06 ZEK
◊ Music
$ Volatile
305.07 Emmanuel Rey
◊ Art/unclassifiable
$ Issur Demsky

306.01 Wissam Shawkat
◊ Art/unclassifiable
$ Hroof Arabia magazine
306.02 THE SKULL DEZAIN
◊ Fashion
$ ROUTEBURN Co., Ltd
306.03 Áron Jancsó
◊ Design

307.04 Like Minded Studio
• Luca Ionescu
◊ Art/unclassifiable
$ ArtsProjekt
307.05 We love moules frites
◊ Music
$ Scampi!

308.01 Tim Bjørn
◊ Corporate
$ Madam Madsen Shop
308.02 Hype Type Studio
• Paul Hutchison
◊ Fashion
$ Steph Ashmore
308.03 Tatiana Arocha
◊ Fashion
$ Burton
308.04 Mash
◊ Fashion
$ Pipsqueek In Saigon

309.01 miniminiaturemouse
• Fumi Mini Nakamura
◊ Fashion
$ Fume Artistry
309.02 Loic Sattler
◊ Fashion
$ Fuse
309.03 Moshik Nadav
◊ Design
$ Noiseappeal Records &
   Division Records
309.05 Deanne Cheuk
◊ Design
$ Gravure Projects
309.06 THE SKULL DEZAIN
◊ Fashion
$ bishop inc.
309.07 Mammal
◊ Art/unclassifiable
$ Venton Manor

310.01 Jared Mirabile
◊ Fashion
$ Extra Mile Merch
310.02 Zion Graphics
• Jonas Kjellberg
◊ Corporate
$ Family Business

310.03 Faith
• Paul Sych
◊ Fashion
$ Bassett Media Group
310.04 Burro Design
• Burro Design
◊ Music
$ Universal Music Singapore
310.05 Dog and Pony
• Dog and Pony
◊ Motion/Games/Media
$ Achtung!
310.06 DTM_INC
◊ Music
$ Home Brew Recordings
310.07 NALINDESIGN™
• Andre Weier
◊ Design
$ Sarp
310.08 Benny Gold
◊ Music
$ interscop records
310.09 THE SKULL DEZAIN
◊ Motion/Games/Media
310.10 DTM_INC
◊ Motion/Games/Media
$ Flabber.nl
310.11 Filmgraphik
◊ Music

311.01 Federico Landini
◊ Music
$ Long Bridge All Starz
© www.myspace.com/longbridge
311.02 Chris Rubino
◊ Motion/Games/Media
$ Ben Nabors/Drank With That
311.03 ATTAK
◊ Music
$ Nuff Said
© ATTAK • Powergestaltung
311.04 Black-Marmalade
◊ Music
$ Tony Jones
© DeChazier Stokes-Johnson &
   Tony Jones
311.05 Philipp Pilz
◊ Music
$ Sebastian Kaufung &
   Leonhard Brandeis Gbr
311.06 Autobahn
◊ Design

312.01 Derek A. Friday
• Derek A. Friday/Finndustry
◊ Design
$ Make My Notebook
© Sara Blette
312.02 Rasmus Snabb
◊ Fashion
312.03 ellenberg-martinez
• Laura Ellenberg & Ale Paul
◊ Corporate
$ küne
312.04 Joshua Distler
◊ Culture
$ Saffron/Visit London
© with Mike Abbink

313.01 Luca Barcellona
◊ Corporate
$ WE-Wedding Events
© www.we-weddingevents.com
313.02 Hula+Hula
• Quique Ollervides
◊ Corporate
$ Floé
313.03 ellenberg-martinez
• Laura Ellenberg - Ale Paul
◊ Fashion
$ Personal work

313.04 NNSS
• Tomás Fliess
◊ Art/unclassifiable
$ Facundo Gallo
© NNSS
313.05 Reaktor Lab
◊ Fashion
$ La Kalandra
© Jorge Aguilar
313.06 Stefan Romanu
◊ Culture
$ Ioan Tomi
313.07 Moxie Sozo
◊ Corporate
$ The Nursery
313.08 Allan Deas
◊ Design
313.09 Allan Deas
◊ Fashion
313.10 Leplancton
◊ Design
$ Barrok
313.11 Project 1000
• Stefan Szakal
◊ Corporate
$ Think Advertising
313.12 Philipp Pilz
◊ Music
$ Sebastian Kaufung &
   Leonhard Brandeis Gbr

314.01 Wissam Shawkat
◊ Culture
$ DCAA, Landor Associates
© DCAA, Landor, Wissam Shawkat
314.02 Wissam Shawkat
◊ Corporate
$ Amina Taher
314.03 Wissam Shawkat
◊ Corporate
$ The Brand Union
© Wissam Shawkat,
   The Brand Union
314.04 Wissam Shawkat
◊ Sports
$ Al Aadeyat Arabians Stud
314.05 Wissam Shawkat
◊ Corporate
$ The Big Blue, Emirates Reit
© Wissam Shawkat, The Big Blue

315.01 Wissam Shawkat
◊ Corporate
$ Pink House Production, Dubai
© Wissam Shawkat, Pink House
   Production
315.02 Wissam Shawkat
◊ Corporate
$ Mr Mashal Al Abdool
315.03 Wissam Shawkat
◊ Design
$ HH Sheikh Mansoor Bin Moham-
   med Bin Rashid Al Maktoum
315.04 Wissam Shawkat
◊ Corporate
$ Siddiqi & Sons
© Wissam Shawkat &
   Siddiqi & Sons
315.05 Wissam Shawkat
◊ Design
$ Linda El Shami
315.06 Alen 'Type08' Pavlovic
◊ Corporate
$ Turabex
315.07 Wissam Shawkat
◊ Design
$ Mr. Obeida Sidani
315.08 Wissam Shawkat
◊ Art/unclassifiable
$ Hroof Arabia magazine

Work Index

316.01 The KDU
- Aerosyn-Lex
- ◊ Design
- $ Diesel—Only The Brave

316.02 Like Minded Studio
- Luca Ionescu
- ◊ Music
- $ Skunkhour

316.03 Tatiana Arocha

316.04
- ◊ Music
- $ Sarah Fimm

316.05 The KDU
- Chow Martin
- ◊ Sports
- $ Reebok

317.01 Base
- ◊ Fashion
- $ CAMPER

317.02 Studio Baum
- ◊ Music
- $ Runtime Records

317.03 The KDU
- Aerosyn-Lex
- ◊ Design
- $ Thugs & Hugs

317.04 Toko
- ◊ Design

317.05 X3 Studios
- Erik Erdokozi
- ◊ Design

318.01 ATTAK
- ◊ Fashion
- $ Angel Age/DEPT.

318.02 The KDU
- Jared Liner
- ◊ Fashion
- $ Amongst Friends

318.03 OMOMMA™
- Daijiro Ohara
- ◊ Music
- $ TONE&CO., Ltd

318.04 Mehdi Saeedi
- ◊ Culture
- $ E.C.O

318.05 Wissam Shawkat
- ◊ Design

319.01 Áron Jancsó
- ◊ Design

319.02 TWhite design
- Troy White
- ◊ Fashion
- $ Nike 6.0
- © Craig Metzger

319.03 Ali Khorshidpour
- ◊ Culture
- $ *Arghanoon* magazine

319.04 xy arts
- Quan
- ◊ Fashion
- $ jala D

319.05 Mehdi Saeedi
- ◊ Corporate
- $ Ali Nateghi

319.06 Mehdi Saeedi
- ◊ Corporate
- $ Talaye Sabz

320.01 Mitchell Paone
- ◊ Design
- $ Twenty 120

320.02 Madhouse
- Alana Twelmeyer
- ◊ Fashion
- $ *The Bliss Book*

320.03 Zion Graphics
- Jonas Kjellberg
- ◊ Corporate
- $ La Venezia

320.04 Studio Output
- Karl Cox
- ◊ Art/unclassifiable
- $ The Curlew

320.05 Andrea Gustafson
- ◊ Art/unclassifiable
- $ Art of Faya Design

320.06 Mitchell Paone
- ◊ Design
- $ North American Wildlife

320.07 Faith
- Paul Sych
- ◊ Corporate
- $ Harlequin

321.01 KalleGraphics
- ◊ Fashion
- $ Carrot Clothing

321.02 Lab2
- ◊ Corporate
- $ Adriani Design

321.03 Base
- ◊ Corporate
- $ LA AMADA hotels and residences

321.04 The Action Designer
- ◊ Fashion
- $ Natasha Borgerli

321.05 Markus Moström
- ◊ Design

321.06 Daniel Blik
- ◊ Design
- $ Suppré Arthouse

321.07 Accident Grotesk!
- Patrick van den Heuvel
- ◊ Art/unclassifiable
- $ Pleasure

321.08 Blake E. Marquis
- ◊ Music
- $ Robyn

322.01 Matthew Manos
- ◊ Design
- $ Black Tea

322.02 Aldo Lugo
- ◊ Music
- $ Hip Hop artist

322.03 Jared Mirabile
- ◊ Music
- $ Know Hope Collective

322.04 Fresh Estudio
- ◊ Motion/Games/Media
- $ Navarra Visual Media

322.05 Face.
- Blast
- ◊ Music
- $ Jaguar House

322.06 No-Domain
- ◊ Motion/Games/Media

323.01 gebrauchsgrafikundso
- ◊ Culture

323.02 A-Side Studio
- ◊ Culture
- $ Projectbase

323.03 Bleed
- ◊ Design

323.04 Áron Jancsó
- ◊ Art/unclassifiable

323.05 LaMarca
- ◊ Music
- $ ROTOR Productions

323.06 The KDU
- Jared Liner
- ◊ Sports
- $ 361 Sports

324.01 Floor Wesseling
- ◊ Sports
- $ Nike Sportswear

324.02 THE SKULL DEZAIN
- ◊ Fashion
- $ ROUTEBURN Co., Ltd

324.03 Áron Jancsó
- ◊ Design

324.04 Zion Graphics
- Jonas Kjellberg
- ◊ Music
- $ Sony Music

324.05 Like Minded Studio
- Luca Ionescu
- ◊ Corporate
- $ Droga 5
- © Luca Ionescu & Yosuke Ando

324.06 Benny Gold
- ◊ Fashion

324.07 Jared Mirabile
- ◊ Fashion
- $ Empire Apparel

324.08 Hype Type Studio
- Paul Hutchison
- ◊ Fashion
- $ Grams&Gods

324.09 ATTAK
- ◊ Music
- $ Def Americans—Johnny Cash Tribute
- © ATTAK • Powergestaltung

325.01 cerotreees
- Carlos Engel
- ◊ Art/unclassifiable

325.02 Andrea Gustafson
- ◊ Music
- $ Clutch

325.03 Inksurge
- ◊ Music
- $ MCA Records Philippines/Urbandub
- © MCA Records, Urbandub, Sonic Boom Productions

325.04 The KDU
- Darren Newman
- ◊ Fashion
- $ SVSV

325.05 Working Format
- ◊ Culture
- $ Love Letters

325.06 Jared Mirabile
- ◊ Fashion
- $ Stuph Clothing

325.07 Jared Mirabile
- ◊ Fashion
- $ Lifeway

325.08 cerotreees
- Carlos Engel
- ◊ Sports
- $ Wrong surfboards

326.01 The KDU

326.02
- Magomed Dovjenko
- ◊ Fashion
- $ Ecko

327.03 The KDU
- Aerosyn-Lex
- ◊ Design
- $ *URB* magazine

327.04 The KDU
- Aerosyn-Lex
- ◊ Music
- $ Ryan Leslie

327.05 The KDU
- Aerosyn-Lex
- ◊ Design
- $ Diesel—Only The Brave

328.06 The KDU
- Aerosyn-Lex
- ◊ Fashion
- $ SVSV

328.07 The KDU
- Aerosyn-Lex
- ◊ Design
- $ R&N

328.08 The KDU
- Aerosyn-Lex
- ◊ Design
- $ Threadless

329.09 The KDU

329.10

329.11
- Magomed Dovjenko
- ◊ Sports
- $ Adidas

329.12 The KDU
- Magomed Dovjenko
- ◊ Sports
- $ Reebok

330.01 Jared Mirabile
- ◊ Music
- $ Third Day

330.02 cerotreees
- Benkee Chang
- ◊ Sports
- $ LMNOP

330.03 Ben Whitla
- ◊ Art/unclassifiable

330.04 Raf Vancampenhoudt
- ◊ Music
- $ Fallen

330.05 Guapo
- ◊ Art/unclassifiable
- $ Virgen Design School

330.06 cerotreees
- Benkee Chang
- ◊ Sports
- $ LMNOP

331.01 Designers United
- ◊ Art/unclassifiable
- $ La Surprise
- © Dimitris Papazoglou

332.01 Like Minded Studio
- Luca Ionescu
- ◊ Fashion
- $ RVCA

332.02 Yucca Studio
- Agnes Tan
- ◊ Fashion
- $ Domanchi

332.03 Like Minded Studio
- Luca Ionescu
- ◊ Fashion
- $ 55DSL

332.04 Jet Black Tribal Ink
- ◊ Fashion
- $ Clair De Lune Dining Couture

332.05 TWhite design
- Troy White
- ◊ Fashion
- $ Ezekiel

332.06 Jared Mirabile
- ◊ Music
- $ Red

332.07 Xavier Barrade
- ◊ Art/unclassifiable
- $ Michaël Sellam

332.08 Jet Black Tribal Ink
- ◊ Fashion
- $ MATTWHITE

332.09 THE SKULL DEZAIN
- ◊ Fashion
- $ ROUTEBURN Co., Ltd

• Designer Name (if not identical with studio name) // ◊ Category // $ Client (if not identical with studio name) // © Credits (if not owned by studio or designer)

Work Index

333.01 KOA
- Olivier Cramm
◊ Sports
$ Black Hole Snowboards

333.02 Luca Barcellona
◊ Music
$ Night Skinny

333.03 DTM_INC
◊ Music
$ Frogbite.nl

333.04 310k
◊ Music
$ MilkMoneyMaffia / Basserk Records

333.05 Aldo Lugo
◊ Culture
$ Odds & Ends

334.01 illDesigns
- Till Könneker
◊ Culture

334.02 Alphabet Arm Design
- Chris Piascik
◊ Culture
$ Second Glass

334.03 Mikey Burton
◊ Corporate
$ Doner / Huner

335.04 Red Box Inc.
335.05
- Tatjana Green
◊ Culture
$ The Shortbread Bakery
© Red Box Inc.

336.06 ilovedust
◊ Corporate
$ Release The Hounds

336.07 Inksurge
◊ Culture
$ The Best Case Scenario
© Inksurge, Camille Vergara

336.08 Superlow
- Halvor Bodin
◊ Culture
$ Oslo International Film Festival
© OIFF 2009

337.01 Mikey Burton
◊ Music
$ Bohemian Foundation
© Design Firm: Little Jacket

337.02 Gustavo de Lacerda & Ricardo Cunha Lima
◊ Corporate
$ Gattopardo Restaurant
© Gustavo de Lacerda (art director and typographer); Ricardo Cunha Lima (illustrator)

337.03 Mikey Burton
◊ Music
$ Wilco

337.04 Blake E. Marquis
◊ Design
$ You Work For Them

337.05 Like Minded Studio
- Luca Ionescu
◊ Motion / Games / Media
$ INK PROJECTS

337.06 illDesigns
- Till Könneker
◊ Art / unclassifiable

337.07 Hexanine
- Tim Lapetino
◊ Culture
$ Park Community Church

338.01 Strohl
- Eric Strohl & Christine Celic Strohl
◊ Corporate
$ 18 Rabbits Granola

338.02 Jesse Kirsch
◊ Art / unclassifiable
$ Terhune Orchards

338.03 Giorgio Paolinelli
◊ Fashion
$ Joewich

338.04 Jesse Kirsch
◊ Art / unclassifiable
$ Three Tablespoons

339.01 Subcommunication
- Sébastien Théraulaz & Valérie Desrochers
◊ Corporate
$ Beautys

339.02 Weather Control
- Josh Oakley
◊ Music
$ Pure Cuban Sugar

339.03 Studio On Fire
◊ Art / unclassifiable
$ Rosenthal Photography

339.04 Irving & Co
- Julian Roberts & Caroline Mee
◊ Corporate
$ Long Barn

339.05 Jesse Kirsch
◊ Art / unclassifiable
$ Four Tines

339.06 Strohl
- Christine Celic Strohl & Eric Strohl
◊ Corporate
$ Vine Ray Farms

339.07 Hatch Design
◊ Corporate
$ Specialty's

339.08 Strohl
- Eric Strohl & Christine Celic Strohl
◊ Corporate
$ Sarah McNally

340.01 Alen 'Type08' Pavlovic
◊ Corporate
$ Buffaleaux

340.02 Ptarmak, Inc.
◊ Culture
$ The Lord
© JR Crosby

340.03 Ptarmak, Inc.
◊ Culture
$ US
© JR Crosby

340.04 Ptarmak, Inc.
◊ Culture
$ Old Faithful Shop
© Christy Carrol

340.05 Ptarmak, Inc.
◊ Culture
$ Nuovo Pasta
© Luke Miller

340.06 Ptarmak, Inc.
◊ Art / unclassifiable

340.07 Ptarmak, Inc.
◊ Culture
$ Black Star Coop
© JR Crosby

340.08 Ptarmak, Inc. & FÖDA Studio
◊ Corporate
$ 1890 Ranch
© JR Crosby

340.09 Trademark™
- Tim Lahan
◊ Fashion
$ Lunch League

341.01 The KDU
- Jared Liner
◊ Fashion
$ Amongst Friends

341.02 Mash
◊ Fashion
$ Basement Salon by Lesley

341.03 Ptarmak, Inc.
◊ Culture
$ Old Faithful Shop
© Ben Hansen

341.04 Andy Mangold
◊ Culture

341.05 Blake E. Marquis
◊ Culture
$ Mistress Creative

341.06 DIE SEINER
- Lain
◊ Motion / Games / Media
$ Amateur Magazine
© www.amateur-magazine.com

341.07 Ptarmak, Inc.
- Luke Miller
◊ Culture
$ Black Star Coop

341.08 Axel Raidt
◊ Corporate
$ Ärztehaus Albert Schweitzer

342.01 44flavours
◊ Corporate

342.02 sellout-industries™
◊ Fashion
$ adidas Originals

342.03 Goldjunge Grafik & Design
342.04
342.05
◊ Sports

342.06 Mikey Burton
◊ Culture
$ Carol & John's Comic Book Shop
© Design Firm: Little Jacket

342.07 Alphabet Arm Design
- Ryan Frease
◊ Fashion
$ Danielle Kupse

342.08 Luke Williams
- Luke Williams (designer); Jessica Lynn White (art director)
◊ Art / unclassifiable

343.01 HUSH
- Laura Alejo
◊ Art / unclassifiable
$ Lima Limon

343.02 The Lousy Livincompany
- Stefan Marx
◊ Fashion
$ Cleptomanicx
© Cleptomanicx

343.03 Mitchell Paone
◊ Motion / Games / Media
$ Centric / Vh1 Networks

343.04 Michael Lashford
◊ Culture
$ Kim S. Davis, Ph.D.

343.05 Red Box Inc.
- Tatjana Green
◊ Art / unclassifiable
$ Belle Fleur Event Planning
© Red Box Inc.

343.06 A-Side Studio
◊ Corporate
$ Trevone Surf Shop Café

343.07 John Beckers
◊ Motion / Games / Media
$ MTV Networks Amsterdam

344.01 Falko Ohlmer
◊ Fashion
$ Ucon Acrobatics

344.02 Mitchell Paone
◊ Motion / Games / Media
$ super Alright!

344.03 Mitchell Paone
◊ Design
$ North American Wildlife

344.04 Mitchell Paone
◊ Motion / Games / Media
$ In Secret Agreement

344.05 A-Side Studio
◊ Culture
$ Loose-Fit

344.06 Andrea Stebler & Thomas Hirter
◊ Music
$ Melonmoon

345.01 Trademark™
- Tim Lahan
◊ Corporate
$ AT&T

345.02 max-o-matic
- Maximo Tuja
◊ Art / unclassifiable
$ Society6
© www.maxomatic.net

345.03 Mitchell Paone
◊ Music
$ Brooklynola

345.04 Toben
◊ Art / unclassifiable
$ Cook My Way

345.05 Weather Control
- Josh Oakley
◊ Fashion
$ Eddie Bauer
© Josh Oakley & Märta Bacon

345.06 Studio On Fire
◊ Culture
$ Falling Deer

345.07 max-o-matic
- Maximo Tuja
◊ Motion / Games / Media
$ EA / Society6
© www.maxomatic.net

346.01 ROMstudio
- Rodrigo Maceda del Río
◊ Music
$ La Lupita

346.02 Philipp Pilz
◊ Sports
$ Fanatic
© 3deluxe

346.03 Allan Deas
- Allan Deas
◊ Fashion
$ Marchpole

346.04 Studio EMMI
- Emmi Salonen
◊ Music
$ Bailes Cubanos

346.05 Weather Control
- Josh Oakley
◊ Fashion
$ Eddie Bauer

Work Index

346.06 Strohl
- Christine Celic Strohl & Eric Strohl
◊ Art/unclassifiable
$ Mudslinger's

346.07 Weather Control
- Josh Oakley
◊ Fashion
$ Eddie Bauer
© Josh Oakley & Märta Bacon

347.01 Mammal
◊ Art/unclassifiable
$ Farmer Guy

347.02 Lapin Studio
- Jorge Navarro Herradón
◊ Culture
$ Lapin Studio

347.03 Moxie Sozo
347.04
◊ Corporate
$ Olomomo Nut Company

348.01 The Pressure
- Adam R Garcia (designer); Dan Shepelavy (art director)
◊ Sports
$ Dan Shepelavy

348.02 Floor Wesseling
◊ Corporate
$ Melly's Cookiebar

348.03 Amy Jo
◊ Corporate
$ Peace Coffee

348.04 Boldº
- Adriano Motta
◊ Music
$ Som Livre
© Boldº

348.05 Uwe Strasser & Maximilian Baud
◊ Art/unclassifiable
$ Brigitte Gombos
© www.waskannstduso.com

348.06 Trademark™
- Tim Lahan
◊ Corporate
$ BBDO New York

349.01 44flavours
◊ Art/unclassifiable

349.02 sellout-industries™
◊ Fashion
$ adidas Originals
© adidas Originals

349.03 Kelly D. Williams
- Kelly D. Williams on behalf of Distrikt Studio
◊ Art/unclassifiable
$ Modern Amusement
© Distrikt Creative Group for respective client(s)

350.01 Achilles Greminger
350.02
350.03
350.04
350.05
350.06
350.07
◊ Sports
$ Alta Rezia
© Achilles Greminger & Allegra Tourismus

350.04 Achilles Greminger
◊ Sports
$ Blenio Bike

350.08 Achilles Greminger
◊ Fashion
$ ShirtCity

350.09 Amy Jo
◊ Music
$ BWNoise

351.01 Achilles Greminger
◊ Art/unclassifiable
$ Internationale Puppensammlung Schweiz
© Achilles Greminger & Roca Puppenbühne

351.02 Bodara
- Alain Scherer
◊ Fashion
$ Cook Couture

351.03 Achilles Greminger
◊ Corporate
$ zoll-kommunikation
© Achilles Greminger & Patrick Zoll

351.04 sellout-industries™
◊ Art/unclassifiable

351.05 Studio On Fire
◊ Design
$ AIGA MN Design Camp
© Illustration by Jenna Brouse

351.06 Matt W. Moore
◊ Music
$ Dagger Or A Dram
© MWM Graphics

351.07 anna-OM-line
- Anna Maria Lopez Lopez
◊ Fashion

352.01 Barnbrook
◊ Culture
$ Biennale of Sydney

353.01 A-Side Studio
◊ Music
$ Hidden Sound

353.02 Celeste Prevost
◊ Corporate
$ Nerdery Interactive Labs
© Agency: Zeus Jones

353.03 Mikey Burton
◊ Culture
$ Carol & John's Comic Book Shop
© Design Firm: Little Jacket

353.04 44flavours
◊ Fashion

353.05 Büro Destruct
- Heiwi
◊ Music
$ Musicians for human rights

353.06 Ptarmak, Inc.
◊ Art/unclassifiable

353.07 INDASTRIACOOLHIDEA
- Luca Forlani
◊ Corporate
$ Italian Building srl

354.01 GWG inc.
◊ Design

354.02 BETA STUDIO
◊ Art/unclassifiable

354.03 Kyle Bean
◊ Design

355.04 We love moules frites
◊ Motion/Games/Media
$ Ladies & Girls

355.05 Meatpack
◊ Music
$ Libertine Supersport Nightclub
© Caracostas Nicolas & Labro Richard

356.06 Pandayoghurt
356.07
◊ Fashion
$ Mayko

357.01 ZEK
◊ Culture

357.02 Gianni Rossi
357.03
◊ Music
$ Valbadia Jazz Festival

358.01 Kyle Bean
◊ Design

358.02 Filmgraphik
◊ Music
$ Electronic Beats/Commandante

359.01 Handverk
◊ Political
$ Nordisk Film og Tv AS
© Eivind S. Platou, Synne Moen Tøften, Helene Ryenbakken & Kåre Martens

359.02 Handverk
◊ Motion/Games/Media
$ Paradox Film AS
© Eivind S. Platou & Synne Moen Tøften

360.01 Fons Hickmann m23
- Fons Hickmann & Gesine Grotrian-Steinweg (art directors); Susanne Stahl & Sabina Keric (designers)
◊ Corporate
$ gerdes

360.02 Toko
◊ Corporate
$ Rainy Day Industries

360.03 Linnea Andersson
◊ Design
$ be my Hero/a`la London

361.01 Ji Lee
362.02
363.03
- Ji Lee/Droga 5
◊ Culture
$ New Museum

364.01 Derek A. Friday & Shawn English
◊ Design
$ Veer

364.02 No-Domain
◊ Music
$ Crashroots Blog

364.03 Dennis Herzog
◊ Music
$ The Water Safety

364.04 Toben
◊ Art/unclassifiable

364.05 Christian Borstlap
◊ Corporate
$ Gramercy Park Music

365.01 Edhv
◊ Corporate
$ De Buitenwereld
© Eric de Haas & Remco van de Craats

366.01 Weather Control
- Josh Oakley
◊ Fashion
$ Ms. Taken
© Kam Martin (apparel designer)

366.02 KalleGraphics
◊ Music
$ TARA
© KalleGraphics™

366.03 Nicklas Hultman
◊ Music
$ DP/Dusty Pink
© Night Club

366.04 Hype Type Studio
- Paul Hutchison
◊ Fashion
$ Thread

366.05 Luca Barcellona & Marco Klefisch
◊ Corporate
$ Circus Srl
© www.circustudios.com

366.06 Red Design
◊ Culture
$ Fondation Carla Bruni-Sarkozy

366.07 Typejockeys
◊ Corporate

367.01 Faith
- Paul Sych
◊ Fashion
$ Bassett Media Group

367.02 MH Grafik
◊ Design

367.03 Projekttriangle Design Studio
◊ Culture
$ Design Report magazine

368.01 dancemade
- Jens Nilsson & Andreas Källbom
◊ Music
$ Dag för Dag

368.02 44flavours
◊ Music
$ Sneaky

368.03 Nico Ammann
◊ Culture
$ Valmann Bar & Club

368.04 Fabian Bertschinger
◊ Art/unclassifiable

369.01 There is
◊ Art/unclassifiable
$ The Talent Business

407

• Designer Name (if not identical with studio name) // ◊ Category // $ Client (if not identical with studio name) // © Credits (if not owned by studio or designer)

LOS LOGOS COMPASS

Edited by Robert Klanten and Adeline Mollard
Preface by Robert Klanten
Text by Sonja Commentz

Layout and cover by Adeline Mollard for Gestalten
Typefaces: Client Mono by O. Lindqvist, S. Wadsted &
Ogaki PRO by Á. Jancsó, Foundry: www.gestalten.com/fonts
Dada Grotesk by deValence, Foundry: www.optimo.ch

Project management by Julian Sorge for Gestalten
Production management by Martin Bretschneider for Gestalten
Proofreading by EnglishExpress
Printed by Offsetdruckerei Grammlich GmbH, Pliezhausen
Made in Germany

Published by Gestalten, Berlin 2010
ISBN 978-3-89955-320-8

© Die Gestalten Verlag GmbH & Co. KG, Berlin 2010
All rights reserved. No part of this publication may be reproduced or transmitted in any form or by any means, electronic or mechanical, including photocopy or any storage and retrieval system, without permission in writing from the publisher.

Respect copyrights, encourage creativity!

For more information, please visit www.gestalten.com

Bibliographic information published by the Deutsche Nationalbibliothek.
The Deutsche Nationalbibliothek lists this publication in the Deutsche Nationalbibliografie; detailed bibliographic data is available online at http://dnb.d-nb.de.

None of the content in this book was published in exchange for payment by commercial parties or designers; Gestalten selected all included work based solely on its artistic merit.

This book was printed according to the internationally accepted FSC standards for environmental protection, which specify requirements for an environmental management system.

Gestalten is a climate-neutral company and so are our products. We collaborate with the non-profit carbon offset provider myclimate (www.myclimate.org) to neutralize the company's carbon footprint produced through our worldwide business activities by investing in projects that reduce CO_2 emissions (www.gestalten.com/myclimate).